WILLIAM IV

WILLIAM IV

THE LAST HANOVERIAN
KING OF BRITAIN

JOHN VAN DER KISTE

PEN & SWORD
HISTORY

AN IMPRINT OF PEN & SWORD BOOKS LTD.
YORKSHIRE - PHILADELPHIA

First published in Great Britain in 2022 by
PEN AND SWORD HISTORY
An imprint of
Pen & Sword Books Ltd
Yorkshire – Philadelphia

ISBN 978 1 39909 857 1

A CIP catalogue record for this book is available from the British Library.

Typeset in Times New Roman 12/16 by
SJmagic DESIGN SERVICES, India.
Printed and bound in the UK by CPI Group (UK) Ltd.

Pen & Sword Books Limited incorporates the imprints of Atlas, Archaeology,
Aviation, Discovery, Family History, Fiction, History, Maritime, Military, Military
Classics, Politics, Select, Transport, True Crime, Air World, Frontline Publishing,
Leo Cooper, Remember When, Seaforth Publishing, The Praetorian Press,
Wharncliffe Local History, Wharncliffe Transport, Wharncliffe True Crime and
White Owl.

For a complete list of Pen & Sword titles please contact
PEN & SWORD BOOKS LIMITED
47 Church Street, Barnsley, South Yorkshire, S70 2AS, England
E-mail: enquiries@pen-and-sword.co.uk
Website: www.pen-and-sword.co.uk

Or
PEN AND SWORD BOOKS
1950 Lawrence Rd, Havertown, PA 19083, USA
E-mail: Uspen-and-sword@casematepublishers.com
Website: www.penandswordbooks.com

Contents

Genealogical Table

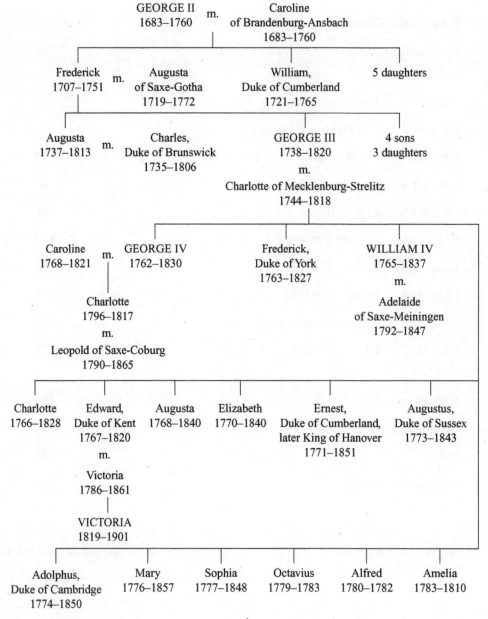

GEORGE II
1683–1760
m.
Caroline
of Brandenburg-Ansbach
1683–1760

Frederick
1707–1751
m.
Augusta
of Saxe-Gotha
1719–1772

William,
Duke of Cumberland
1721–1765

5 daughters

Augusta
1737–1813
m.
Charles,
Duke of Brunswick
1735–1806

GEORGE III
1738–1820
m.
Charlotte of Mecklenburg-Strelitz
1744–1818

4 sons
3 daughters

Caroline
1768–1821
m.
GEORGE IV
1762–1830

Frederick,
Duke of York
1763–1827

WILLIAM IV
1765–1837
m.
Adelaide
of Saxe-Meiningen
1792–1847

Charlotte
1796–1817
m.
Leopold of Saxe-Coburg
1790–1865

Charlotte
1766–1828

Edward,
Duke of Kent
1767–1820
m.
Victoria
1786–1861
|
VICTORIA
1819–1901

Augusta
1768–1840

Elizabeth
1770–1840

Ernest,
Duke of Cumberland,
later King of Hanover
1771–1851

Augustus,
Duke of Sussex
1773–1843

Adolphus,
Duke of Cambridge
1774–1850

Mary
1776–1857

Sophia
1777–1848

Octavius
1779–1783

Alfred
1780–1782

Amelia
1783–1810

Introduction

'Look at that idiot!' King George IV exclaimed to a dinner guest one evening in June 1826. 'They will remember me, if ever he is in my place.' He was speaking of his brother William, Duke of Clarence, who was sitting close to them. At that time, William was second in succession to the throne and a few months later, after the death of their brother Frederick, Duke of York, he became heir to the throne.

Four years later to the week, King George died. He had hoped to go down in history as a man of good taste and was indeed among the most noted royal connoisseurs of the arts. One of his few redeeming features was exquisite taste in paintings and furniture, and he did as much as any other member of royalty to enhance the Royal Collection. Despite this, for many years he was dismissed as an extravagant glutton, and the ungracious husband of a grossly mismatched wife. 'That idiot', William IV, the man whose head had been described by some as being shaped like a pineapple, and by others as being akin to a frog's head carved on a coconut, turned out to be a thoroughly likeable if sometimes unpredictable human being. This monarch who enjoyed strolling along the streets of London in broad daylight with a friendly grin to passers-by and with scant regard for his own safety, who swore like a trooper, was given to telling indelicate stories about his naval past with a reputation for drinking well rather than wisely in his unrestrained youth, and who cheerfully listened to his ministers and took note of public opinion, reigned for barely seven years at a critical time in Britain's history.

In retrospect, Britain was a country whose radicals had been inspired by the example of France, and who were openly talking about establishing a republic in Britain for the second time within less than two centuries. Yet the country had weathered the storms of the Great Reform Act, a measure that the sometimes-hesitant King William had been pleased to help his government facilitate. Several of the royal family had urged him to exercise his prerogative and block the measure, but he knew better. To use a cliché, he who dares wins. He did not listen to the fainthearts and the diehards – one of whom was the wife he loved and deeply respected – but followed the advice of those people whom he believed were more in tune with the mood of the people. As a result, he bequeathed to his niece, Victoria, a throne that was considerably more secure than it had been when he himself was called upon to reign.

His two predecessors, his father (George III) and eldest brother (George IV), had been strongly authoritarian figures, monarchs whom their chief ministers would think twice about daring to argue with or oppose in any way. By contrast, King William relished discussion and argument within reasonable bounds. Moreover, in treading a delicate path with his chief ministers during the convoluted passage of the Act during the first two years of his reign, he strongly expected to be remembered as the first constitutional monarch of Britain. Admittedly, in his last years he sullied his good reputation somewhat, by turning into an ill-tempered autocrat, and his ministers found him increasingly obstinate and difficult to work with. While this was a blemish on his earlier record, it should not detract from the fact that he bowed, no matter how reluctantly, to the democratic winds of change that had begun sweeping throughout mainland Europe and then across the shores of Britain.

History has always remembered William IV as 'the sailor king'. In fact, he entered the navy as a midshipman at the age of thirteen, and his naval career on board ship was over by the time he reached twenty-five. Because he reigned for barely seven years there is an unusually small number of statues in England to commemorate him. The first was erected in central London in 1844 at the junction of King William Street and Cannon Street, facing down towards

London Bridge. He and Queen Adelaide had opened the Bridge in 1831, but with the constant increase in traffic it had to be moved, and was reinstalled at Greenwich Park, close to the National Maritime Museum, in 1935. Other statues can be seen in the Royal William Victualling Yard, Plymouth, which was completed during his reign, and at Montpellier Gardens, Cheltenham.

On a more light-hearted note, one of the first pieces of legislation to be passed during the reign of William IV was the Beerhouse Act which came into force in October 1830, four months after he ascended the throne. The Act aimed to 'permit the general Sale of Beer and Cyder by retail in England' or to promote free trade and encourage the drinking of beer rather than spirits, and also to try and thwart the monopoly that local breweries had with regard to tied rather than free houses. There was an immediate rush to take advantage of the new legislation and more than 24,000 new licensed premises commenced trading within the next six months. It explains why King William IV was for some time the most common name of a monarch used by English pubs, many of whom named themselves after the king in whose name the legislation had been passed. In 1872 the city of York had three different King William IV inns, which must have been confusing for any local patrons asking their friends to meet them in the 'King William' or 'King Billy' for a pint at the weekend. However, it is perhaps not an inappropriate way to remember a man who in his unrestrained youth once had a reputation for drinking enthusiastically, if not sensibly. Kings after all are only human, like the rest of us.

William IV has been the subject of a few – surprisingly few – biographies over the years. Such a state of affairs might have pleased him, for he once allegedly had said that there was 'no person so perfectly disagreeable and even dangerous as an author'. (Biographers beware.) He has perhaps suffered from being perceived as no more than a short interlude between the reigns of his brother, King George IV, and his niece, Queen Victoria, whose sixty-three years on the throne ensured that her name was given to the age in which she lived and reigned. Surprisingly, the only really comprehensive biography to date is a well-rounded personal and political life, *King William IV*, published by Philip Ziegler in 1971, supplemented in part by Tom Pocock's *Sailor King: The life of King William IV*, published in 1991, which dwells almost completely on his naval career, and a short introductory essay, *William IV: A King at Sea*, by Roger Knight which appeared in 2015. The only in-depth nineteenth-century study, useful in its own way, although inevitably now very dated, is a two-volume work by Percy Fitzgerald from 1884.

I am glad to add to their number in portraying the life of an often under-rated monarch, a flawed but endearingly human character, who has perhaps not received full recognition for his achievements in strengthening the British monarchy as we know it today.

Chapter 1

The Sailor Prince

Born on 4 June 1738, the future King George III was the eldest of nine children, five sons and four daughters, born to Frederick, Prince of Wales, and his wife Augusta, a princess of Saxe-Gotha. Frederick died suddenly in 1751, without ever having become king. Under the upbringing of his widowed mother George grew up to be a likeable, gentle-natured young man, but somewhat reserved, immature, inexperienced and full of prejudices. Educated by private tutors, he could read and write in both English and German by the age of eight and was the first English monarch to make a thorough study of the sciences as a child. His grandfather, King George II, died on 25 October 1760, and the next day the young George was proclaimed king, at the age of twenty-two.

On 8 September 1761 King George III married Princess Charlotte of Mecklenburg-Strelitz at the Chapel Royal, at St James's Palace. The groom had previously lost his heart to Lady Sarah Lennox, who was descended from an illegitimate son of King Charles II by his mistress Louise de Kérouaille, Duchess of Portsmouth. Having been told that marriage to Lady Sarah was impossible, the young bachelor king had no choice but to submit to a suitably arranged marriage with some Protestant European princess. Aged seventeen, Charlotte was not particularly clever or attractive, but was well-educated and dutiful. By ducal standards, the duchy of Mecklenburg-Strelitz was not rich, and for one of the duke's daughters to be chosen as Queen of England was no mean prize. Like several arranged royal marriages of the time, it did not start as a love match, but both partners were very alike in several respects. They were domestically-minded and home-loving, George was a model of marital fidelity – unlike his father, grandfather and great-grandfather – and they remained happy together until the king's bouts of mental illness in middle and old age.

Eleven months after the wedding of King George III and Queen Charlotte, on 12 August 1762, their first son, George (the future King George IV), was born at St James's Palace. As the eldest son of a sovereign he automatically became Duke of Cornwall and Duke of Rothesay at birth. A few days later he was created Prince of Wales and Earl of Chester. Fourteen more children were to follow at intervals over the next twenty-one years. Frederick appeared one year later, in 1763. In 1764 the queen had a miscarriage but recovered quickly and was expecting a third child by the end of the year.

On 21 August 1765 a third prince was born at Buckingham House, and on 20 September he was baptised with the names William Henry. Of the younger siblings who were yet to come, six would be princes, two of whom died in early childhood, and six would be princesses. For the prince, who always got on well with his siblings, it may have been a source of sadness that he never had more than a fleeting opportunity to know his two youngest brothers. He had gone to sea and, to a certain extent, had left home by the time Octavius, appropriately named as the eighth son, was born in February 1779, followed by Alfred in September 1780. Both were sickly infants; the former died at the age of four, and the latter at twenty-three months.

At the time of his birth William was third in succession to the throne, but it was taken for granted that he would move further down the order once his elder brothers were married and had produced families of their own. Nobody ever envisaged that William Henry would have any chance of becoming king one day.

As far as is known, William made his first public appearance in October 1769, on the ninth anniversary of his father's accession to the throne. At the age of four, he attended a drawing room event at St James's Palace. George and Frederick wore splendid uniforms, while William and Edward, the fourth brother who was then a mere two years old, were both attired in Roman togas. At this stage the three eldest brothers shared the nursery under the care of Lady Charlotte Finch, known as 'Lady Cha'. In 1772 they were separated when the two elder boys were given their own establishment in the Dutch House at Kew.

William and Edward were 'boarded out' in the house on the south side of the Green, later known as Kew Palace. From this time, William's education was supervised by Major-General Jacob de Budé, a Swiss tutor from the Hanoverian army, and Dr James Majendie, a classical scholar who had taught English to Queen Charlotte. All the children were expected to join their parents for breakfast at the Queen's House, at nine o'clock sharp. By this time the boys had already risen three hours earlier and spent two of those hours at their lessons. At breakfast they had milk or sometimes tea and dry toast, and then returned to their houses for at least two further hours of lessons, followed by a walk in the gardens, regardless of weather. Luncheon, a simple course of meat and vegetables, was followed by a session of games, including cricket, hockey and football, in the garden. At five o'clock they met at their parents' apartments to read, write or make conversation. They were given a light supper except on alternate Mondays, when they had their bath in a tub of tepid water, and the governesses took them off to bed at about half-past six. Occasionally they enjoyed a rare treat when their elderly unmarried great-aunt, Princess Amelia, the last surviving daughter of King George II, invited the boys to come over to her house for afternoons of games and good food; her tables were laden with fruit and biscuits, of which the hungry youngsters made short work.

Aware of his family's tendency towards obesity, King George III had a horror of becoming overweight. He always adhered to a strict diet in order to keep his weight down and insisted that his sons should do the same. Some but not all inevitably disregarded any thought of such self-control when they became adults, but William was among those who managed to stay relatively slim throughout his life. He also enjoyed good health on the whole, until he was plagued with asthma from middle age, a complaint that worsened in his last years. It was perhaps significant that King George and his fifth son, Ernest, later Duke of Cumberland and King of Hanover, both refrained from gluttony and lived to see their eightieth birthdays, which none of the other princes managed. William and Adolphus, later Duke of Cambridge, who also lived quite temperate lives (the former, admittedly, only once he had calmed down in middle age), were the only princes to reach their seventies.

With two healthy elder brothers, it seemed most unlikely that William would ever succeed to the throne. By the time he reached adolescence, the King had decided what the destiny of his three eldest sons was to be. George, the eldest, would become king, Frederick was to be a soldier, and William would join the royal navy. William was an affectionate boy, much loved by his sisters in particular. King George's two eldest daughters, Charlotte and Augusta, were born one and three years respectively after William, and always remained his favourites. Augusta later commented that they had been devoted friends since early childhood. 'I had known every secret of his heart, the same when he was quite a lad, that I could believe and pity all his worries.'[1] As a boy he was amiable and unpretentious if at the same time rather impressionable, undisciplined and hot-tempered, shorter and less handsome than the two eldest. There was much good in him, his father believed, although he feared that his insubordinate, often unruly and sometimes downright irritating eldest son (the Prince of Wales) might become a bad influence on the others. He was sure the navy, with its tough discipline and sense of order, would be able to bring about some improvement in William's character.

In June 1779, at the age of thirteen, William entered the service as a midshipman. Queen Charlotte was pleased to notice that he went to join his ship very happily, 'and undertakes his profession with a great deal of zeal'.[2] King George wrote to Captain Samuel Hood, Resident Commissioner at Portsmouth Dockyard, that it was important 'no marks of distinction' or any favours were to be shown to William.

Accordingly, William was left in no doubt that even though he was the son of the sovereign, he was not to expect any special privileges and would be treated just like all the other young men on board. He had been given no real choice in the matter, but as he would claim later in life, nothing had ever made him happier than the parental decision to make a sailor of him, so it was indeed a fortunate choice.

After joining the 98-gun *Prince George* as a midshipman, he was destined to see action within a year. Although life in the navy was often harsh, he soon proved equal to the demands made of him by such an exacting regime. Until then he had led a very sheltered existence and meeting new shipmates from a wider circle may have come as rather a shock to him, at first. Fortunately, he was not of a quiet, retiring nature. It is said that when his peers asked how they should address him, he told them that he had been entered as Prince William Henry, but his father's name was Guelph, and if they pleased, they could call him William Guelph, as he was 'nothing more than a sailor like yourselves'. On his first day aboard, he saw another recent recruit being flogged for some misdemeanour, but such displays of discipline, cruel though they might have been, left him unmoved and he accepted them as part of the naval way of life. Many anecdotes about his verbal (and physical) exchanges, which may or may not be true, have been passed down to posterity.

Being hot-tempered, inclined to speak or use his fists first and think afterwards, meant that he was bound to be involved in altercations from time to time. It is said that he had a fight with a Lieutenant George Moodie of the Royal Marines, who told him that if it was not for his coat, 'I would give you a basting.' William immediately took off his coat. Their fisticuffs were stopped by an officer who was passing by and ordered them to shake hands, and the prince said, 'You are a brave fellow though you are a marine.'[3] During an argument with another midshipman, the latter said, 'If you were not the King's son, sir, I would teach you better manners.' William told him sharply not to let that be any hindrance and offered to fight him over a sea-chest.

The other lad declined, saying it would be unfair on the prince as he was the elder and stronger of the two.[4]

Many 'middies' who joined at a similar age were enrolled in the royal navy by their parents, and were drawn from the nobility, the landed gentry or professional classes, so there was nothing unusual about the prince's introduction to his profession. He found himself in the company of many who were from a relatively comfortable if not royal background. They were billeted on board in the midshipmen's mess and served with food that was almost inedible. Despite the king's request that he should not be singled out for special attention because of who he was, his privileged status ensured that he was sometimes invited to dine at the admiral's table, where the fare was inevitably much more palatable, and a cabin was set aside for him to continue his course of studies with Dr Henry Majendie.

At the time, the country was almost in a state of war. The American War of Independence had broken out in 1775, and the French had declared war on Britain, in support of the American colonists, in March 1778. Early the following year the Spanish followed their example, and during the summer the Channel Fleet was placed under the command of Sir Charles Hardy. The navy had to keep ships continuously at sea to supply the garrisons in America, as well as fighting the French in the West Indies, supplying Gibraltar, which was besieged by the Spaniards, guarding the Channel, and trying to keep the French fleet confined to their own ports. The service's worst fears were almost realized when a strong Franco-Spanish fleet intent on invading Britain approached the south-west coast at Plymouth. William could see it from the masthead and was as eager for action as the rest of the force. They were to be disappointed but perhaps relieved at the same time, for the enemy fleet had to withdraw owing to a shortage of supplies. Once the crisis was over William was granted a period of leave and spent the Christmas of 1779 at Windsor with his parents.

Returning to his duties on board early in January 1780, he was present when the fleet, under Admiral Sir George Rodney, captured a

Spanish convoy and its escort. The Spanish flagship was occupied by British crew and named the *Prince William*, in respect of the prince in whose presence the operation had taken place. Continuing along the coast of Portugal, in mid-January the fleet caught sight of the Spanish at Cape St Vincent, pursued them and battle was joined. Although his ship was in some danger from enemy action, the prince's earnest hope that they would 'give these dons a sound thrashing' was fulfilled. He witnessed the explosion that destroyed the Spanish ship *Santo Domingo*, with a crew of about 600 men, and wrote to his father that it was 'a most shocking and dreadful sight. Being not certain whether it was an enemy or a friend, I felt a horror all over me'.[5] The defeated Spanish commander, Don Juan de Langara, was astonished to see that the youthful midshipman in command of the barge to take him ashore was none other than Prince William. 'Well does Great Britain merit the empire of the sea,' he commented, 'when the humblest stations in her Navy are filled by Princes of the blood!'[6] William was excited to find himself so close to the theatre of war, so soon after having joined the service. Admiral Digby noticed that when they were preparing for action, his spirits suddenly rose, and once the fleets were separated afterwards, he appeared almost dejected. His mother was very proud of him, and wrote to her brother Charles that her son had been in the midst of fire, 'and the Admiral told me he behaved bravely and spiritedly'.[7]

The fleet sailed on to Gibraltar to relieve a besieged garrison. Like many of the other naval ratings William too was given the opportunity to relax and visit the pubs, and when he overheard a group of soldiers making insulting comments about the navy, he became involved in a brawl. He was arrested and briefly placed in custody, but the Admiral's urgent intervention ensured that he was soon released. They set off back to England in February, and on the journey home the ship intercepted and captured a French convoy, taking a booty of about £100,000 from the flagship in the process. William was very pleased, writing to his father that so far that year they had had nothing but success, as if providence was punishing their enemies 'for having begun the war so unjustly'.[8] Once back in London, he was charged with the ceremonial duty of handing the captured flags of the Spanish and French admirals to his father. It was not only his parents who, for perhaps the only time in their lives, were proud of and delighted with the conduct of their third son.

Although still only fourteen years of age, he found himself treated almost as a hero by the public, who seemed to think he had personally won the battle, with a little assistance from Rodney. When King George and Queen Charlotte took him to Drury Lane to see a performance of *The Tempest*, the audience cheered him so loudly as he stepped to the front of the royal box that the curtain for the start of the play had to be delayed for a quarter of an hour, and in the excitement several people narrowly escaped being trampled in the rush to come and take a look at him.

This hero-worship was to be short-lived. Within a few weeks William was at sea again, and from May to August he was engaged in the more mundane business of cruising in the Channel without seeing anything of excitement, interspersed with periods of leave at Kew and Windsor. The novelty of going to sea had now worn off, and he was frustrated by his parents' continual fault-finding with him. It was as if they were never satisfied, being reluctant to offer him any praise but instead continually taking him to task for his bad temper, his thoughtlessness, and resistance to accept criticism.

In spite of this he was granted leave at Christmas, which he spent at home with his parents, and during this holiday it was seen that he had apparently fallen in love, or at least begun his first serious infatuation. At a ball at St James's Palace, he danced all evening with Miss Julia Fortescue, who lived with her parents at Green Park. Supposedly secret assignations in the park, evidently not so secret if other people knew about them, and rumours of his hopes of being able to marry her, soon reached the ears of the king and queen. Whether they took such aspirations seriously is open to doubt, for apart from all the other objections he was still only fifteen and far too young to think of committing himself for life. Even so, before he could entangle himself any further, he was sent back to his ship. His father believed that service on waters close to home provided him with too much scope for amorous liaisons, particularly with the Prince of Wales and his potentially corrupting influence close at hand.

The eldest son and heir was something of a hero to his younger brothers, and at that time he was in particularly bad odour with King George for having fallen very much under the spell of his uncle Henry, Duke of Cumberland. The latter had been notorious for his scandalous behaviour on more than one occasion and was considered the black sheep of the family. His 'unsuitable' marriage with Anne Horton, a commoner who had previously been married and then widowed, had been the main catalyst for the king's determination to see an Act of Parliament passed as a bulwark against any more royal *mésalliances*. Determined to ensure that such a thing should never happen again, in 1772 he insisted on the passage through parliament of the Royal Marriages Act, by which no member of the British royal family under the age of twenty-five could marry without the consent of the sovereign. Moreover, even once that age had been attained, twelve months' notice had to be given to the Privy Council, or the sanction of parliament secured, before a valid marriage could be contracted. Only after the Act became law did King George realize that another of his brothers, William, Duke of Gloucester, had also contracted an 'unsuitable' marriage, with Maria Walpole, Dowager Countess of Waldegrave, an illegitimate granddaughter of Sir Robert Walpole. To make matters worse, William of Gloucester did not even inform his brother and sovereign until long after the event.

The very least the king could do under the circumstances was to try and see to it that young impressionable William did not become a disciple of his mischievous eldest brother and their notorious uncles. A more remote posting to foreign waters for the boy, he decided, would be the best course of action. By the end of January 1781 William was back on board *Prince George*, which cruised the English Channel for several weeks, then sailed south to take part in the relief of Gibraltar. During the summer the ship returned to Spithead in Hampshire. Having William so close to home disturbed the king, who still felt it would give him too much opportunity for unsuitable liaisons, as well as the possibility of meeting up with the Prince of Wales.

Accordingly, William was sent overseas again, to serve under Admiral Robert Digby, who had been placed in command of the North American Station. In August 1781, the week of his sixteenth birthday, he arrived in New York, at that time the last stronghold of royalist America. The citizens felt that King George III had sent his son there to soften the hearts of the rebels and hoped that perhaps his presence would help to end the war. At first, he found the city terribly dull. One mild excitement, of a somewhat dubious kind, was provided by talk of a conspiracy being planned by the American rebels, who seemed hopeful that he might become their first king. He knew that such a project would never come to anything, and was undoubtedly aware that even if he was ever persuaded to lend any support to it, his father would never countenance such a treacherous scheme.

Early the following year, one of George Washington's staff officers, Colonel Ogden, devised a plot to lead a small force that would sail from New Jersey in whaleboats, and capture the young prince and Admiral Digby, who were known regularly to take a stroll along the streets of New York, quite unguarded. Holding them as hostages could be a useful bargaining counter when the time came to make peace with Britain. The British authorities were alerted to the potential danger, and immediately sent orders for an extra guard to be placed on the Admiral's house. Their intervention ensured that it would come to nothing, and the prince was thus spared some embarrassment in the process.

King George and Queen Charlotte believed that it would be unwise to let the young man stay for a long time in New York, partly because of the threat to his safety and partly as he was bound to seek out disreputable company in his leisure time. He was therefore sent back to sea in the *Warwick*, a ship of fifty guns, under the command of Captain George Elphinstone. The latter was a firm disciplinarian who would accept no nonsense from his young charge. Fortunately for both, he and the prince quickly came to like and respect one another. In due course the captain would not only remain his friend and adviser, but also become his treasurer and comptroller of the household after both had retired from active naval service.

The orders were for them to cruise off Chesapeake Bay under French control, and intercept any enemy ships that might try to enter. His hopes of being involved in any action were quashed when he injured his arm in a fall from the rigging on board ship, and was thus prevented from joining the chase and capture of two French blockade runners. Once he had recovered, in November 1782 he was transferred in the *Barfleur* under the command of Sir Samuel Hood, who was asked to keep a strict eye on him. As the ship sailed for Jamaica, William heard with some disappointment that peace had been concluded with all combatants in the American war in a treaty signed at Versailles, and any more chances he might have had of covering himself with glory in combat were therefore over. In addition, the prince and Hood both quarrelled with Captain Napier, who had been chosen to supervise him. When he was told, the king remarked sadly that William was 'ever violent when controlled' and he 'had hoped that by this time he would have been conscious of his own levity'.[9]

William returned from sea in June 1783. After several years in the navy, he sorely lacked the polish and graces so cherished by society, particularly those of his eldest brother. Undignified but uproarious practical jokes in the midshipman's mess were more his style. Even so, he was growing up to be a good-hearted, companionable young man with an outgoing manner, and took to London society at once. The king was unimpressed, finding he had become rather loud and boorish, and told him that he had an excellent example in his brother

Frederick which he would be well advised to follow. He was convinced that William should be removed from the corrupting influences of the capital, and his eldest brother, without further delay. As a result, he was sent to Hanover, ostensibly to learn languages and undergo a spell of military training, but above all to learn the manners that service on board ship had plainly failed to teach him. A short period of stricter supervision might make an officer and a gentleman out of him, instead of a mere sailor. William had enjoyed his life at sea and was disappointed at this interruption to his naval service, in which he was accompanied by Captain William Merrick, and General Budé. The latter's presence was unwelcome to him, as he associated him with his childhood days and resented what seemed like a refusal to acknowledge that he was now almost an adult. He must have felt that his father was treating him like a tiresome little child and was sending him back to school.

The much-favoured Frederick was already in Hanover, having been sent to Germany for military training, and was proving himself a loyal, dutiful and affectionate son. The king hoped that he would help to keep William on the paths of righteousness. Frederick and their father agreed that the young midshipman sailor was too fond of practical jokes, and 'excessively rough and rude'. Even so, any hopes that his second son would soon make a gentleman out of the younger brother were to be dashed. Not the saint that his father might have supposed, Frederick soon introduced William to the thrills of gambling, even though the elder brother was a poor card-player and lost money heavily, losses that he never liked to make good. William likewise had little success when it came to enjoying a flutter or two, and an annual allowance of £100 proved insufficient to cover his cost of living and clothing as well as his betting activities. Within a year of his arrival in Hanover, he was heavily in debt. Budé asked the King for permission to settle his losses, and the king agreed with a heavy heart, at the same time cautioning his son that he could not go through life spending so heavily and making himself wretched in the process. With thirteen children, the king was responsible for making ends meet, and could not be expected to have to pay those children's debts.

William arrived in Hanover in July 1783, with Budé and Merrick. The king had outlined to Budé a curriculum that William was supposed to pursue while he was abroad, explaining that he hoped his son would return home with a good mastery of the German language, as well as a thorough knowledge of civil law, engineering, artillery and military tactics. It was also intended that he should visit some of the foreign courts in Europe, and thus absorb something of their elegance and refinement.

William found his two years in Hanover just as tedious as he had expected them to be. He had no interest whatsoever in horses and found the routine daily inspections of the royal stables boring. Having been encouraged to take up boar-hunting, he disliked it once he discovered that the recoil of the gun gave him pain in his shoulder. With his poor command of German, he never enjoyed visiting the theatre as he found it almost impossible to follow the plots of the plays. He was irritated by having Budé, a reminder of his childhood when he had been treated as an ignorant young boy, as part of his entourage. He tended to ignore him and made it plain that he much preferred the company of Merrick, who knew better than to try and discourage the prince from his carousing, and occasionally became something of a willing accomplice in his activities.

Moreover, society life in the kingdom was too formal for his liking, and he greatly preferred the more relaxed, if less respectable, life of naval officers and whores. Although he used to patronise the brothel on a regular basis, contracting venereal disease in the process, he also had a couple of brief affairs, and also a fling with his cousin, Princess Charlotte of Mecklenburg-Strelitz. This attachment to her namesake niece did not alarm the queen in England, or surprise her at all, as she appreciated that William was of an age when he was bound to be attracted to the company of young girls. For a while he also courted

Maria Schindbach, the daughter of a merchant, until she became betrothed to Captain Merrick instead. Rumour suggested that he had made a secret marriage with Caroline von Linsingen, the daughter of a general in the Hanoverian infantry, and that she either gave him a son or else miscarried his child. It was subsequently proved that he was in England at the time that he was supposed to have met and proposed to her. A son called William, born to an unknown mother, was born at around this time. His mother brought him to England a few years later when Prince William was obliged to accept his paternity of the boy, and had him brought up in his household. The boy William joined the navy, served aboard HMS *Blenheim*, and was drowned off the coast of Madagascar in 1807.

Several attempts were made to broaden the mind of the sailor prince, but without success. At Göttingen he attended a lecture given by the historian Johann Michaelis, which turned out to be more an impromptu harangue on the sovereignty of the people, and some less than respectful comments on royalty in general. He naïvely commented on it with approval to his father, suggesting that it ought to be translated into English. King George was horrified at the thought of his impressionable young son being inculcated with such subversive ideas, and Michaelis was dismissed from his post.

In the summer and autumn of 1784, Prince William paid brief visits to Silesia, Prussia and Switzerland. In Berlin he met Frederick the Great, King of Prussia, who scolded him when he admitted he had never read Voltaire's *Candide*. That autumn he and his brother Frederick attended the imperial review at Prague, travelling under the aliases of Lord Fielding and Count Hoya. Yet as the months wore on, he became increasingly miserable in Hanover, which he called 'this damnable country'. This should have been his chance to make the most of his time on shore, regardless of which country he found himself in, but by the spring of 1785 he was desperate to leave. Frederick was tiring of the presence of this unpolished younger brother, and wrote to their father to say that it would be wise to recall him to England

and send him back to the navy, 'under severe discipline, which alone can be done on board of ship, for his natural inclination for all kinds of dissipation will make him, either here or indeed any place by land, run into any society where he can form to himself only an idea of pleasure'.[10]

The king accordingly summoned William home and he was in London again on 10 June. His happiness at returning to familiar surroundings did not last long, for he was under strict instructions to stay at the Queen's House at Kew, where he would be under stringent supervision. The Prince of Wales had planned to hold a fete at Carlton House on the evening of his arrival, and naturally intended to invite his brother. When told of this, the king insisted that William could not possibly attend as he ought to be spending the evening quietly with his parents, ostensibly on the grounds that he was keen to find out how matters were at Hanover, but really because he wanted to keep the brothers apart. William's fury at being incarcerated can be imagined.

One week later the full Board of Admiralty, instead of the customary panel consisting of three captains, and presided over by Admiral Earl Howe, First Lord, assembled for William's lieutenant's examination. He produced his midshipman's journals and certificates of competence and was duly promoted to the rank of Lieutenant. Howe told the King that his son was 'every inch a sailor', and on 17 June he was sent back to sea without further delay. A junior Admiralty Board member, Captain John Leveson-Gower, as commodore of the 38-gun frigate *Hebe*, which sailed from Portsmouth later in June, followed by a small squadron, took William on a training cruise around the British Isles and he was appointed third lieutenant. They sailed up the eastern coast and went ashore briefly at Hull, where he was thrown from his horse and knocked unconscious but soon recovered. After a cruise around the Scottish coast and down to Wales, they moored at Milford Haven in August and later at Portsmouth. He spent some time ashore, during which he fell in love with Commissioner Martin's daughter Sarah, but the romance was doomed and they had to part.

For several months he took part in short cruises on *Hebe*, but before long he became bored and discontented with his lot. In February 1786 he wrote to the Prince of Wales, bemoaning his fruitless existence, complaining that everything was against him, and he was not allowed to enjoy himself like any other person of his age. 'What is to become of a young man of one and twenty years old [sic], who has neither profession nor money? A pretty situation indeed, add to all this, a King's son.'[11] He did not want to return to the West Indies, and was considering writing to Howe, offering his resignation from the navy. When he returned to Windsor to tell his parents how unhappy he was, the queen was quite anxious about his situation, although the king had less patience. Howe put forward a plan to have William promoted from third to first lieutenant but was overruled by the king.

In April he was made Post-Captain and given the command of the 28-gun frigate *Pegasus*, serving in the North American stations and the West Indies. It was some encouragement to him after his recent disappointments. However, he had been promoted above his competence, and it did not bode well for his future in the service. As a captain, albeit a very young and inexperienced one, he enjoyed considerable power over the officers and seamen aboard ship. Having been granted such power by the Admiralty commission that appointed him, he proved himself ill-suited to the job, imposing discipline and frequent floggings, demanding unquestioning obedience all the while. To restrain him, Howe appointed a first lieutenant, Isaac Schomberg, aged thirty-three and with some experience, who had already served during the war with America. It would be a difficult experience for both men over the next two years. William had accepted the instruction of Leveson-Gower, but he felt that a mere lieutenant, however senior, was ill-qualified to give him advice. With his years of experience, Schomberg considered it was his duty to guide the young captain during his first period of command, but William had taken an instant dislike to him and strongly resented being told what to do. On one occasion Schomberg intervened as

William was about to discipline a seaman for some trifling offence, saying that if a man was to be punished for every misdemeanour, no matter how small, as officers they would make themselves very unpopular on the ship. Further, the *Pegasus* cruise took the ship away from the calming influence of very senior officers. Whenever the friction between Schomberg and William threatened to get out of hand, William would argue bitterly with him, which proved harmful to discipline on board ship.

In June 1786, the vessel set off for Newfoundland, arriving there at the end of the month. William carried out various civic duties, and in August he celebrated his twenty-first birthday riotously aboard ship. Prince, officers and men all became very drunk, and in the revelry, he was hoisted on to the shoulders of the sailors and paraded from one end of the ship to the other. Apart from such social life, he found Newfoundland exceptionally tedious, writing to his father that 'the face of the country is truly deplorable … a small brushwood for the first five hundred yards inshore and then a most dreadful, inhospitable and barren country'.[12]

They left at the end of September, and sailed for Halifax, Nova Scotia, where they stopped for a month. One of William's companions was a young army officer, Lieutenant William Dyott, and both got on very well, although the latter was quick to observe that if ever any man tried to take the most trifling liberty with the prince, 'he cuts instantly'. Also, William was not above taking liberties of another sort. He became a regular caller at the house of Lieutenant-Governor Sir John Wentworth of Nova Scotia, who was frequently away on business, although his wife was not. She had a reputation in the neighbourhood for entertaining men at home, and as Dyott discreetly inferred, William did not hesitate to take advantage of any temptation that might have been offered.

Once again, the endless round of parties and his love of good living took their toll on his inadequate finances. In January 1787, he found it necessary to write to Captain George Elphinstone in London, asking him to lobby for a further allowance to be paid to him. With a rather naïve sense of honesty, he apologised for not having written for so long, his excuse being that he had been 'in a constant round of dissipation' ever since his arrival in the West Indies and feared that it would continue as long as he remained there. He was sure that it would not hurt his health, but he feared lest he might 'fall a sacrifice to this feasting'. There was no immediate response.

On 11 March 1787 Captain Horatio Nelson married Fanny Nisbet, the young widow of a physician. Born on the island of Nevis into a plantation family, she had been orphaned at an early age, and William gladly accepted the invitation to give her away at the wedding. Nevertheless, the next few months were not a happy time for him. He had become the best of friends with Nelson, who was almost six years older, to a degree bordering on hero-worship. When the newly-married captain and his bride sailed for England in July, he was so sorry to see him go that his mood almost bordered on depression.

His notoriously short temper became even more so, due partly to health reasons. He suffered from various fevers, with large blotches forming on his skin that became inflamed boils when he moved to a cooler climate, and from rheumatic pains on his right side and thigh. Prickly heat prevented him from sleeping properly, something he sought to alleviate by staying up at balls almost until dawn, when he inevitably drank more than was good for him, and had to be treated for venereal disease. He became ever more irritable and was continually giving petty instructions to those below him, for example, giving orders that any seamen who were unduly noisy should be punished. Having become notorious for drinking too much and making plenty of noise himself, he was ill-placed to order the punishment of those who behaved in similar fashion.

As he rose in rank he became quite a martinet, and as a captain serving on HMS *Pegasus* in the West Indies, he often fell out with his fellow officers. Maybe they had an exceptionally liberal attitude in advance of their time. Nelson, who was known to flatter those above him when it suited him to do so, had praised the prince's ship as one of the best disciplined vessels in the service. Any honeyed words, lavished on him by an officer who realized that there might be something to be gained by befriending senior royalty, should have been treated with caution. Nevertheless, it was clear that William had become a competent naval officer with courage aplenty, and a likeable young man of a boisterous kind. Yet, as the son of a sovereign, he encountered peculiar difficulties in learning how to work well with others, and a foolish quarrel with his first lieutenant soon soured his regard for his profession and showed his incapacity for high naval command.

Meanwhile, relations between William and Schomberg had steadily deteriorated even further. William was in the habit of placing petty restrictions on the officers, and when Schomberg continued to point out gently how bad this policy was for morale on board, William had him arrested. Schomberg was placed in confinement for three weeks and then released, but the arguments continued until he felt that the situation was untenable and requested a court-martial to examine the arguments in detail and clear his name. Nelson was annoyed at what he thought was a rather frivolous and unnecessary appeal for justice, and he ordered Schomberg's confinement. To have held a court-martial would have needed five captains to sit in judgment, and there were not enough at the Leeward Islands station. William suggested to Nelson that *Pegasus* should leave the Leeward Islands station without orders from the Admiralty and go to Jamaica, where the minimum number of captains would be available for the purpose. Commodore Alan Gardner, Commander-in-Chief of the Jamaica station, persuaded Schomberg to withdraw his request for a court-martial, offer his royal captain a suitable apology, and return to England.

In the autumn of 1787 *Pegasus* headed south and sailed to Jamaica, then to Bridgetown in Barbados. There was no senior officer there to restrain the prince, and reportedly he had a riotous time – balls and entertainment were put on for his enjoyment, and once again he made good use of the available brothels. *Pegasus* returned to Halifax at the end of October 1787 and sailed to Quebec before crossing the Atlantic. That autumn there was a risk of war between Holland and Britain over the issue of navigation of the Scheldt river, and in November William was ordered to proceed secretly to Ireland, to be ready to serve in any naval action. The dispute was settled by the time he had crossed the Atlantic and sailed into Cork in December.

The king had been annoyed by regular reports of his son's dissipation and debts abroad and insisted on his being recalled to England. William feared that once he was at home, he would again receive a lecture from his father on immorality, vice and other dissipations. However, the latter had no wish to see him this time. He gave orders that once *Pegasus* had arrived at Plymouth the Admiralty should ensure that William remained in port until further notice. At around the same time, he received a letter from Lord Hood, now Commander-in-Chief at Portsmouth, to inform him that he had appointed Lieutenant Schomberg to be the first lieutenant of his flagship, *Barfleur*. It was a demonstration of official support for his enemy. The furious William wrote Hood a letter calling it 'an attack on [his] personal character' and threatened to resign from the service if he did not receive a satisfactory explanation for the appointment. Hood replied that he could not imagine that anyone of the prince's 'humanity and condescending goodness' would wish to be the ruin of another officer, even if the latter inadvertently might have offended him.[13]

Pegasus left Cork on Christmas Eve 1787 and arrived at Plymouth three days later, after being delayed by a severe storm. William's wandering eye had been caught by a local belle, Sally Wynne, the pretty daughter of a merchant in Plymouth. George Wynne knew that the provisions of the Royal Marriages Act would prevent him from ever becoming father-in-law to the king's son, but he hoped that a romantic connection between the two young people might help him to further his business and his ambitions by becoming Agent Victualler, or principal contractor, for naval provisions in the town. Prince William was therefore welcome in his house at any time. Wynne noted in his diary that the prince had sent his purser, Mr Whitehead, to inquire after the health of his family, and to say he would be with them shortly, 'which he was accordingly soon after the departure of Mr Whitehead, who breakfasted at my House. The Prince also dined, drank Tea, supped and slept this night under my roof'.[14] Next day William returned to his ship after breakfast but continued to dine with them regularly for the next few days. He spent New Year's Eve with them and they stayed up until after 2:00 to see in the New Year.

This pleasant situation continued until William received letters from the Prince of Wales and the Duke of York, saying that they were on their way to come and see him. Their motives were not social so much as political, for they were united in opposition to their father, and believed that to have a third brother on their side would help their cause. The heir to the throne was running up huge debts because of the courts he was establishing at Carlton House and Brighton, which an increased allowance from the Civil List and a new parliamentary grant had only partly alleviated. He was also spending generously on Maria Fitzherbert, a Catholic widow with whom he had contracted a clandestine marriage, as well as entertaining his fast-living political friends and fellow gamblers. Several of the leading Whig politicians (a British political group in the late 17th to early 19th centuries, which sought to limit royal authority and increase parliamentary power) had become his friends, not because of their policies but because they were good company, and naturally eager to solicit the support of the heir, who could be a useful ally against their Tory-minded father. The Duke of York had not yet become so deeply mired in debt, but there was every indication that he would follow the elder brother he admired so much.

They must have realized that it would be pointless trying to persuade William to help bring some pressure upon their father to grant them more money, but on the principle of 'unity is strength', the three brothers thought that making a joint stand might succeed in wearing down their father's resistance. The pleasure-loving trio accordingly devoted themselves to two days of dinners, balls, and, remembering their royal duties, a few miscellaneous inspections to demonstrate they were not idling all the time. George Wynne recorded details of another ball in the town attended by the princes, his daughter Sally, and the cream of local society, with the company not dispersing until the small hours of the following morning – and the promise of another ball the following evening. Before the two elder brothers returned to London at the end of the week, they spent a morning with William viewing the Marine Corps and Barracks, the Royal Hospital, and the Plymouth Citadel, then went to Cornwall where they rode at Mount Edgcumbe and Maker Heights. Returning to Plymouth, William accompanied his brothers as far as Ivybridge on their return journey to London, then reported for tea with the Wynne family. As the elder princes had hoped, William was more than ready to close ranks with them in support against their parents and align himself with the Prince of Wales's Whig friends. He was sure they would help to ensure that William did not have to wait too long for a dukedom and the subsequent increased allowance. Their visit, short though it was, whetted his appetite for society life, and taught him not to take their father's regular scoldings so much to heart. Lightheartedly he wrote to the Prince of Wales in February that they need not be alarmed by any parental commands; 'the old boy is exceedingly out of humour,' and 'fatherly admonitions at our time of life are very unpleasant and of no use; it is a pity he should expend his breath or his time in such fruitless labour'.[15]

Although the king could hardly have been surprised, he was angry to hear of his son's latest romantic entanglement. William, he said angrily, was 'playing the fool again', spending too much time with the family and being seen in public with their daughter. For the next few months, William and Sally were regularly seen in Plymouth, and he spent a good deal of time at the family home. In March 1788 the crew of *Pegasus* was turned over to a 32-gun frigate, commanding the frigate *Andromeda*, with William still in command. Having been disappointed not to be given command of the larger *Melampus*, he was less than anxious to leave Plymouth, and Sir Richard Bickerton, the port admiral, was reportedly 'too much of a courtier to question the Prince about the progress of the ship'. In June the vessel was part of a squadron taking part in sailing tactics and manoeuvres off Plymouth, occasionally venturing as far as the Scilly Isles and the coast of Ireland. However, King George was annoyed that his son should still be enamoured with Miss Wynne. During William's brief return to Plymouth, Sally Wynne celebrated her twenty-first birthday, on 8 June, and William was invited to dine with her and her parents to celebrate the occasion. To George Wynne's embarrassment, there was no champagne in his house at the time, and William had to send to his ship for half a dozen bottles to be despatched forthwith so they could toast her. The king decided that his errant son must return to America without further delay, and ordered that *Andromeda* should proceed to Halifax, where she anchored in August and stayed for five weeks. It marked the end of the happy but short romance between William and Sally, and with it the end of George Wynne's business aspirations where any royal patronage might be concerned.

A bored and homesick William was glad to be reunited with his old friend Dyott. It did not bode well that he was serving under Commodore Charles Sandys, an incorrigible drunkard. Dyott was happy to enjoy them in their carousing and regular dinners where the alcohol flowed freely. At one banquet, the guests dined so well that they failed to hear the booming distress signals from a ship that was foundering very close to them. With no active service to concentrate their minds, the men led an aimless, tedious existence, enlivened only by the customary distractions of good living and whoring.

Another event, four days after William's arrival, was the occasion of his twenty-third birthday. For this, they hoisted the royal standard and a salute of twenty-one guns was fired, while a series of parades, receptions and dinners continued throughout the week. It came to an end with a ball on board the *Andromeda*. Dyott wrote in his diary, after a dinner at the Chief Justice's House, that he had never seen a man get as drunk as the prince did that night.

William's romantic inclinations and strong sexual appetites were also liable to cause difficulties. In Hanover he started by courting the daughter of a rich merchant, but was soon sighing for a return to 'the pretty girls of Westminster'. At Halifax, in 1788 he fathered a son, William Henry Courtney, and was said by a friend who was serving in the same station to be 'well acquainted with every house of a certain description in the town'.

In November the ship sailed for Jamaica, where William was entertained by sugar planters, merchants and ship-owners and given expensive presents. The most precious gift, his Star of the Order of the Garter set in diamonds, was presented to him by the Executive Council of the island. He was also taken on tours of the sugar fields and factories and noticed that the slaves seemed cheerful, healthy and contented with their lot. It created in him the lifelong impression that the practice of slavery was beneficial to both parties involved.

On 15 December *Andromeda* set sail from Kingston Bay for Bridgetown, Barbados, and arrived early in the new year. William was greeted with disquieting tidings from various merchant ships as they arrived from England.

Chapter 2

The Duke of Clarence

In June 1788, a few days after his fiftieth birthday, King George III had fallen seriously ill with abdominal spasms and a bilious attack. The doctors were puzzled by his condition, which they initially thought was gout. After a few days his physical health improved, and on medical advice he spent a few days taking the waters at Cheltenham, followed by visits to Tewkesbury, Gloucester and Worcester. While he was there his behaviour became increasingly eccentric. He began greeting passers-by as old friends, and visiting private houses to speak to the occupants as if he had known them for years. When he, Queen Charlotte and their daughters returned to Windsor in August he was taken ill with severe stomach pains. He looked alarmingly ill, complained that his feet were swollen, his eyesight was deteriorating, and he could not send letters to his ministers on the grounds that he was 'not quite in a state to write at present'. In October his doctors, with whom he was arguing violently, said that 'agitation and flurry of spirits gave him hardly any rest'.[1] Two weeks later William Pitt, the Prime Minister, came to visit him and the Prince of Wales at Windsor, where he was told there was 'more ground to fear than to hope, and more reason to apprehend durable insanity than death'.[2] Around that time he spent two hours in a coma, on one occasion, and when he was conscious he talked incessantly during the day and slept badly at night. 'I am not ill, but I am nervous,' he told those around him. 'If you would know what is the matter with me, I am nervous.'[3] Two of the doctors were convinced that he was 'in a state of lunacy' from which there might be no recovery. It proved to be the onset of porphyria, initially misdiagnosed as madness, which provoked a political crisis. The Whig opposition, who regarded the Prince of Wales as their champion at court, demanded that he should be created Prince Regent. On behalf of the Government Pitt dismissed such demands, indicating that His Majesty's indisposition might be only temporary.

Although relations between father and son had been difficult for some time, with the latter grumbling at a ceaseless tirade of fierce parental admonitions, William was genuinely distressed. At once he wrote back to the Prince of Wales, expressing his sympathy with the plight of their parents. 'Sincerely do I love this good and worthy man and long may he yet with his usual firmness reign over us,'[4] he remarked. He also felt great sympathy for their mother, knowing how worried she would be. It would have been possible for his ship to sail home at an hour's notice if required, and he immediately begged the Admiralty for permission to return home. In the meantime, he felt duty-bound to continue complying with naval orders, cruising to the Leeward Islands, then to Antigua and then on to Dominica.

At the beginning of April, he received permission to set sail for England. On 29 April 1789 *Andromeda* arrived at Spithead, and three days later he was at Windsor. To the delight of the family, King George had made a remarkable recovery, and a few days earlier a service of thanksgiving had been held at St Paul's Cathedral. When William saw the father whom he had so recently doubted he might meet again, still very weak but convalescent and looking better than he had dared to hope, he confessed afterwards that he was so overcome by emotion that he could hardly stand. Queen Charlotte had lost much weight and looked alarmingly thin. To add to her worries, she had quarrelled fiercely with the Prince of Wales over his demands for unlimited royal powers, which would have enabled him to secure additional funds and pay off his ever-mounting debts. In this he had been strongly supported by the Duke of York and the Whigs. Harassed almost beyond endurance, Queen Charlotte had insisted that the king would soon be restored to health, and she was proved right.

Although Prince William was relieved to see his father so much better, it brought him one temporary disappointment. He had known that one of the Prince of Wales's first actions, once he had secured suitable powers for himself, was to have been the offer of a ducal title for William, but Pitt told him that any ennoblement could not possibly be considered until the king was better.

Within a few days of William's return, it was announced that he had decided to offer himself for election to the House of Commons, as an independent candidate. The death of Sir Philip Jennings-Clerke earlier that year had left the seat of Totnes in Devon vacant, and William was persuaded to see if he could exploit the situation to his advantage. As a mere prince he was dependent on his father's bounty, but as soon as he was made a duke he would receive a parliamentary grant. Sharing the spendthrift tendencies of his brothers, he was heavily in debt. Had a title been conferred on him at the age of twenty-one, as in the case of Frederick, now Duke of York, he would by now have been at least £30,000 better off. Indignant at what he saw as an undue delay in receiving a title, he decided the time had come to make a stand.

As a prince of the blood royal any election to parliament would have doubtless been declared invalid, but the gesture in itself was enough to alarm the king who perceived it as a warning that William would make trouble in any way he could, until he could get his own way. On 16 May he signed the patent creating his third son Duke of Clarence and of St Andrews, and Earl of Munster in the peerage of Ireland, remarking gloomily as he did so that he knew it was 'another vote added to the Opposition'.[5] For the next forty years William would be known as the Duke of Clarence, a title that was said to originate from the castle and manor of Clare in Suffolk. It had previously been conferred on three princes in the fourteenth and fifteenth centuries, namely sons of King Edward III and King Henry IV, and a brother of King Edward IV. He was now given £12,000 a year and apartments in St James's Palace, and sent his father a grudging letter of thanks, adding ungraciously that this new income would not be enough to keep him solvent.

Turning a blind eye to this ingratitude, the king agreed to a ministerial request to pay off *Andromeda* on 8 June, especially as he was aware that his son intended to remain on shore for the time being. He was reluctant to promote him beyond the rank of captain, mainly because of his regular defiance of orders from senior officers that suggested he was still too immature for such responsibility, and also because he was foolish enough to associate with the unfilial and mischievous Prince of Wales and the Duke of York. Yet William was thrilled to have the title for which he had thirsted for so long, and on 1 June 1789 he threw a party at Willis's Subscription Rooms to celebrate his new status. As guests wandered through the rooms, they were allowed to look through an open door into a room where their host was sitting beside the Prince of Wales and the Duke of York. On the wall behind them was a transparency of their arms, and underneath in large letters, 'UNITED FOR EVER'. The Duke of Clarence was thus informing the world that he was supporting his brothers against the King. It was done out of thoughtlessness rather than malice, for William was at heart a good-natured character, but he was still young and all too easily swayed by the combined persuasions of his two elder brothers.

In the autumn of 1789 William rented Ivy Lodge, on Richmond Hill, where he settled down with Miss Polly Finch, a courtesan from Berkeley Square. Her craving for society was at odds with her royal paramour's recent preference for a quiet domestic life. Although William was not known for any great love of literature, and was alleged to have said dismissively that he knew 'no person so perfectly disagreeable and even dangerous as an author',[6] he enjoyed descriptions of the battle scenes in Homer's *Iliad*, which he found quite stirring, and he could not resist the lure of books on naval history. His idea of an enjoyable domestic evening was for him to read aloud to Polly from the first volume of *Lives of the Admirals*.

Having reluctantly subjected herself to this at first, it was said, she then realized to her dismay that after the first tome there were still several volumes to come. Having not the slightest interest in the subject, she was unable to resign herself to any more such purgatory, took her farewell of him and returned to Berkeley Square. He left Ivy Lodge soon afterwards, spent the next few months living in his apartments at St James's, and then purchased Petersham Lodge at Roehampton, spent a considerable sum on embellishments, and renamed it Clarence Lodge.

However, it was not quite the end of his days at sea. In 1790 there was discord between England and Spain over an incident near Vancouver Island, and in May that year the Cabinet decided to mobilise the Channel fleet to threaten Spanish ports. William was appointed to the 74-gun *Valiant* and arrived at Plymouth to take up his command on 13 May. The ship left port for Spithead to join the main fleet in June. This proved to be a difficult time for him. The other captains on board ship cold-shouldered him, and he continued to be a strict and unpopular disciplinarian. In August Earl Howe arrived to take command of the whole fleet. William remained critical of Howe, but the latter took the fleet to sea, the Spaniards backed down and the dispute was soon settled. The fleet sailed back towards its home ports in September. *Valiant* returned to Plymouth where William took his final leave of Sally Wynne and her family, their passion having cooled, and he sailed *Valiant* back to Spithead.

In December 1790 he was made a rear-admiral but in view of his lack of experience, it was only an honorary rank, and in peacetime there would be no chance of a sea appointment. His return to Clarence Lodge effectively marked the end of his active naval career. Any hopes he may have nursed of being appointed to the command of a ship during a mobilisation of the fleet against the Russians the following year, under Lord Hood, were to be disappointed.

Some thirty-seven years later he would be appointed Lord High Admiral in what turned out to be an experiment that brought mixed success and failure in its wake. Sir Thomas Byam Martin, who had gone to sea for the first time as a captain's servant, aboard HMS *Pegasus*, and later ended his naval career as Admiral of the Fleet, shrewdly summed up the achievements of the man who would go down in posterity as Britain's sailor king. He noted that, of the fifty-one years that had elapsed between the date of the prince entering the navy and his accession to the throne, the man who became King William had been professionally employed for ten years, nine months and three weeks, including more than a year when he had been on leave of absence in Germany.[7] During the next few years, Britain would be involved in action at sea, but to William's disappointment he would never again be called upon to serve on board ship.

In spite of this, his years in the navy had had a lasting and beneficial effect on his character. They had brought him into close contact with men from all classes, helped to give him a colourful if somewhat indelicate vocabulary, and ensured that he would lose any trace of a German accent that he might have acquired in childhood. Moreover, his naval journeys to distant continents led to William being the most widely travelled monarch at the time, until the next man to wear the British crown, his great-nephew King Edward VII, ascended the throne. (By contrast, during his fourscore lifespan, King George III neither left England nor set foot any further south or west than East Cornwall, or further north than Worcester.) Yet despite frequent appeals to the Admiralty for an active command during the Napoleonic wars, even making clear that he was prepared to accept demotion if his rank should prevent his being given the command of a ship without a squadron, the Duke of Clarence was kept unemployed for several years. Because of his position as a senior member of the royal family, it was almost impossible for him to be offered or accept anything but a fairly high-ranking post, one for which he might not be suitably qualified. At the age of twenty-five, his regular career at sea was over.

William, Duke of Clarence, had repeatedly prejudiced and more or less put an end to his naval career, due largely to his ill-considered behaviour. Yet in the years to come, he would show himself a devoted family man and good father. On the whole, despite a rebellious streak and his not unnatural youthful desire to flout authority, at heart he was a more loyal son than his elder brothers. At Windsor he still showed great affection for his father and respect for his mother, and he always remained on excellent terms with his sisters. Although fond of the Prince of Wales, he was not altogether at ease in his home, Carlton House, as George liked to surround himself always with elegant, witty company. In such an environment he perhaps inadvertently made his less polished, less intellectual, sailor brother feel slightly his inferior. Some of these people, such as the politician Charles Fox and the playwright Richard Brinsley Sheridan, were accomplished, sophisticated personalities who enjoyed making fun of the bluff and ignorant sailor who had spent so much of his time abroad and was so ill at ease in smart society.

The time would undoubtedly come when William would be required to marry, but his matrimonial options basically amounted to foreign royal women who were not Roman Catholic. Apart from the restrictions imposed by the Royal Marriages Act almost twenty years earlier, a wife from the ranks of the British aristocracy would bring with her unacceptable political implications. As ever, he was deeply in debt, and the House of Commons would have been disinclined to make him a large marriage grant to alleviate the situation. In true Hanoverian fashion he was a hot-blooded young man who fell in love regularly, but during his mid-twenties, after a few short-lived flirtations, he met the woman with whom he would share several happy years and also raise a large family.

Dorothea Bland, better known as Dorothy Jordan, had been born in London to an Irish father and a Welsh mother. She was about four years older than William, and had long made for herself a reputation as one of the most distinguished comic actresses of her age on the

London stage. She was already a friend of the Prince of Wales, and her acting skills were much admired by the royal family. As a young woman she had produced at least two children through other brief liaisons, none of which had led to marriage. Shortly after making her debut on the London stage, she began living with Richard Ford, the son of a physician, and they had a couple of daughters together, but her hopes of becoming his wife came to naught. It is thought that the Duke of Clarence had become bored with his life of inactivity at home, something he sought to alleviate by developing an interest in going to the theatre instead. *The Spoil'd Child: A Farce in Two Acts*, not only had William roaring with laughter, but he was also captivated by Dorothy's performance in a role that required her to wear boy's clothes. Having been spurned by the fathers of her children, she was longing for a man who would not cast her aside. An introduction from one to the other soon led to more than friendship, and sometime around the autumn of 1791 she agreed to set up house with William.

Being the mistress of a prince who was relatively close to the throne did not alleviate Dorothy's financial problems, and William's indebtedness showed no improvement. Every quarter he made out to her a payment of 200 guineas, while she continued to earn her living on the stage. Both were unfailingly generous to those around them, being kind-hearted souls who were reluctant to discharge faithful servants, and also *bon vivants* who loved to entertain regularly on a lavish scale. Yet, despite the regular provision he was making to her, there was some speculation that she actually saved him from financial disaster, her earnings being on a scale that somehow managed to mitigate his lavish expenditure. In 1797 it was estimated that his debts, though less substantial than those of his profligate elder brothers, were at least £45,000 and probably more. Not even her income as a hard-working actress could support the family adequately. Dorothy was committed to providing for her elder children, the two by Ford and an elder child by Richard Daly, a theatre stage manager with whom she had had an affair during the first years of her career in Dublin, before she returned to England to settle. Between 1794 and 1807 she and the duke produced a large family between them, five boys and five girls, no mean feat in view of her career. All of them survived to maturity and were given the name FitzClarence.

Believing firmly in the sanctity of marriage, King George could hardly have been expected wholeheartedly to endorse his son's relationship. Yet he was broadminded enough – or at any rate resigned to accepting the inevitable – to joke good-naturedly with him about Mrs Jordan on occasion, as well as ask after her as a matter of courtesy, and he continued to attend her performances at the theatre. Some eighteenth-century moralists were inclined to frown upon 'play-going' as a sin, but their views were not shared by the king and his consort. Queen Charlotte, who seemed even less tolerant than her husband of extra-marital affairs and grandchildren born outside a wedding ring, accompanied him on visits to Drury Lane when Mrs Jordan was on the stage there. For several years the couple shared Clarence Lodge, Roehampton, and after the duke was made Ranger of Bushy Park in June 1797, they moved to Bushy House, Teddington, which his father had given them. Yet thanks to the legislation that had been enacted at the behest of this same father, there could never be any hope of a marriage between them.

At the beginning of 1793, hostilities threatened yet again in what would turn out to be several years of war with the French, and the whole fleet was mobilised. In February an order was received at Plymouth dockyard to fit the 98-gun *London* for the Channel Fleet to receive the flag of Rear Admiral His Royal Highness the Duke of Clarence, with Richard Goodwin Keats as his flag captain. If William had hoped to set sail immediately, he was doomed to disappointment, with various delays preventing his early departure. On 27 June he unwisely spoke in the House of Lords against the war, pointing out that Holland, the endangered state which had been the original cause of British hostility towards France, was now secure. He reproached the Government for its policy and urged the ministers to make peace. In doing so he might have been motivated in part not only by not having been able to join the ship, but also by his resentment of William Pitt, who he believed had been more responsible than anybody else for delaying the granting of his dukedom. Pitt advised King George to veto the duke's appointment on the grounds that it would never do to have a political Admiral in the Channel Fleet. William's foolish behaviour in the past, particularly his public criticism of senior officers on board ship, still counted strongly against him, and now he had further prejudiced his case by arguing for peace. It was certainly inconsistent of him, bearing in mind how eager he had been to take part in naval actions against any of the enemy powers while on active service, and particularly as he was never remotely a Francophile. Like the rest of his family, he looked with horror on the state of affairs in revolutionary France, especially after the executions of King Louis XVI and Queen Marie-Antoinette, and he never shared the views of those Whigs in parliament who welcomed the new political climate of republicanism across the Channel. He had made his views plain to Nelson, to whom he wrote in 1792 that 'this pernicious and fallacious system of equality and universal liberty must be checked, or else we shall here have the most dreadful consequences'.[8]

While he had previously been a vehement critic of the Government's war policy he now recanted, presumably because he realized that a change of heart would be greatly to his advantage. Yet it still failed to bring him that much longed-for command. In March 1794 he wrote to the Lords of the Admiralty Board to seek appropriate employment. At a time when his country was engaged in war with a powerful and active enemy whose aim appeared to be the subversion of all the ancient European monarchies, he said it was up to every man who valued the Constitution 'under which he enjoys so many blessings, to rally round the throne and protect it from dangers by which it is so imminently threatened'. During his naval career, he insisted, he had never committed an act that had tarnished the flag under which it was his pride and glory to fight. In conclusion, he emphasised that all he wanted was to serve, and especially at a time when his gallant countrymen were fighting for their country and their sovereign. The last thing he wanted was to be accused of living a life of inglorious ease when it was his duty to be in the front line of danger.

Ten days later, having received neither a reply nor an acknowledgement, William wrote to his father. He enclosed a copy of what he had written, with a covering note adding that, 'To neglect, they have added insult insomuch as they have withheld from me, even that courtesy, which is due to every individual who makes a respectful tender of his service at a momentous period, like the present, when everything that is valuable to an Englishman is at stake and the throne on which you sit is endangered by the machination of regicides and revolutionists.'[9] His father did not reply directly and the only result was a promotion the following month to the rank of Vice-Admiral. He was still desperate for naval responsibilities and when he compared himself to his brother, the Duke of York, who had been appointed Commander-in Chief of the army, he felt entitled to some commensurate position himself. In June 1796 he wrote to his father asking if he could be promoted to Head of the Admiralty, either as First Lord, or in any other way which His Majesty might consider becoming of the son of a king of Great Britain. He may have considered that a political role was more suitable than a fighting command. Throughout these years, he continued to receive automatic promotion in rank, and in 1798 he was made an Admiral. However, this did nothing to increase his already slender chances of active employment.

In March 1801 William Pitt resigned as prime minister, to be succeeded by Henry Addington, Viscount Sidmouth. When the time came for the new ministry to appoint a new First Lord of the Admiralty, it was expected that the most likely candidates would be the Duke of Clarence and the Marquess of Buckingham. Nevertheless, the choice fell upon the Earl of St Vincent instead.

Despite this setback, the Duke of Clarence continued to hope that some fitting reward would be found for him, in the form of official employment, but for this he would have to wait some twenty years. It was as well for his peace of mind that he and his wife, in all but name, were able to lead a relatively contented, peaceful life at Bushy with their ever-growing family, without the distractions of being called to fight for his country. Mrs Jordan continued her career on the stage out of necessity, and he undoubtedly lived largely off her money for some time. 'Mrs Jordan is getting both fame and money,' he wrote to his bank, Thomas Coutts, in October 1797; 'to her I owe very much, and lately she has insisted on my accepting four and twenty hundred which I am to repay as I think proper.'[10] Perhaps pride prevented Dorothy from being able to consider retiring and relying on his income, although he remained as much a spendthrift as ever. However, she was also determined to do her best for her three eldest daughters when the time came, and ensure that she would be able to provide a generous dowry for them as well. She and the duke were always conscientious, devoted parents to the children they had together, and observers noted with approval what a contented family they made.

Increasingly eccentric, he never failed to speak his mind in public, and not without frequent embarrassment to some of those around him. Any political reputation he might have had was not helped by his confused, ill-thought-out interjections in the House of Lords, where his appearances attracted much attention. When William Wilberforce, Member of Parliament for Yorkshire, introduced the Slave Trade Bill to abolish what many regarded as a barbarous and degrading practice, William's speech brought him much criticism. To a later age, such an attitude is regarded as inhumane beyond measure, but his views should be seen in the context of the time in which he lived, and he was not by any means alone in his opinions. During his time in Jamaica and other outposts of the Empire he had seen during his naval days, he had formed the opinion that a steady supply of slave labour was essential to the economy of the island. A sudden termination of the practice, he argued, would not merely imperil the Government's investment, but also destroy the livelihood of those it had planned to assist. He was convinced that the slaves were happy, contented and well cared for, and that most of the planters who were responsible for their well-being were aware of their obligations to ensure that they were properly cared for.

His apparent blindness to the more distasteful aspects of such activity was an unwelcome reflection on his attitude, but like many of his class he was woefully ignorant of the degrading conditions in which slaves were kept. Moreover, as a senior officer of the royal navy, he maintained that a strong navy in wartime depended on a strong merchant fleet during peacetime, and that the prosperity of the trade was largely reliant on the merchant navy. When the bill was debated in the House of Lords in April 1793, he asserted that the proposal to put an end to a business that had been so beneficial to the country had been '*philosophised* by those new-fangled principles of liberty, which had deluged Europe with blood' and the promoters of abolition 'were either fanatics or hypocrites; and in one of these classes he ranked Mr Wilberforce.[11]

His participation in other debates in the Lords suggests that on other issues his outlook was relatively liberal. In April 1800 a debate had been held on a Divorce Bill moved by William Eden, Baron Auckland, to prevent anyone who had been divorced for adultery from marrying the other guilty party. The duke spoke firmly against it; to him, an adulterer was 'an insidious and designing villain, who would ever be held in disgrace and abhorrence by an enlightened and civilised society',[12] but that did not alter the fact that the woman in such a situation was thus left with no alternative but suicide or prostitution. He said he did not believe the bill would do anything to suppress the vice it was intended to suppress, but on the contrary would only encourage it. If it could help discourage 'a growing and a lamentable evil' nobody in the House could give it more wholehearted support than him. It would, however, merely 'add to the misery and the misfortunes of the unfortunate female', while doing nothing to discourage the male. By passing a law to prevent the parties from marrying, 'that only reparation which the seducer could make; that reparation which, since there was still some virtue and honour left in him, he might wish to make [for] the poor female would be denied, were the present measure adopted'.[13]

It was fortunate for the Duke of Clarence that he was able to occupy himself with such matters from time to time. He did not always have the gift of expressing himself succinctly, although when he made contributions to debates on issues of the day, his views were always passionately held and he possessed a great deal of common sense, but at heart he yearned to return to active service with the navy. During the temporary lull in hostilities with France as a result of the Treaty of Amiens, signed in March 1802, which brought about the end of what became known as the French revolutionary wars, he travelled to Sweden, Denmark and Russia with Captain Thomas Baker. The European peace lasted only for a year before Britain found herself at war again with Napoleon Bonaparte and the French empire, but the duke's hopes of a suitable fighting role commensurate with his status were not to be realized.

Nevertheless, he followed the course of Britain's role with interest. Like the rest of the nation, he rejoiced at the victory of the Battle of Trafalgar, in October 1805, but was deeply grieved when news reached England that Admiral Nelson had been fatally wounded on board ship in the fighting. He attended the funeral at St Paul's Cathedral in January 1806 alongside the Prince of Wales, and the Dukes of Kent, Cumberland and Sussex, and burst into tears during the obsequies for the man he had known and greatly respected as an old friend.

By the end of 1810, the state of King George III's health was to bring about changes for the family, and not necessarily for the better. The health of his youngest daughter, Amelia, had always been poor. She had never really recovered from a severe attack of measles in 1808, and shortly afterwards the doctors diagnosed pulmonary tuberculosis. Her father had always been particularly devoted to her, and when it was evident that she seemed to be fading fast, he was inconsolable. By the summer of 1810 everyone knew she did not have long to live, and all the doctors could do was try to make her as comfortable as they could, during what little time she had left. The king was now aged seventy-two, his behaviour was increasingly odd and his eyesight was deteriorating. His grasp on reality was faltering, and the family were horrified at the change in him.

Although the Duke of Clarence had often chafed at parental authority, he had always been devoted to his father, and he was profoundly moved by the changes in him. In October he wrote to his eldest son George that it was 'impossible to know the King and not to love him'. After spending a little time with him, he reported that the elder man's conversation 'was perfection itself, and I wish the whole world could have heard it'.[14]

Nevertheless, there was no disguising the decline in the mental health of King George III. His family and entourage knew that Amelia would not last long and feared that he would take the news of her death very badly when it came. She died on 2 November, aged twenty-seven, and not for another nine days could they bring themselves to tell him the sad news. He took it better than they had expected, and assured people at court that she could be brought to life again. Later he told everyone that she was living in Hanover, where she would always be well and never grow older. It was as if, in his confused mind, the German ancestral home which he had never visited, had become a synonym for heaven.

King George III was never the same man after the death of his youngest daughter, and from then on, the decline in his mental health was noticeable. Within a few weeks he was considered incapable of governing, and unlikely to recover. Early in the new year of 1811 the Government decided to introduce a Regency Bill with restrictions, which would lapse if the king had not made a full recovery within twelve months, as they had come close to doing at the time of the king's previous severe illness in 1788. On 6 February 1811 the Prince of Wales took the oaths of office as Regent, thus formally assuming charge of the Government, in place of his father.

Chapter 3

The Regency

Now that his eldest brother, the Prince of Wales, held the reins of power, the Duke of Clarence may have been hoping for the additional responsibilities and commensurate financial reward to which he felt he was entitled. These would surely come to him under a new, more sympathetic regime than that of their father. As a young man he had held the Tories responsible for thwarting some of his aspirations, such as not granting him a command or commands during the wars against Napoleon, for which he felt he was well suited, and also for delaying his dukedom. By default, he looked more benignly on the Whigs, whom he thought might prove more amenable. He was sure that the Prince Regent and sovereign-in-waiting would dispense with the Tories in government and favour the opposition, but this did not happen. It was perhaps partly as a result of this that what had always been a strong relationship between the first and third brothers began to weaken. From then on William would be seen less often at Carlton House with the Prince Regent, his friends and associates, and would spend more time at Bushy.

This was not the only imminent change ahead in the life of the Duke of Clarence. Mrs Jordan was now relatively wealthy, but only because she had been obliged to commit herself to a demanding schedule as a busy actress, between her regular pregnancies. She was committed to help maintain the man who had become her husband in all but name, in the style to which he was accustomed, and also to provide for her ever-demanding children, several of whom had clearly inherited their father's spendthrift outlook.

The birth in January 1796 of his niece, Princess Charlotte, only child of the Prince Regent and his wife, Caroline, had moved him as well as the Duke of York one place further down in the order of succession to the throne. Like most other Englishmen, he assumed that in due course Princess Charlotte would marry and help to perpetuate the dynasty, thus making him unlikely to inherit his father's crown at home. The Prince Regent's marriage had been little short of a disaster for Caroline, one of his Brunswick cousins, an unladylike figure whose boisterous manners, poor dress sense and scant attention to personal hygiene made her the very opposite of what her husband expected in a female companion. Most of the rest of his family were similarly unimpressed by her, although they felt that the Prince of Wales should have made more of an effort to accommodate his wife and try to accept her shortcomings as something to be endured. He had behaved very unwisely, the Duke of Clarence admitted in 1796, having 'married a foolish, disagreeable woman, but he should not have treated her as he has done, but made the best of a bad bargain as my father had done'.[1] Queen Charlotte had proved an acceptable bargain, the cynics felt, but the niece who had also become her daughter-in-law never did. Ironically, some were sure that it was the Duke of Clarence who had first suggested the marriage in the first place, on the grounds that 'it would plague the Duke and Duchess of York, whom he hates, and whom the Prince [of Wales] no longer likes'.[2]

In Hanover, where the Salic Law barred a princess from succeeding, it was a different matter entirely. For this reason, and as the Duke and Duchess of York were still childless after almost twenty years of marriage, which was unlikely to change, William knew that one day he might be obliged to find a more suitable partner. She would almost certainly have to be an eligible European Protestant princess. A wealthy heiress would suit him ideally, if was not for the fact that he could hardly disobey the terms of the Royal Marriage Act and marry a commoner. From that time on, the idea gradually took hold in his mind that it would be advisable to find himself an officially-approved wife. What hastened a solution to the issue was the matter of his debts, not only in terms of maintaining a lifestyle that befitted a senior son of the monarch, but also the wearisome business of providing for ten adult children and their ever-growing demands. His eldest son George, who had served with distinction in the army during the Peninsula War, had developed a taste for drinking and gambling and was more than a little disconcerted to find that many of his fellow-officers, despite not being of royal blood, had more plentiful incomes than he did. He demanded more money from his father, who had to remind him sternly that he had nine siblings, all of whom had to be provided for as well. Even though he was the king, he had made great sacrifices and was ready to make more, but there were limits to what the prince and his brothers could expect.

In June 1811 the duke attended a fete at Carlton House to which Mrs Jordan had not been invited, as she was on a provincial tour at the time. Also in attendance was Miss Catherine Tylney-Long, an attractive, vivacious lady who was young enough to be his daughter. According to contemporaries she was not particularly intelligent, but was reputed to have an annual income of at least £40,000 from her family, as well as about £300,000 in her bank account. Having made her acquaintance and found her pleasing as a personality, the duke then discovered that not only was she one of the wealthiest heiresses in the country, but she was also under the guardianship of her aunt, Lady de Crespigny. He accordingly opened negotiations with the latter through an intermediary. Before long he found to his chagrin that she would never consent to becoming his mistress, and certainly not while he was living with Mrs Jordan and their family of ten. He assured the young woman that the Prince Regent intended to withdraw all restrictions on royal marriages as soon as he had the authority to do so. If he had ever really believed such a thing, it was a pious hope that would never be realized. Miss Tylney-Long soon put an end to any hopes he might have entertained when she became betrothed to William Wellesley-Pole, a nephew of the Duke of Wellington.

Meanwhile, Mrs Jordan remained on tour in the provinces. While she was probably unaware of the imminent changes to her destiny, she was plainly aggrieved at receiving no letters from other members of her family. Ageing and exhausted, she was also increasingly weary with her profession, 'this disagreeable drudgery'. To the Duke of Clarence, she wrote resignedly that she believed 'when I am out of the gate at Bushy Park I am very soon *forgot*. Well, I cannot help it – it is only a continuation of my strange fate'.[3]

Her strange fate was not destined for a happy ending. Two months later, while at Cheltenham on another provincial tour, she was handed a letter from the duke, asking her to meet him at Maidenhead so they could discuss terms of separation. It was a profound shock. During her performance in the play in which she was appearing that night, at one point she was supposed to laugh uncontrollably, to which another character would respond that the conjurer 'has not only made you drunk, but he has made you laughing drunk'. When they reached that moment of the drama, instead of laughing she wept bitterly. As a result, the actor swiftly improvised, 'The conjurer has not only made thee drunk, he has made thee *crying* drunk.'[4] Although she was deeply distressed, she could see matters from the duke's point of view. Money, or the want of it, she wrote to her friend, James Boaden, a playwright and in time her first biographer, 'made HIM at this moment the most *wretched* of MEN'.[5] A deed of separation was drawn up on 23 December 1811, a day before the duke became an Admiral of the Fleet, and Dorothy Jordan left Bushy a month later, to install herself in a house in Cadogan Place.

It was followed by a settlement drawn up in January 1812 by which she was given an annual allowance of £1,500, plus £600 towards a house and coach, and £800 for her daughters by her two previous liaisons. An additional £1,500 was provided for the maintenance of her youngest daughters, but in the event of her returning to the stage, she would forfeit this sum, and the daughters would return to their father's custody. Yet she never allowed one word of criticism to pass her lips. The duke, she always maintained, magnanimously, had done wrong and was now suffering for his actions. Yet for some years, the British newspapers were full of invective against the royal prince who had treated her so ungallantly. He had lived on her earnings and now, it was asserted, he was choosing to fling her aside to fend for herself when she could no longer earn her (and his) keep.

The duke's conduct in terminating his liaison with her was not easy to excuse, but as with his views on the slave trade, it was understandable and unexceptional in the light of conventions of the time. The role of a royal mistress was never meant to be a permanent arrangement, until death removed one of the partners, but strictly temporary; the duke and the actress were doing no more than conforming to the expected standard, and he was as generous in terminating the matter as he could afford to be. William was almost certainly not aware of the true, pitiful state of her finances and subsequent living conditions. Always a kindly man by nature, had he realized how badly off she was, it was unlikely that he would not have made some effort to ameliorate matters. He had undoubtedly assumed that certain persons in his employ would have kept him informed, and if so, they shared at least some of the blame for Dorothy's subsequent hardship.

By this time, he had thrown himself with enthusiasm into a series of brief, doomed courtships with English aristocratic ladies and foreign princesses. Spurned by all of them, he looked further afield and in 1813 he decided to offer himself to Grand Duchess Catherine, younger sister of Tsar Alexander I of Russia. At twenty-five, she was a widow whose brief marriage to George, Duke of Oldenburg, had ended with his death from typhoid fever the previous year and left her with two small sons.

At the end of 1813 William had requested permission to be allowed to visit the British army, who were fighting in the Low Countries, and the Prime Minister, Lord Liverpool, could see no reason why not. This was in fact something of a smokescreen for William's journey to Holland in January 1814, with the full approval of the Prince Regent, to go and meet Catherine at The Hague. He was full of confidence and wrote to John Bourke, Earl of Mayo, 'Nothing that is human is certain: but from the favourable state of affairs in Russia and the good understanding between the Prince Regent and the Emperor Alexander, there is every probability of my marriage taking place.'[6]

While in Holland, for a brief moment he found himself very near the battlefront. While the British army under Sir Thomas Graham was engaged in driving the French army out of the Netherlands, the Duke of Clarence climbed up a church steeple to watch the bombardment of Antwerp. The church was struck by several shells, and he narrowly missed being hit himself when a bullet pierced his coat. To his delight when the Dutch soldiers saw how close he had come to being wounded himself, they treated him like a hero.

It was an unexpected adventure, but the same good fortune would prove lacking in his attempts to woo Grand Duchess Catherine. He thought that she seemed pleased with him at first, but everything began to unravel when the time came for him to escort her across the Channel to visit England. She was angry when she found there was no British ship of the line ready to take her, her suite of thirty-seven and her four carriages across the North Sea. When a vessel finally arrived, it was a single-masted cutter, hardly larger than a fishing boat and certainly beneath the dignity of the sister of the Tsar of Russia. He therefore had his own ship converted so as to provide her with a more fitting passage. She was mollified, but not for long. By the time she reached England, any ideas she may ever have entertained of his making a suitable husband had long since evaporated. She complained of 'the assiduities of the Duke of Clarence, of his vulgar familiarity, and of his want of delicacy,' and was repelled even more by the Prince Regent, whom she thought '*un voluptueux*'.[7]

Perhaps fortunately for William, before he had time to dwell on his disappointment, he was allowed to assume his naval career briefly, once again, at last. At the end of March, the allies entered Paris, the monarchy was restored with a Bourbon prince on the throne as King Louis XVIII, and the war with Napoleon was over. The duke was asked to escort the new sovereign to his kingdom, and on 23 April they set sail from Dover in the yacht *Royal Sovereign*, which flew the flag of the duke of Clarence. After this mission was accomplished he transferred his flag to the 98-gun HMS *Impregnable* in which he was ordered to collect the monarchs of the victorious alliance, Francis II, Emperor of Austria and Frederick William III, King of Prussia, and escort them to London for victory celebrations. For this, he had HMS *Impregnable* as his flagship with *Royal Sovereign* and another yacht, *Royal Charlotte*, as well as several Russian warships under his command. He was thrilled to be given such an important ceremonial task, and all went smoothly until the Admiralty countermanded an order he had given for fifty extra beds on board. To avoid having to subject his guests to the indignity of sleeping in hammocks, he had to send a cutter to collect the extra accommodation from Deal. Initially he planned to take his passengers there, but it was decided it would be too dangerous to put them ashore in boats, so they had to proceed to Dover instead where their carriages could wait on the quay and the Tsar's escort of Cossacks could be stabled at the local barracks.

The sovereigns arrived for the celebrations held in London in June, which lasted for several days, following which there was a naval review at Spithead. The Duke of Clarence, who had been created Admiral of the Fleet, or Commander-in-Chief of the Navy in 1811, hoisted his flag on HMS *Impregnable*, from which the Regent, Tsar and King of Prussia were to witness proceedings. As the duke came on board with his visitors, he saw something wrong with the top-gallant yard, and was not one to conceal his anger, particularly on such an important occasion and in front of such esteemed guests. Putting his hand to his mouth, he shouted out a stream of only too audible profanities to the sailors up there. Being ignorant of naval life, the Tsar and King thought this was part of the entertainment. The Regent, who was long since used to covering up for his brother at embarrassing moments, remarked solemnly, 'What a good sailor William is.'[8]

William's two eldest sons also heeded the call to serve their country. George and Henry FitzClarence had joined the army and served in the Peninsula War with some distinction. Unfortunately, they paid no heed to their father's advice that they should not regard themselves as privileged, should not expect to be promoted too quickly, and if they were patient their merits would be recognized and rewarded in due course. Having every confidence in their ability as junior officers, the young FitzClarences constantly chafed against their uncertain status and comparative poverty, surrounded as they were by more affluent officers with well-established families who had purchased their commissions for them. They did not appreciate that the highest powers in the land would resent their actions, interpreting such behaviour as brazen ambition by two spoilt young semi-royals who were nursing ideas evidently above their station.

Without giving thought to the inevitable consequences, they joined a group of officers of the Tenth Hussars who brought a series of accusations against their commanding officer, Colonel Sir George Quentin, for incompetence, misconduct, cowardice and neglect of duty, and failing to maintain proper discipline during the French campaign earlier in 1814. Quentin's court-martial that autumn was presided over by Frederick, Duke of York, as Commander-in-Chief of the British Army. He agreed with the Prince Regent that the real offence had not been committed by Colonel Quentin, but by the 'impudent young officers' who had brought these charges, which had evidently been invented by the latter in retaliation for Quentin's attempt to impose discipline on what he called disdainfully the 'aristocratic rabble' under his command. The Prince Regent and the Duke of York believed it was necessary to make an example of Quentin's accusers in order to discourage others from doing the same thing in future, and the two FitzClarence brothers and twenty-three other officers were ordered to return their swords, dismissed from the regiment and told that they would be duly appointed to different regiments of cavalry. Thoroughly disgraced, George and Henry contemplated leaving the army altogether, but the Prince Regent decided instead to send them to serve with the British forces in India for about four years. It was tantamount to temporary banishment, but less humiliating than dishonourable discharge. Fearful of offending his brothers and powerless to protest, the Duke of Clarence told his sons that India was a land of opportunity and could offer them both a golden future.

While they were in India their mother, Dorothy Jordan, was reaching the end of her unhappy road. Her allowance had proved inadequate for somebody as deeply in debt as she was, and depredations by two of her spendthrift sons-in-law only magnified her plight. In 1815 she found herself obliged to move to France in order to escape her creditors. She found lodgings near Paris, where she died alone in July 1816, aged fifty-four.

Her second son was not long in following her to the grave. Henry's health had never been robust, and in the summer of 1817 when it became apparent that he was suffering in the heat of the Indian climate, he was allowed to be sent home on compassionate grounds. The decision came too late and he succumbed to fever that September, the first of the FitzClarences to die. His commanding officer, fearing the possibility of another untimely death within the family, allowed George to travel back to England as soon as possible, and he returned in June 1818.

Meanwhile, William was continuing in his quest for a suitable wife. It was suggested, perhaps by the Prince Regent, that he ought to consider his cousin Sophia, daughter of the Duke of Gloucester and Edinburgh, the late younger brother of King George III. William liked her as a person but she had no enthusiasm for such a match. Moreover, at the age of forty-two she was unlikely to bear him a child. Even if she was to have a son, he would not be able to succeed his father as King of Hanover, as her mother was a commoner by birth, having been an illegitimate daughter of the politician Sir Edward Walpole. Under these circumstances, he wrote to his brother, he could see no advantage in such a marriage. He was transparently honest in his matrimonial aims; his sole purpose for finding a wife was to beget an heir to the throne, and secure a parliamentary grant. Not for the first time, he tried to woo Miss Mercer Elphinstone, then aged twenty-seven and a close friend and confidante of Princess Charlotte of Wales, the Prince Regent's daughter. When she heard about William's intentions, Charlotte responded indignantly to Miss Elphinstone that '[his] conduct to *you* is just what it *ever* is, ungentlemanlike and blackguard. It is not worth thinking or caring for a second. He deserves being treated with due contempt'.[9]

Some thought that William gave the impression of being obsessed with his pursuit of a wife, until gossips whispered behind his back that soon his father's 'mad' doctors might find they had another patient from the family on their hands. In August 1815 he had been among the guests at the wedding of Ernest, Duke of Cumberland, who was fifth in line to the throne, William being fourth at the time, which might have provided him with additional thoughts of marriage. Ernest's choice of a bride, his cousin Frederica of Mecklenburg-Strelitz, had been controversial. She was already twice married and twice widowed, and had been on the point of divorcing her second husband, Frederick William of Solms-Braunfels (whom she was obliged to marry when seven months pregnant with his child), until alcoholism brought about his early death. Moreover, a year after her first husband had suddenly died, she had become unofficially engaged to the Duke of Cambridge, and then suddenly ended their relationship. While Queen Charlotte admitted to her brother Charles that she preferred her niece to be a widow rather than a divorced woman,[10] she made it plain to Ernest that the unfavourable publicity in England caused by her breaking off the engagement placed her 'under the disagreeable necessity of refusing to receive her'. She could not 'but rejoice' that the princess would not be accompanying him to England,[11] and on no account would she consent to the marriage or attend the wedding of this daughter-in-law whom she considered had behaved so badly.

Accordingly, the hopes of the dynasty rested on Princess Charlotte, the only legitimate grandchild of King George III and Queen Charlotte. On 2 May 1816, at the age of twenty, she married Prince Leopold of Saxe-Coburg-Saalfeld at a ceremony held at Carlton House. Among the royal guests present were the Dukes of Clarence, York and Kent, and it was to the former that the honour fell of escorting his niece to the altar, where she was received and then given away by the Prince Regent. Although she had often been less than complimentary about her uncle William in correspondence with her friends, he had always remained very fond of her and thought she had managed remarkably well, despite a difficult childhood with divided loyalties to parents who genuinely hated each other. She had grown into a very level-headed, vivacious young princess. The young couple settled at Claremont House, near Esher.

When the wedding took place, Charlotte was second in succession to the throne after her father, the Prince of Wales, who was unlikely to have any further children. It was assumed that she and Leopold would soon have a family of their own. Should this not be the case, her heirs would be her uncles, Frederick and then William, but few people – themselves included – thought their chances of becoming Kings of England were likely. It could not be taken for granted that the royal dukes would all live to a ripe old age. Although his life was not thought to be in danger, in the summer of 1817 the Duke of Clarence was ill with a particularly bad bout of asthma, as well as gout and suspected food poisoning. However, he had recovered in time for the dinner to celebrate his fifty-second birthday in August, given by Queen Charlotte at Frogmore.

During the first few months of her marriage to Leopold, the younger Charlotte had two miscarriages. Yet time was on her side and everyone, not least she and her husband, assumed that an heir would soon be forthcoming. The following year she was expecting again and her impending confinement was to be in the autumn of 1817, but the joy of the family and nation alike at a new prince or princess in the next generation was about to be shattered.

On the evening of 5 November, she produced a stillborn son, yet far worse was to come. The Duke of Clarence and Queen Charlotte were together at Bath the following day where they had been invited to a reception by the Mayor and Corporation, to be followed by a banquet given in their honour that evening. Shortly before members of the Corporation were presented to the Queen, a messenger arrived with the news that the expected newly-born heir had been stillborn, but it was assumed that the young mother would recover. Although everyone present was deeply affected, they decided to proceed with the banquet as arranged. As the tables were about to be cleared, one of Queen Charlotte's pages arrived and handed a letter to the doctor, Sir Henry Halford. He passed it immediately to the Duke of Clarence who struck his forehead as he read it and then hurried from the room, a look of utter despair on his face. The princess had become seriously ill and had died, early that morning. Once the full distressing news was known to the main dignitaries, the Marquis of Camden, Recorder of the City, in a faltering voice, proposed the suspension of any further entertainment, and within seconds the Guildhall was empty.[12]

This tragedy left George III without any legitimate grandchildren to inherit the throne, after his by now middle-aged sons, made the prospect of a suitable marriage essential for the Duke of Clarence and his still unofficially married brothers. After having already experienced several rejections, it was clear that his prospects were not good, but the duty still lay before him. The next English heiress who came within his sights was a Miss Sophia Wykeham, and although she appeared respectable enough, the Prince Regent and the Government likewise thought she would not be suitable, and they forbade the match. (When he became king, William created her a peeress in her own right with the title Baroness Wenman, and she died unmarried in 1870.) William knew that it was almost impossible for either the Prince Regent and the Duke of York, the only people who stood between him and the throne, at the time, to leave an heir that would displace him in the succession.

At once, the other members of the family and the Government began to look carefully at such eligible unmarried princesses as there were in the royal and ducal houses of Europe, for the duke and his still unmarried brothers, particularly the Dukes of Kent and Cambridge. William knew there was no choice but to acquiesce in any plans being made for him, but not unconditionally. In December he wrote to Queen Charlotte, stating his terms. Should the cabinet consider his marriage to anybody of consequence, he stated, they ought to inform him what provision there would be for his establishment. With several children who were entirely dependent on him, and with his existing debts plus the interest payable on them, it was impossible for him to consider marriage without knowing beforehand what the financial settlement would be. Lord Liverpool accordingly proposed that the duke's parliamentary grant should be raised from £18,000 to £40,000 a year, and that parliament would provide £22,000 for outfit upon his marriage and also cancel £17,000 pounds of his debts.

Marie of Hesse-Cassel and a princess from Denmark were both considered as brides for the Duke of Clarence, but no betrothals followed. During the winter of 1817 the Duke of Cambridge, who had recently been appointed Viceroy of Hanover and was now living there as representative of the Prince Regent, was also in search of a bride and sent home a description of Marie's younger sister, Augusta. To a friend, he wrote that Princess Augusta would make an ideal Queen of England, and as his brother William was much more likely to reign in England than he ever was, he considered it his duty to the nation, as well as to his brother, that William should have 'the first opportunity of making his advances'. When the Duke of Clarence was told, he was at first rather puzzled and then burst out laughing, and he told the others that Adolphus was in love with her himself. 'I'll write and tell him to take her, bless him!'[13] When it was again pointed out to him what a suitable Duchess of Clarence Augusta would surely make, he observed that queens were not easily chosen, especially for thrones such as that of England. But it would be easier to find a future queen than to chance upon the one and only mate for any particular human being, so Adolphus would have her if she would have him. Adolphus accordingly 'took her' and they went to the altar in May 1818.

By that time, an appropriate lady had been chosen in the plain but gentle-natured Princess Adelaide of Saxe-Meiningen, who was twenty-seven years younger than William. She had been brought up in a small German duchy, covering a little more than 400 square miles, but it was probably the most liberal of the German states. Her father, George, who succeeded his childless brother Charles as Duke in 1782, was a learned and enlightened ruler, who published philosophical treatises under a pseudonym, took a passionate interest in education, and opened the ducal library to the public. He died suddenly of a fever in 1803 when Adelaide, his elder surviving daughter, was only eleven years old, leaving his widow, Louise Eleonore, to rule as Regent until their only son, Bernhard, attained his majority. The family were never prosperous, and a man who had seen the room in which Adelaide spent her childhood had said that he would not kennel his dog there.[14] It may have been a humble upbringing, but despite losing her father at such an early age, Adelaide had a happy childhood as part of a very close family.

On 21 March 1818 William wrote to his eldest son, George FitzClarence, that he could at last reveal to him who was going to become the Duchess of Clarence. 'It is to be the Princess of Saxe-Meiningen, whose *beauty* and *character* are *universally* acknowledged. She is doomed *poor, dear, innocent young* creature to be my wife. I *cannot,* I *will not,* I *must not* ill use her ....'[15]

Although Lord Liverpool had rashly promised the duke a greatly increased income on his marriage, his ministers had other ideas. George Canning, President of the Board of Control, told parliament that the duke would not have thought of contracting such a marriage had he not been obliged to do so as an act of public duty. Aware that parliament was in no mood to countenance large expenditure, he reduced a proposed increase to £10,000 a year, but when several backbenchers protested, it was cut further to £6,000. Grossly insulted, the duke claimed that such an increase was so irrelevant to his needs that he intended to refuse it altogether, and the marriage as well. Viscount Castlereagh, Leader of the House of Commons, then informed the House that all hope of the marriage was over.

However, when William heard that the diffident Princess Adelaide (perhaps less than confident of attracting a more dashing suitor) was unwilling to give up her chance of marriage, and upon being told that the reports of her character had not been exaggerated and she really would make a gentle, home-loving wife, he was persuaded to reconsider. A Duchess of Clarence who would also willingly accept his family as her stepchildren surely would be a rare find. His description of her as 'beautiful' was an exaggeration, but with regard to devotion to duty, and, above all, when it came to proving a loyal wife, her future husband could hardly have wished for more. Beneath the gentle exterior was a firm, steady character with great capacity for affection, loyalty, kindness and devotion to duty. Moreover, Bushy had become much less homely since the departure and death of Dorothy Jordan, and a wife and helpmeet would surely suit him very well. William had searched high and low, met with several rejections, and at his time of life he knew this might be his last chance.

Even so, he approached the wedding in a sombre frame of mind. Far from enthusiastically making preparations to cross the North Sea in order to meet his future bride, he stayed in England, while Adelaide and her mother made the journey and installed themselves at Grillon's Hotel, Albemarle Street, London. Their initial reception was anything but hospitable, as only the proprietor was ready to welcome them. The first member of the royal family to come and make their acquaintance in person was the Prince Regent. He arrived that evening after dinner, and a little later the Duke of Clarence joined them. Mother and daughter had travelled from their duchy across the North Sea for several days and both were tired as well as uncomfortable at finding themselves in a land they did not know at all. For Adelaide, meeting her future husband for the very first time in such circumstances must have been a daunting prospect.

William was doubtless quite ill at ease himself, and although none of those present left any impressions of the meeting, it cannot have been a comfortable occasion for any of them. The general impression, based partly on hearsay and the considered, if not necessarily accurate, impressions of subsequent diarists and such biographers who have dared to speculate on the basis of slender evidence, is that Adelaide differed considerably from his expectations. She was small, slight, modestly dressed, graceful and apprehensive, as different from the buxom, self-assured and outgoing Dorothy Jordan as it was possible to be. Yet she was also quiet (although overawed might be a better word), attentive, and above all spoke very good English. William's command of foreign languages was almost non-existent, apart from some indelicate French phraseology.[16] Neither of them had any illusions about the future; this was strictly the most arranged of arranged royal marriages. How confident William was at coming face to face at last with the person whom he had written of in unintentionally comic terms as this '*poor, dear, innocent young creature*' can hardly be imagined. He knew that he was generally regarded as the ugliest and least sophisticated of his father's sons, and the thought may have crossed his mind that he was not worthy of her, or, perhaps, she of him.

Seven days later, the marriages of the Dukes of Clarence and Kent took place. A double wedding was to have been celebrated on 11 July at Kew Palace, where the increasingly infirm Queen Charlotte had been staying for the last few weeks and was now too unwell to travel any further distance. As she was ill on the proposed date it was postponed, but two days later she was well enough to attend.

A temporary chapel was arranged for the purpose in the drawing room on the first floor of the Dutch House, where an altar covered with crimson velvet, adorned with large Communion plates borrowed from the Chapel Royal and Whitehall Chapel, and four velvet cushions, was put in front of the fireplace. The service, printed in English and German, had been shortened for the queen's benefit. The royal family began to assemble at three o'clock in the afternoon. They included the Duke of York, the Dukes and Duchesses of Cambridge (married only a few weeks earlier), and Gloucester, Princess Sophia of Gloucester, the bride's mother Louise, Dowager Duchess and Regent of Saxe-Meiningen, and Frederick, Landgrave of Hesse-Cassel, father of the new Duchess of Cambridge.

The political presence was restricted to the Earl of Liverpool, the Earl of Eldon, Lord Chancellor and Viscount Sidmouth, the Home Secretary, and clergy to the Archbishop of Canterbury and the Bishop of London. A little later, Queen Charlotte was brought into the room by the Prince Regent and took her place to the right of the altar. Adelaide wore a robe of silver tissue trimmed with Brussels lace and silver tassels, fastened at the waist with a diamond clasp, and a wreath of diamonds as a head-dress, while the Duchess of Kent wore a dress of gold tissue. Both brides were given away by the Prince Regent. They knelt to receive the blessing of their mother-in-law, who answered in a cracked, unemotional voice, and signed the registers, it was noted, with a firm hand. She retired to her boudoir as soon as she could afterwards, leaving the rest of the family party to a large dinner presided over by the Regent, with turtle and other soups, fish and venison, followed by several varieties of fruit for dessert.

After the meal the Kents left for Claremont, while the rest of the royal party drove in open carriages to Kew Cottage, where they drank tea until they dispersed. William had assumed that his mother-in-law would be spending the night at Kew, but as Queen Charlotte had not invited her, she accompanied the young couple when they retired for the night to his quarters at St James's Palace.

As yet William and Adelaide hardly knew each other, having met each other only once before the ceremony. Yet both were determined to make a success of the marriage, and against all the odds it proved to be one of the most successful of matches, lasting until the bridegroom's death a little less than nineteen years later. Two days after the wedding the Prince Regent called upon them in their London home and found them sitting together 'just like Darby and Joan'. It gradually became evident to William that his new wife was every bit as home-loving and domestically minded as he was. The prince, whom his family and closest associates had long known as an impetuous, sometimes hard-drinking and foul-mouthed sailor, was now about to mellow almost beyond recognition. Being more than prepared to settle down, he could not have found a better partner, notwithstanding the disparity in their ages.

The only great disadvantage was that, as the House of Commons had declined to grant him the financial settlement he had expected, the duke felt that he would be unable to live in England in a style that befitted his status as one of the king's elder sons. It would therefore be necessary to move to the continent for a year or two, and the only logical place was Hanover, the ancestral home in which he had spent such a tedious existence as a young man. Adolphus, Duke of Cambridge, was settled and living in the official palace, and William would be obliged to yield precedence to him on official occasions.

Later in August, the newly-married couple left to settle in Hanover for a few months. The Duke of Clarence had indignantly refused the meagre increase of £6,000 in his allowance on the grounds that it was niggardly, and they settled at Fürstenhof, Hanover, where they spent much of the first year of their marriage. This was done largely for reasons of economy and to escape his creditors, and with a less eventful social life, their finances soon improved. After a few months the duchess was known to be with child. They had intended to return to London for the birth, as the duke thought it only right that a child directly in line of succession to the English throne should be born in the kingdom. However, the duchess was warned that her health and that of the unborn child would not be equal to a journey across the North Sea.

The baby was due in April, and a couple of weeks earlier she went for a walk in the garden where she caught a cold that turned into pleurisy. Her doctors accordingly prescribed a course of bleeding that resulted in a premature delivery. Early in the morning of 26 March 1819 she gave birth to a daughter, whom they immediately named Charlotte Augusta. It was immediately apparent that she was very sickly and unlikely to survive, and she was baptised at once. She died a few hours later and was laid to rest beside the body of her ancestor, King George I, in the palace crypt. For several days, the life of the gravely weakened duchess was also in some danger.

She recovered slowly but surely, and by August 1819 they knew that she was expecting again. The duke decided that this time the child should certainly be born in England. On their way back, they paid visits to the duke's sisters, Elizabeth in Hesse-Homburg and Charlotte in Württemberg, and to the duchess's mother in Ghent. Unfortunately, the protracted journey was uncomfortable and proved too demanding for the duchess in her condition. When they reached Calais in September she miscarried, and on their arrival at Dover on the 22nd it was decided that they should spend about six weeks at Walmer Castle so that she would have time to convalesce and rest properly after her ordeal.

An anonymous correspondent's letter, published in *The Times* in October, commented approvingly on their homely existence in the town, leading very retired lives and seeing little or no company. It was noted that 'a very plain carriage and a pair of horses constitute the whole of their equipage, and even of this they make very little use. They walk almost daily through the town and its vicinity, dressed in the simplest style.' The duchess's main female companion was a young German countess of about her own age. Her main mode of travel was either riding on a donkey, or in a little carriage built by a local tradesman that was named the *Clarence Fly*. Her main recreation was sea bathing, 'in which she appears to take the light; her health also appears to be greatly benefitted by it,' and even 'the roughest and most blowing weather' did not keep her out of the water.[17] On their way from Dover back to London, they broke the journey by paying a visit to Canterbury Cathedral and inspecting the engineering works under construction at Chatham. They returned to St James's Palace in the middle of November.

Despite the Duchess of Clarence's sad inability to produce a living child, the year 1819 had been a year of births for the family. On 26 March the Duchess of Cambridge had a son, George, at Hanover, while on 24 May Victoria, daughter of the Duchess of Kent, was born at Kensington Palace. Three days later George, destined to be the last King of Hanover, completed the trio of royal babies when he was born to the Duchess of Cumberland at Berlin. He proved a particular source of joy to his parents, as his mother had produced nine children altogether by her two previous husbands, followed by two stillborn daughters since her marriage to the Duke of Cumberland.

Yet these additions to the family came between two years of deaths. On 17 November 1818 Queen Charlotte died at the age of seventy-four, her hand in that of the Prince of Wales. The Duke of York and their sisters, Mary, Duchess of Gloucester and the unmarried Augusta, were also present. Later, only a few days into the new year of 1820, the family were shocked to learn that the Duke of Kent, who had often boasted that he would outlive his brothers, was seriously ill. He, the duchess and their baby daughter, Victoria, had been staying at Sidmouth on the coast of Devon during Christmas and into the new year, when he had caught pneumonia which rapidly worsened. The Duke of Kent died on 23 January 1820.

By this time, the royal physicians in charge of King George III at Windsor Castle had reported that, without any apparent illness, at the age of eighty-one 'His Majesty appears declining fast'. The Duke of York, who had assumed responsibility for the care of his blind and deranged father, wrote to the Prince Regent on 20 January that he had become much worse in the last few days; 'the degree of weakness and languor in his looks and the emaciation of his face struck me more than I can describe'.[18] Six days after the death of the Duke of Kent, the pitiful existence of the sovereign came to an end, and the Prince Regent succeeded him as King George IV. Now aged 57, the new King George was not in the best of health. At this point, only his life and that of Frederick, Duke of York, stood between William, Duke of Clarence, and the English throne.

Chapter 4

Brother of the King

The accession of King George IV brought to a head the increasingly disturbing matter and behaviour of his estranged wife, now Queen Caroline. Now that she was no longer Princess of Wales, she could no longer be treated as a tiresome nuisance, best left to her own devices. She had spent the previous few years in Europe, attracting scandal wherever she went, but in June 1820 she returned to England to demand what she considered was now rightfully hers as the first lady of the kingdom. Up until that time the Duke of Clarence had kept his opinions of his sister-in-law and her actions to himself, and on the rare occasions when her name was mentioned, during the first few months of the reign of George IV, he had spoken of her in a friendly fashion. Yet from the moment she set foot on English soil once again, without hesitation he joined ranks with his brother. It was a display of solidarity with his sovereign that made him deeply unpopular.

The queen's Attorney-General, Lord Brougham, alleged that the Duke of Clarence had written to the captain on whose ship the then Princess Caroline had sailed, from England in 1814, that she and the Prince Regent would both be very glad if the captain himself was to attempt to seduce her during the voyage. It was an astonishing claim to make. Much as William privately might have deprecated the lack of moral compass of the Princess of Wales, with his sense of fair play it was most unlikely that he would have stooped to such depths. Brougham and her Solicitor-General, Lord Denman, both offered to prove the existence of the incriminating letter that testified to this suggestion, but the Secret Committee that had been set up to examine the pertinent evidence ruled that it was no business of theirs.

Thwarted, Denman had to content himself with an attack on the Duke of Clarence in the House of Lords. He claimed that certain people in the highest circles had been industriously circulating 'the most odious and atrocious calumnies'[1] against Her Majesty. Those who were present knew exactly to whom he was referring.

In July a Bill of Pains and Penalties was brought before parliament, to deprive the queen of her titles and dissolve her marriage to the king, on the grounds that she had committed adultery with Bartolomeo Pergami, 'a foreigner of low station', and thus forfeited her rights as queen consort. The politician and diarist, Thomas Creevey, noted that when the Duke of Clarence's name was called at the final reading, he leaned over the rail of the gallery 'and halloed 'Content!' with a yell that would have quite become a savage.'[2] Nevertheless, the king's action against his wife proved unsuccessful and the divorce was never granted. She considered herself fully vindicated and thus entitled to be crowned as queen when the time came. The coronation of King George IV was held in July 1821, and although she was advised to stay away she presented herself at Westminster Abbey, demanding admittance. Guards had been posted at every door, forewarned that she was likely to try to force an entrance, and refused to allow her entry. By this time she was already ill, and died a few weeks later, the probable cause being either cancer or an intestinal obstruction.

When the Duchess of Clarence became *enceinte* again, the physicians recommended that the couple should move from their draughty quarters at St James's Palace, so she could have her confinement at the more spacious Bushy with its country air. Although the house was indelibly associated with his life with Dorothy Jordan, the Duchess had transformed it into a homely dwelling for them both, and as they preferred it to London, they spent the majority of their time there. As she had promised at the time of their marriage, she made an admirable stepmother to the FitzClarences, and shared in William's pleasure when he became a grandfather for the first time.

Mary, wife of his eldest son, George, presented him with a daughter on 28 August 1820. The baby girl was named Adelaide in honour of William's wife. The Duchess of Clarence was also happy to join the guests who attended the wedding of the duke's third daughter, Elizabeth, to William Carr, Earl of Erroll at St George's Church, Hanover Square, on 4 December, although she was more than seven months pregnant at the time. The doctors had said that it would be inadvisable to travel in her condition, and she was forced to stay at St James's Palace for the birth.

Although William had been taking the greatest possible care of his wife, on 10 December she gave birth six weeks prematurely to a daughter, weighing nearly eleven pounds. Sir Henry Halford remarked rather coldly that the mother was a 'poor wishy-washy thing', yet he expected the baby would probably thrive as long as she could survive the dangerous first few weeks. The duchess was left in a delicate state of health after the birth, and for a while she was again in danger. Once she recovered, the papers were able to give the customary news that mother and infant were 'doing very well'.

The parents wanted to name the baby Georgina, but they deferred to the king's requests that she should be called Elizabeth instead. That Christmas was a happy one for them, and the baby princess seemed to thrive for the first few weeks. However, on 1 March 1821 she became feverish, and the doctors were called the following day. She became progressively weaker but there was nothing they could do, and on the morning of 4 March she died after suffering a convulsive fit. The Duchess of Clarence had been watching over her for most of the last distressing hours. She had left the room briefly and was called back just in time to see her baby take her last breath. Overcome with fatigue and shock, she fainted in her husband's arms. A post-mortem confirmed that the cause of death was 'an entanglement of the bowels'.

The Duke and Duchess had not yet given up all hope of parenthood. By autumn 1821 they knew she Duchess was expecting again, yet it all came to nothing when on 8 April 1822 she was delivered of twin sons, both stillborn. Her husband was just as broken-hearted as she was 'at these repeated misfortunes to this beloved and superior woman'.[3] These infant deaths darkened the lives of the Duke and Duchess of Clarence, yet their shared grief brought them closer together. All the family could see that since his marriage William had evidently mellowed into a much more sympathetic, more likeable character.

King George IV had given the impression that he resented the presence of his niece, Victoria of Kent, a reminder of the daughter whom he had so tragically lost in 1817. Princess Victoria would inherit the throne of Britain (but not of Hanover, where the Salic Law that barred women from succeeding to the crown was in force), if the Clarences had no surviving children. Yet the Duke and Duchess of Clarence were genuinely fond of the little girl. 'My children are dead,' the Duchess wrote sorrowfully to the Duchess of Kent, 'but your child lives, and she is mine too.'[4] While some might have seen such a comment as bordering on the possessive, such a trait had no place in the character of kindly Adelaide, and it was well-meant. She was aged thirty-seven when her husband ascended the throne and she became queen, and from time to time the papers speculated that she might be with child again. 'Damned stuff,' was William's bitter comment every time he saw such a report.

Since William had somewhat grudgingly agreed to marry on condition of a considerably increased allowance, and in furtherance of producing at least one heir to the throne, and that the marriage had succeeded in neither, he was all solicitude to his wife. As his twenty years with Dorothy Jordan had shown, he was more home-loving than most of his brothers and having a wife to help make home and hearth comfortable enough for the retired naval officer appealed strongly to his sense of domestic virtues, in which he greatly resembled his father. Early in the new reign, he swallowed his pride and accepted the £6,000 allowance that he had indignantly refused at first. It was backdated to 1818, so he found himself in receipt of an additional £18,000 that allowed him to settle some of his outstanding debts.

Though Adelaide was plain, prudish, and gave people the impression of being dull and lacking in personality, her gentle but firm influence on him had been all to the good. After having met the duke for dinner at Portsmouth, on an occasion in January 1822, Lord Lyttelton found it difficult to believe the change in him; 'To our astonishment [he] behaved perfectly well, was civil to everybody, even gentlemanlike in his manner, did not say a single indecent or improper thing.'[5] It was by no means an isolated occurrence, as other dignitaries who attended dinners at which William was a fellow guest noticed how quiet and well behaved he had become. They were sure that it was entirely because of his wife's influence. It was all the more remarkable as he was now in his mid-fifties, had not found it easy to change the habits of a lifetime and was still too readily inclined to say the first thing that came into his head, especially when his temper was aroused. Yet as a husband he had cleaned up his language considerably, and now he appreciated the importance of not offending other people's susceptibilities so much. From time to time his outbursts would still embarrass people, but much less frequently than before.

For a while William took hardly any part in public life. He spent most of his time with the duchess at Bushy Park or St James's, it was said, 'poring over naval histories, confusing the farm manager and playing Pope Joan for one-shilling stakes'. At home he regularly called on his brothers and sisters, and attended dinners as well as occasional functions in London, such as a visit to the Royal Academy which, with his total lack of interest in the arts, can have interested him but little. Neighbours and others who saw the couple together were very impressed by the change in him. He had become not only less uncouth but also less eccentric than formerly, ate and drank more sparingly, and was more conscientious about settling his debts promptly.

This middle-aged country gentleman, it was considered, had now become a model husband. Every day he maintained a strict routine, rising early and being dressed by seven o'clock in the morning. After breakfast he went for a walk, then spent two or three hours dealing with his correspondence, answering letters in his own hand. A close friend, Dr William Beattie, tried to persuade him that he did not need to do so much, to which he replied that it was important for him to keep up the practices, because one day, 'I may still have more occasion for it.' Luncheon comprised cold fowl, ham, veal or game. Later he would take another, generally longer walk, sometimes up to four hours long if the mood took him. Companions might innocently suggest a short walk with the duke and find themselves taken on an exhausting two-hour stride. He never ventured out in the rain without his galoshes, and in severe weather, he would pace briskly up and down the drawing room with the windows wide open. Dinner was generally a dish of roast or boiled mutton. He enjoyed sherry and wine, but his most regular drink was barley water and lemon. For most of the time his health was good, apart from pain in his legs which was probably gout, and an annual attack of asthma, which generally arrived to torment him at the end of May or early in June, sometimes quite severely.

During the first few years of his brother's reign the Duke and Duchess of Clarence paid three visits to Europe, mainly so they could visit members of their families, spending about three or four months there at a time. These generally passed without incident, and the most exciting thing that ever occurred was the odd minor carriage mishap which might mean a sharp intake of breath but from which they ultimately emerged unscathed. While travelling they ate as sparingly as ever, enjoying a breakfast consisting simply of tea and a slice of dry toast, a picnic of cold meat for luncheon, and a pot of green tea in place of dinner. The duke found little to interest him in the German resorts that the duchess enjoyed so much, but he took it all in his stride.

On the first of these continental excursions, during the summer of 1822, they called on his sister Charlotte, Queen of Württemberg, and she took them on various excursions. William Beattie was impressed by the memory recall of brother and sister, who were both in their late fifties but could still remember the exact day and month as well as the year on which various childhood happenings at Kew had taken place, so long before. 'This might appear unimportant to anyone not accustomed to place implicit reliance upon this faculty,' he wrote, 'but with these royal personages, the memory is almost an infallible book of reference.' An elderly admiral who dined with them at about this time said afterwards that he was astonished at the thorough knowledge which the duke retained of naval affairs, correct in every detail. He had often heard people mention His Royal Highness's excellent memory, but confessed he was not prepared to find that he still remembered every officer of a particular ship on which they had served some forty years before, and not only their names but also those of their family.

Whereas William formerly had been a spendthrift, getting through far more money than he had or could ever hope to afford, and giving the impression that he would meet the costs somehow, he now became slightly parsimonious. On their travels, Beattie noticed, 'he looks over all the accounts himself, sums up, calculates, adjusts, and compares, nicely balancing every item'.[6] In at least one instance, William was surprised to see the cost was much less than he had anticipated, and asked for it to be returned for correction. At around this time, he also acquired a London residence. Clarence House was built between 1825 and 1827 as the new home in the capital for the Duke and Duchess of Clarence, constructed in a somewhat cramped nook adjoining the west side of St James's in Stable Yard.

In August 1825, during one of the continental sojourns, William celebrated his sixtieth birthday. For the last few years, he and the duchess had led a relatively quiet, semi-retired life, but he could never refrain from thinking that before long the inheritance he had never imagined might be his, until less than a decade ago, would soon come to pass. King George IV was now an indolent, bloated recluse, suffering especially from severe attacks of breathlessness and increasingly dependent on large doses of laudanum. He was rarely seen in public and now spent most of his time at Windsor Castle, well away from the public gaze. By the summer of 1826 the Duke of York, who was first in succession to the throne, was also seriously ill, similarly overweight, racked with gout and dropsy, and the doctors warned that he was unlikely to last much longer. The king had always been fond of him and was not alone in his conviction that he would make a much better sovereign than their brother, the Duke of Clarence. Princess Dorothea von Lieven, wife of Prince Christopher von Lieven, the Russian ambassador in London, noted the king's misgivings as to the abilities of the man likely to succeed him. 'The Duke of Clarence will be a fine king!' she commented sarcastically to Prince Metternich, regarding the man whose red face she had likened to that of a frog's head carved on a coconut, adding that King George had told her at table a few days ago, 'Look at that idiot! They will remember me, if ever he is in my place.'[7] At the time, the king was arranging for a substantial payment to the Duke of Clarence from the privy purse, so there can have been no malice in his words, even if he seriously believed that Frederick would be a more worthy occupant of the throne.

The doctors were proved correct in supposing that England would not see the accession of a King Frederick. On New Year's Day in January 1827, the Dukes of Clarence and Sussex called upon Frederick for what they knew might be the last time. By then he had lost the power of speech and died four days later, aged sixty-three. While he was saddened at the loss of yet another brother, the Duke of Clarence could hardly pretend that he was not excited by the knowledge that now only one life stood between him and the throne. He made a shamelessly cheerful chief mourner at the funeral, speaking to everyone as if they were attending a dinner party or reception. Thomas Creevey, the

English politician and diarist, noticed that several peers were now paying more interest in and attention to the duke than they had in the past, as if looking to their own futures. At a gap in the proceedings, he turned to the Duke of Sussex, and remarked that now they would be treated 'very differently from what we have been'.[8] Sir Robert Peel, who was Home Secretary at the time, noted disapprovingly that William spoke to everyone around him much as usual, and at one stage asked the Marquess of Hertford 'how many head of game he had killed at Sudburn'.[9]

As king-in-waiting, William's financial position immediately had been improved. Lord Liverpool was in favour of substantially increasing his income and that of the duchess, who had been more responsible than anyone else for teaching him the value of money. The sums ultimately agreed by ministers fell short of these figures, but he was content with an additional £3,000 a year, and his wife an annual jointure of £6,000, which enabled him to reduce his debts still further. His financial position was more comfortable than it had been for some time. He had already been given the sinecure post of General of the Royal Marines, at £4,000 a year, some years earlier. After a decade of Adelaide's management, enhanced by these new provisions, he was able to reduce his debts accordingly. In terms of money values at the end of the twentieth century, the couple's joint income had risen to some £2,000,000 a year. Marriage had thoroughly domesticated William, and husband and wife were content to live quite frugally. Such a way of life was warmly appreciated and approved of by the Government of a nation that had been impoverished by years of war.

In February 1827 Lord Liverpool had a stroke. He managed to continue in office for a few weeks, but by April he realized that he could no longer continue as prime minister and resigned. On his departure, the king asked George Canning to form a government. Several other politicians, including Viscount Melville, Liverpool's first Lord of the Admiralty, distrusted Canning and were reluctant to serve in his cabinet. Believing that his grip on the highest office of state would be strengthened if he had the support of the heir to the throne, Melville decided to revive the long-dormant office of Lord High Admiral, which had been vacant for more than a hundred years, since the death of Prince George of Denmark, husband of Queen Anne, with the specific aim of appointing the Duke of Clarence to the post.

The intention was that the heir to the throne should act as a nominal President of the Board of Admiralty. In theory, the holder of such a position was the supreme commander of the Royal Navy, and the head of naval administration at Whitehall, with a seat in the cabinet. However, by the nineteenth century, the Government thought that such powers would be excessive, even for the man who would be their next sovereign. Such a post, simply as a figurehead with very limited responsibilities, would be a suitable way of allowing him some direct practical insight into public affairs, or, in more modern parlance, the equivalent of a few months of work experience, no matter how slight. Any mistakes William might make, and the lessons he would thus learn from them, were best made in such a situation rather than once he became monarch, when the results could be unfortunate, if not worse, for the Government, the country and his own reputation.

Although he had mellowed considerably in recent years, William's reputation for being somewhat excitable had not been forgotten, and it was feared that too much power and responsibility might go to his head. Any personal initiatives and room for manoeuvre on his part had to be carefully curtailed, and it was made clear that his office would be little more than an honorary post. It was unanimously decided that he should not be a member of the cabinet, and that the majority of his powers should be exercised through a council drawn from officers at the Admiralty. His patent restricted him, while in London, to act only with the knowledge and approval of the High Admiral's council, and when he was at sea, he would need the endorsement of the council for any orders he might give, unless he was accompanied by a council member.

It had been designed to flatter him by giving him the impression that after almost four decades of retirement from active service he now had some genuine responsibility. Some contemporaries thought the new appointment would flatter and therefore conciliate the duke as the heir presumptive, while Sir William Knighton, King George IV's private secretary, saw it as no more than an empty gesture, calling it 'sad and foolish'.

John Wilson Croker, secretary to the Admiralty Council, was thought to have been the person who initially had the idea of offering William the job. Having done so, he preceded to write in less than flattering terms of the Lord High Admiral's unsuitability for the post. The Duke of Clarence suspected him of being an uncertain ally at best, and there was little love lost between both men. On one occasion, when they had been at the Royal Pavilion in Brighton, in the presence of the king, the duke was particularly annoyed with Croker, and told him sharply that if he was king, he would be his own First Lord, and 'you should *not* be my secretary'. Croker then reminded him that the last person to fill both roles, that of Lord High Admiral and subsequently King, was James II, and the precedent was hardly an auspicious one. When everybody else within earshot laughed, King George asked what the joke was. Croker assured him it was nothing, apart from the fact that his royal brother was saying what he would do 'when Your Majesty is no longer King'.[10] Clearly less than pleased, the king walked away without saying anything.

At first, everyone had the impression that the duke was undaunted by the terms set out in his letters of appointment. Initially, his term of office was free from trouble. He made an excellent start when he requested at once that all the present councillors should be retained in their posts to assist him with his new responsibilities. For some time he kept himself cheerfully occupied by sailing around southern ports, while the duchess, always a poor sailor, travelled overland to attend the receptions he hosted in the evenings. Yet, as some had anticipated if not even feared, he soon showed he was not content to be a mere rubber stamp or a nonentity who would confine himself to hospitality and making speeches. During the daytime he would often poke his head around the corners of the dockyards at Portsmouth, Plymouth and anywhere else that he happened to be at the time. The dockers were startled but flattered to see this elderly gentleman going around the docks quite unattended, chattering away to everybody. They guessed that he must be somebody important and were startled to realize that this was the heir to the throne. A royal prince or duke, they had assumed, would be insufferably pompous, and this affable character was quite the opposite. When he was not inspecting or visiting such establishments, he would hurry around to the Admiralty with a volley of questions on matters with which nobody had occupied their minds for a long time. In the evenings he often held balls on board his yacht. A kindly, approachable, enthusiastic and even generous man at heart, his presence was responsible for raising the morale of a service that had declined since the end of the Napoleonic wars.

The most important condition of his appointment, as far as the councillors were concerned, was that whenever he was at sea, he would need their endorsement of any orders he might give unless he was accompanied by at least one of them. They knew that he was quite capable of issuing instructions off the cuff with barely a second thought. Yet he was ready to take a quite relaxed view of this restriction. All might have been well had it not been for the presence of their senior member, Sir George Cockburn. From the outset, it was clear that both men would be unable to function in harmony. Cockburn was extremely knowledgeable on the subject of naval law, very obstinate and set in his ways, and exactly the kind of person who would fiercely object to the mere possibility of any encroachment on his powers by a member of the royal family. As for the duke, he had disliked and distrusted Cockburn for some years, regarding him as hopelessly unqualified for his position and telling others rather tactlessly that such a man was no more suited to be at the Admiralty than his old grandmother. Both were headstrong personalities, and it was only to be expected that sooner or later conflict would arise.

Canning had been seriously ill for some time, and died on 8 August 1827, after only 119 days in office. Frederick Robinson, Viscount Goderich, was appointed as his successor. His tenure of office would be a mere 125 days longer than that of his predecessor. Unable to command the confidences of his sovereign and fellow ministers, he resigned in January 1828 and was succeeded by the Duke of Wellington. The Duke of Clarence did not anticipate any problems and was confident that they would be able to work harmoniously together. He had not considered that the new prime minister would prove far more sympathetic to the councillors than to the enthusiastic, but somewhat eccentric, and sometimes headstrong heir to the throne. Neither had they appreciated that an event of the previous year was destined to have consequences that would place great strain on their working relationship.

Three months later, on 20 October 1827, Admiral Sir Edward Codrington, who was stationed in the Eastern Mediterranean in order to assist the French and Russian fleets defend the Greeks and prevent any massacres by the Turks, engaged the Turkish fleet in battle at the Bay of Navarino without explicit orders from the Admiralty. A belief that the duke had encouraged Codrington by adding a codicil to his written orders, encouraging him to go in and 'smash those Turks', was probably the result of an exaggeration, but news of any conflict that resulted in English victory certainly delighted the patriot in him. He promoted several of Codrington's senior officers and recommended to the king that the Admiral himself deserved to be awarded the Grand Cross of the Order of the Bath. The enthusiastic praise Codrington received from the Lord High Admiral had not been preceded by consultations with the latter's council, and it did not reflect the Government's policy. The Admiralty was embarrassed by Codrington's precipitate actions and received the Lord High Admiral coldly. The king's speech at the next session of parliament, in January

1828, was the first during Wellington's term of office and referred to Navarino as 'this untoward event', while Codrington was recalled and dismissed from his post. Wellington felt obliged to make it clear that the Lord High Admiral's enthusiastic reception of the victory may have been a heartfelt gesture, indisputably a patriotic one, but it represented his own view only, and neither that of the Government nor the nation.

In July 1828 the first major disagreement arose between the Lord High Admiral and his council. Having been shocked by the poor standard of naval gunnery, William set up a standing commission of naval officers to ameliorate the problem. It was a sensible and long-overdue measure, and he chose experienced officers who recommended several practical improvements. All the same, council members were annoyed that he had not thought to consult them first and was taking matters into his own hands in this way, and they complained that his terms of reference were too wide. Cockburn insisted that the order was neither in accordance with the spirit of the Act of Parliament, nor consistent with the real nature of his office. He referred the issue to Wellington and his ministers, who decided without hesitation to side with Cockburn and the council. Feeling unsupported, the duke wrote an angry letter to Cockburn, pointing out that the function of the council was merely to advise, not to dictate to him. When this had no effect, he demanded that Cockburn be dismissed. Wellington found himself in a difficult position as he did not wish to clash with the Duke of Clarence, but he felt that Cockburn had acted correctly. He knew that other members of the council would resign if the Lord High Admiral was permitted to have his own way, and such a situation would place the ailing King George IV in a very difficult position. He decided that the wisest course was to ask the sovereign to reason with his brother.

The king realized at once that duty to country and government had to take precedence over family solidarity. His beloved brother was in the wrong, and there was only one person in the kingdom who had the authority to tell him. With a heavy heart, he wrote to his brother gently but firmly that he regretted the embarrassment in which William had placed himself, but he was in the wrong. Sir George Cockburn, he reminded him, was a Privy Councillor, and it was his duty to advise the Lord High Admiral where necessary. As the king, he could hardly be called on to dismiss the most useful, even the most important naval officer in his service, for doing his duty. William would have to give way.

On receiving this letter, the duke realized there was no alternative but to concede defeat as gracefully as possible. At London, he spoke to Cockburn who refused to back down. Next, he had a meeting with Wellington, who similarly stood firm in his views. A few days later he visited Wellington and Cockburn at what proved on the surface an amicable enough meeting. Nevertheless, it soon became apparent that both men (Cockburn and the Duke of Clarence) could not work together, and before long one of them had to go.

A further episode during William's term of office bordered on farce, although it might have been trivial enough in isolation. It was unfortunate that he had already weakened his position, and the second ill-advised action was enough to prove his undoing. On another inspection of outlying ports, at the end of July, the Lord High Admiral came across a squadron of ships at Plymouth due for manoeuvres and awaiting the arrival of Admiral Sir Henry Blackwood. Without more ado he hoisted his flag in *Royal Sovereign*, ordered the ships out to sea, and requested that the council to come and meet him at Portsmouth.

Cockburn argued that the Duke of Clarence had no right to hoist his flag at sea in this way, and in doing so had exceeded his responsibilities. Yet William sailed to Plymouth, supervising exercises for the guard ships in manoeuvres and gunnery as they went. As the vessels generally never left their moorings in peacetime, their captains and crew enjoyed this departure from their customary routine, as well as the pomp and circumstance, notably the receptions, that punctuated their journey. On 27 July, the duchess arrived in Plymouth to join William, and troops lined the streets to welcome her. After the reception the new 120-gun *Britannia* was unmoored and proceeded majestically down the harbour to take up her station in Plymouth Sound. Meanwhile, irritation was mounting at the fact that William had not told either the council or ministers in government what he was doing and where he was. The Earl of Ellenborough, Lord Privy Seal, noted after a cabinet meeting at the beginning of August that the Lord High Admiral was 'gone to sea with two three-deckers and some small vessels, and is not to reappear till August 9. Nobody knows where he is gone.'[11]

The royal truant and his fleet returned to Greenwich on the morning of 7 August. While everyone else was relieved to see them safe and sound, they could not conceal their extreme annoyance at what had happened, and the king wrote sadly to Knighton that his 'poor brother' had placed himself in a situation from which it would be difficult to disengage. Meanwhile, the Lord High Admiral proceeded to promote more than sixty members of the navy to the rank of captain or lieutenant, in four weeks. The action certainly made him popular with those on the receiving end of such rewards, but the authorities were not pleased. Croker thought he was planning to create his own power base within the service and thus strengthen his position against the members of the council, who were probably thirsting for his resignation.

For the despairing Duke of Wellington this was more than enough. He reported these various misdeeds in detail to the king, who replied sadly that he had already had occasion to write to his brother 'that he was in error from beginning to the end'. When he had appointed the Duke of Clarence, he went on, 'I had reasonably hoped that I should have derived comfort, peace, and tranquillity from such an appointment; but from what has hitherto taken place, it would seem as if the very reverse were to happen … Can the Lord High Admiral suppose that the laws are to be infringed, the rules of true discipline (which he knows so well how to uphold) are to be broken in upon? And that these things are to pass without notice or remonstrance by the responsible advisers of the Crown?' Much as he loved his brother, he had to leave him the example of what the inherent duty of a king of this country really was. The Lord High Admiral was obliged to obey the laws enacted by parliament, otherwise, as sovereign, he would have to insist on his resignation.[12]

When the Lord High Admiral returned to shore, he found a letter addressed to him, pointing out in the most uncompromising terms that he was once again violating the terms of his office. William pleaded that his council was competent to advise him only on financial matters. Only when it became clear that the prime minister had already made it clear that his understanding was exactly the contrary, and that he had the full support of the king, did he realize that his position was no longer tenable.

Domestic matters briefly commanded the Duke of Clarence's attention, for 13 August was his wife's thirty-sixth birthday, an occasion they planned to mark with a grand dinner at Bushy at which the Duke of Cambridge would be one of their guests. More in sorrow than in anger, the duke visited the Admiralty Office and spent much of the day there. He presided over his final council meeting, solemnly informed everyone present that he was taking the chair merely as a replacement had not yet been selected, and announced that he would be resigning with immediate effect although he did not intend to give his reasons. At first, he treated Cockburn with coldness, but then became less distant and, regarding it as business as usual while he was still there, asked him if he would take some communications to various departments. Afterwards he shook hands magnanimously with the man who had been such a thorn in his flesh, and invited him and several of the other council members who had regularly opposed him, to come and join him at the birthday celebrations a week later at Bushy. Although he may have had the hasty Hanoverian temper, he was just as quick to forgive, and never bore a grudge against either Cockburn or the Duke of Wellington for his departure from office. Perhaps he realized, as they did, that it had been an experiment doomed to probable failure, but he was prepared to put a brave face on it and concede that everyone involved had learned something from the experience.

William's eldest son, George FitzClarence, had been convinced that his frustrated father was close to a nervous breakdown, irritated beyond endurance with the resistance that his well-intentioned and largely very sensible reforming zeal had met with, from the Admiralty diehards. Ever one to savour and even propagate gossip, Princess Lieven said that William was about to end up in a straitjacket, like his father before him. *The Times* was guarded in its opinion as to why the Lord High Admiral had left office, although it did not hesitate to offer its opinions on what it regarded as the unsatisfactory, even unnecessary appointment of a man who had proved himself quite unfit for such a task:

> At present, it would be mere impertinence to repeat the various conjectures and absurdities which have been thrown into circulation by way of accounting for an occurrence by no means unexpected ... What now most nearly concerns the state, is the mode in which the navy ought to be furnished with an official chieftain. A steadily-working First Lord of the Admiralty may prove a more profitable head of the office than a slap-dash Prince of the Blood. Had the author or approvers of the Duke of Clarence's promotion continued in power to this day, we do not know that they would have felt themselves able to maintain His Royal Highness in a post which cannot, we apprehend, be suitably administered without a share of tact and discretion, not possessed by the average of men or Princes.[13]

On balance, how good or bad a Lord High Admiral had William been? Sir John Barrow, one of the secretaries at the Admiralty who worked closely with him, noted that 'After a daily intercourse of fifteen or sixteen months, I never met with a more kind-hearted man, more benevolent, or more desirous of relieving distress'.[14] Barrow had been a staunch ally during the last eighteen months, and thought that the Duke of Clarence's misdemeanours or, rather, mistakes had been brought about by others who expected him to have unlimited power.[15] The duke gave him an especially warm farewell and presented him with a small silver inkstand, engraved, as a small testimonial of his esteem and regard. One modern, rather critical biographer, Roger Knight, stated that his tenure of office 'had been disastrous', that he had tried to accomplish too much, had regarded his council as mere advisers when he required their advice and ignored them the rest of the time, and had issued orders outside the powers of his patent when they should have been agreed by members of his council instead.[16] The more kindly verdict of another biographer, Philip Ziegler, suggests that William had been much more successful than he is generally given credit for.[17] While William was not a great administrator, and would never have claimed to be one, he was by no means the ignoramus or buffoon that his detractors tried to claim. In the face of indifference or even active opposition of the council, some of whom had not really expected an enthusiastic prince to turn into a new broom, sweeping clean and bringing fresh thinking to an institution that deserved a good shake-up, he had brought some worthwhile new ideas with him, and his achievements deserved recognition.

Anyone who knew anything about the duke as a personality would have taken it for granted that with his little eccentricities, he was bound to display a sense of the farcical during his appointment. He was a thoughtful man (if sometimes too impulsive) and proved responsible for several long-overdue reforms. Among them were an overhaul and streamlining of the anachronistic system of promotion, a system of reports every six months for each ship in the navy on their state of readiness for battle, and quarterly reports on gunnery exercises and the expenditure of ammunition. Nobody could argue that such measures had been badly needed. Although William had always been a spendthrift, he was not by nature a selfish man. It was said that he had been responsible for expenditure of about £23,000 for entertaining during his period of office, something he did not deny, but many officers and also ordinary seamen had enjoyed his largesse, extravagant though it may have been. Yet at the same time, he declared that he 'hated presents'. It says much for his integrity that he did not want to profit unduly from his office, and he ordered that certain luxurious gifts sent to him, such as a cask of fine wine and a box of truffles, were to be returned to their donors. Most humanely of all, he reduced the severity of punishments to much milder chastisements, and in particular he abolished the use of the cat-o'nine tails for all but the most serious misdemeanours, such as mutiny at sea.

After William had left office, his good-natured departure gave the king some food for thought. He studied the terms of the patent of Lord High Admiral and concluded that they appeared to place excessive restrictions on the occupant of the post. When he suggested to Wellington that they might be modified, the latter said he was reluctant to open the matter again and could not see any reason to recommend change. It would have been a purely academic exercise, for the office was henceforth abolished and that of First Lord of the Admiralty restored in its stead. The Duke of Wellington reappointed Lord Melville, with Admiral Cockburn as a senior naval member of the reconstituted Board of Admiralty.

For the next year or so, there was little for the sovereign-in-waiting to do but to bide his time. Six months later, William made what would be his last foray into public life as the Duke of Clarence. While he was less radical than some of his younger brothers, he could never be dismissed as a diehard reactionary.

The cause that returned him briefly to the public eye was that of the relaxation of restrictions placed on Roman Catholics in England.

In the past, William had not been noted for his consistency on the issue. In 1820 he had told the Duke of Norfolk who, being a Catholic, was prevented from sitting in the House of Lords, that he hoped to see him there before long, yet he would vote against emancipation a year later. This had been in solidarity with the Duke of York, who strongly opposed any change to the status quo, but the latter's death left William free to think about the matter again. On a couple of occasions during his brother's reign, he had spoken about his sympathies for Catholics and his belief that their pursuit of emancipation should be taken seriously. Yet, at a dinner of the Society for the Promotion of Christian Knowledge, he had given his word that he was 'unalterably attached' to the principles of the Church of England and saw it as his duty to maintain those principles. A few days later, at a naval dinner, he had declared unequivocally that he was 'for the Catholics – heart and soul to the very backbone'. Although he was less than consistent, gradually he became a vocal if not altogether dependable supporter of the measure. He confided in a friend that he had previously been a staunch defender of the Church of England and the status quo, mainly out of respect for King George IV and the late Duke of York, and their strongly held opinions on the matter. Frederick had been regarded as an arch-reactionary who would never have countenanced any change to the established order, but William recognised that the public mood was shifting. If His Majesty's senior ministers had good reason to favour lifting restrictions on the Catholics, he would give the issue some thought and change his mind if he thought it right to do so. In the process he would deliver a fierce attack on the most fervent champion of Protestants in the royal family, his brother Ernest, Duke of Cumberland.

In February 1829, the Duke of Wellington and his ministers brought the Catholic Relief Act before parliament. As an Irishman by birth, the prime minister had a clear understanding of the grievances held by the Catholic communities and their anger at the restrictions imposed on them. Also, he had never forgotten that a large number of them had enlisted in the army during the Napoleonic wars to fight on behalf of the British. When the issue was debated, the Duke of Cumberland spoke passionately in the Lords. While he conceded that there were many Roman Catholics who were 'just and worthy men', it was their lordships' responsibility to decide whether the country was to remain a Protestant country with a Protestant government, or not. The moment that Catholics were admitted into either the Commons or the Lords, it would cease to be so.

Later that week he called upon the Duke and Duchess of Clarence at home, and they had a long conversation. 'Nothing could be more friendly or more amicable than he had been towards me,' the Duke of Cumberland said later, 'we talked of indifferent things, but not one word of politics.' After that he visited their sister Mary, Duchess of Gloucester, who asked if he had seen William, and how had he found him. When Ernest told him that everything had gone very well, she was astonished. She told him that William had recently been to visit her 'and he has frightened me to death'. Because Ernest had made a declaration strongly in favour of the Church and the Protestant cause, she continued, William had insisted that 'he must go down and avow his opinion to be completely *for* the measure [emancipation].' When she asked him whether he had the king's consent to do so, he replied that he certainly had not, and he needed nobody's consent.[18]

Their apprehensions were justified. When the Duke of Clarence went to the Lords, he had delivered a somewhat long-winded speech in which he praised the service of the Irishmen and declared firmly that it would be 'merely an act of justice to raise the Roman Catholics from their state of degradation'. Neither he nor the Duke of Wellington would ever forget their bravery, valour or devotion in recent years, and that when the Act was passed, 'it would have the effect of uniting and quieting eight millions of His Majesty's subjects'.[19] He then proceeded to speak in 'such strong and violent language against all those who had declared themselves *adverse* to the measure and resolved to impose it,'[20] and criticised those who persisted in opposing the measure. Stung by his words and '*this unjustifiable attack*', the Duke of Cumberland, a firm believer in keeping the legislation as it was, rose to his feet and said that he objected strongly to having his conduct described as 'factious', and he had forgotten the other epithet his brother had used. 'Infamous,' the Duke of Clarence responded, helpfully.

The Act was passed with a majority of more than a hundred, despite the votes of many Tories. For this the Duke of Clarence had found himself hailed briefly as a forward-looking liberal. If nothing else, his speech endorsing emancipation had demonstrated that he was capable of changing his mind, and to some extent moving with the times, taking note of what the ministers had said and believed was for the good of the country. He found a staunch ally in the Duke of Sussex, who said that Catholic emancipation would immortalise the Duke of Wellington more than all his victories in Spain or at Waterloo.

As the health of King George IV declined the Duke of Clarence was increasingly sympathetic, visiting him regularly at Windsor and always returning deeply saddened, if not actually moved to tears. Yet he would not have been human if he had not felt some sense of excitement at what the future might hold for him. Occasionally he overreached himself. He had been unable to resist writing to the Duke of Wellington to tell him that he meant to confirm him in office in due course. This was nothing less than an assurance that, as sovereign, William would without hesitation retain the present prime minister in office.

The Duke of Wellington recognized that this could place him in rather an awkward situation, and responded that it would be improper of him to pay any heed to such a letter. The Duke of Clarence became indignant and complained to his friends that he had been very rudely treated. 'He was very cold in his manner,' the Duke of Wellington noted, 'but I took no notice, and went on as before.'[21] The situation was not lost on others, some of whom had repeatedly snubbed their sailor prince and treated him like a fool. Politicians and aristocrats likewise came forward to proffer their admiration for the man whom they often had not taken seriously, yet who would surely be their sovereign before long.

Although William might have been relishing the prospect of ascending the throne, the Duchess of Clarence was increasingly apprehensive, and did not share his enthusiasm. In her diary on 11 June 1830, she wrote that their position 'keeps getting more trying, and we are passing through a very dark time'.[22] While her husband genuinely felt every sympathy with the sufferings of his brother, he found his eagerness as he contemplated the future difficult to conceal. He was ready for the challenge.

Chapter 5

King William

As dawn broke on 26 June 1830, Sir Henry Halford rode along the chestnut avenue of Bushy Park. William was woken at six o' clock that morning by his servants and told that the doctor wished to see him. The long-ailing King George IV, who had spent most of his time in bed at Windsor Castle for the last few months of his sixty-seven years, had just died. Legend – and probably no more than that – has it that the man who had just become King William IV told the doctor that he must return to bed forthwith, as he had never yet slept with a queen. Adelaide's immediate reaction was more measured; in her own words, 'God helped us to master the shock of that moment.'[1] Once Halford had taken his leave to go and inform other members of the royal family, in person, she burst into tears. She was not looking forward to the publicity, ceremony and fatigue to which she knew they would now be subjected.

Although William knew that Adelaide was right to dread the imminent changes they faced, for several months he had been eagerly preparing himself for the day when he would assume his sovereign rights. Aged almost sixty-five at the time, he was the oldest prince ever to succeed to the British throne. Having been anxious to keep himself as fit and healthy as possible for a man of his years, he had made a point of gargling two gallons of water every morning and always wearing galoshes in bad weather, to protect himself from chills. He had never lost an opportunity to tell family, friends and acquaintances alike that he was perfectly well and in the very best of health.

Having generally preferred his second Christian name, Henry, some had supposed that William would rule as King Henry IX.

However, the lords spiritual and others recommended that he should reign as William IV, perhaps to avoid any possible confusion or even argument, as supporters of the Stuart dynasty had regarded Cardinal York, the grandson of King James II, as the true Henry IX.

Within hours the new monarch was on his way to Windsor in a coach. A long piece of black crepe to signify mourning for the deceased flowed from the crown of his white hat, while he grinned and bowed to everybody as he passed. Very few people yet knew that the previous sovereign had passed away, and still fewer had any idea about the appearance of his successor. A small crowd had heard the news and gathered outside St James's Palace and as he drove towards the entrance, shortly after half past nine that morning, a faint, dutiful cheer was heard. At ten o' clock the firing of a double salute announced the start of the ceremony of the proclamation of King William IV, and the public were admitted into the courtyard to watch. A few minutes later, the window of the Presence Chamber was thrown open, and the king walked forward alone, dressed in mourning and wearing the Order of the Garter. He bowed gracefully three times to the crowd, who cheered vigorously as a band of fifteen trumpet players struck up the National Anthem. A group of cabinet ministers, various officers of state, and senior male members of the royal family, including the Dukes of Cumberland, Sussex, Gloucester and Prince Leopold, formed themselves into a semi-circle around the window.

The Privy Councillors had all assembled to be sworn in by their new lord and master. For the last couple of years William had lived such a secluded life that few of them really knew anything about him, beyond his reputation for eccentricity and indelicate language. Some who had worked with him knew that he was affable, good-natured, if prone to occasional outbursts of anger, and he was expected to be less remote and less pompous than his predecessor. The meeting was due to begin at midday, and as they stood waiting in groups, talking solemnly together, the doors suddenly were flung open and a short, red-faced figure dressed in naval uniform bustled in. William spoke respectfully to them of the passing of the late sovereign, and said he was sure they would:

> fully participate in the affliction which I am suffering on account of the loss of a sovereign under whose auspices, as Regent and as King, this country has maintained during war, its ancient reputation and glory, has enjoyed a long period of happiness and internal peace, and has possessed the friendship, respect, and confidence of foreign Powers. In addition to that loss which I sustain in common with you, and with all who lived under the government of a most beneficent and gracious King, I have to lament the death of a beloved and affectionate brother, with whom I have lived from my earliest years on terms of the most cordial and uninterrupted friendship, and to whose favour and kindness I have been most deeply indebted.[2]

The councillors were asked to swear their allegiance to 'King George IV', which was quickly corrected to 'William IV', amid the sound of laughter. After this the new king was handed a pen with which to sign his declaration of accession and did so, rather spoiling the solemnity of the moment by remarking immediately afterwards, 'This is a damned bad pen you've given me.' One by one the councillors knelt to kiss his hand and render him their allegiance. He peered at them as they did so, startling Henry Goulburn, his Chancellor of the Exchequer, when he told him he had become so near-sighted that he did not recognise him, and he must tell him his name.

King George IV's funeral at Windsor Castle took place at night on 15 July, with much solemnity but little grief. At the ceremony King William, the chief mourner, dressed in a long purple cloak relieved only by the brilliance of the Star of the Order of the Garter, walked behind the two-ton coffin up the length of St George's Chapel. He alarmed some of the people around him, and amused others, by recognizing various friends, giving several a hearty handshake, and nodding with a grin to others. An observer noted afterwards that His Majesty talked incessantly and loudly throughout the service 'so that the most frivolous things were overheard', while another regretted that a coronation could hardly have seemed more jovial. After two hours, as the anthem was being sung, King William rose from his seat, thanked the Earl Marshal genially for having made all the arrangements, and walked out. Only after his departure was the body of his brother lowered into its grave.

It was soon evident that William was a very different kind of monarch, arguably less dignified, but far more informal. This was a man who seemed to welcome the chance to be at one with the people over whom he reigned. There could hardly have been a starker contrast for His Majesty's loyal subjects between the new king and his late brother. The diarist Emily Eden noted that their adored sovereign was 'either mad or very foolish' but at any rate 'an immense improvement on the last unforgiving animal, who died growling sulkily in his den at Windsor. This man at least wishes to make everybody happy, and everything he has done has been benevolent.'[3] He would be the first British monarch who made some effort to behave like an ordinary citizen, choosing to walk around his capital unescorted. There were times when his natural bonhomie was slightly misplaced, he was not bothered by upsetting the traditionalists, seemed impatient with ceremony and preferred to do things as simply as possible, and revealed a thin line between affability or informality and a lack of dignity. Once, when William was staying at Bushy, the Duke of Norfolk called upon him to discuss some minor matter. As he was about to leave, the king insisted that he could not go without seeing Her Majesty first and rang a bell himself. When a servant came to see what he wanted, the king said, 'Tell the Queen I want her.'[4]

William's demeanour brought a reassuringly human touch to the monarchy, at a time when it was held in low esteem. He started his reign with a large measure of approval, as noted by Charles Greville, Clerk to the Council and renowned diarist, who said: 'King George had not been dead three days, before everybody discovered that he was no loss, and King William a great gain. Certainly, nobody ever was less regretted than the late King ... Altogether he seems a kind-hearted, well-meaning, not stupid, burlesque, bustling old fellow, and if he doesn't go mad may make a very decent King.'[5]

Not everybody was quite so impressed. Sir Thomas Creevey had noted a little acidly on the day they lost one monarch and gained another, 'Poor Prinney [George IV] put on a dramatic, royal, distant dignity to all.'[6] Yet distant dignity had never been William's way, and he did not see fit to change, even though he was now the mightiest in the land. It had been anticipated that there might be a lack of ease between the new monarch and his prime minister, the Duke of Wellington. Both men had not seen eye to eye on occasion. While King William had long since forgotten the part he had played in asking for Wellington's resignation as Lord High Admiral, he perhaps regarded him with some coolness after Wellington had scorned his somewhat clumsily-expressed willingness to retain his services as prime minister, on his accession. Alternately, William may have had second thoughts as to the impropriety of such behaviour, and therefore felt a little embarrassed. The former military commander turned politician had not always found William easy to work with in the past, but within a few days Wellington observed sagely to Princess Lieven that this was 'not a new reign; it is a new dynasty'.[7] There might have been occasional murmurings that repeated old allegations that William was slightly mad, but by and large they were made with a smile rather than as a gloomy forecast that he was about to go the unfortunate way of his father.

King William IV had never been a stickler for standing on ceremony, and just because he had succeeded to the highest position in the land, he was not about to change the habits of a lifetime. His touches of informality, an unerring affability, were commonplace. On 19 July he made his first official public appearance reviewing the Coldstream Guards, wearing military uniform for the first time in his life, with a pair of gold spurs halfway up his legs, although the chalkstones in his hands made it impossible for him to ride on horseback as he could not hold the reins. Queen Adelaide watched from the window of a nearby house and afterwards held an informal drawing-room at which ministers, wives and various officials were presented to her. They thought her rather plain and timid, going somewhat nervously through her part 'as if she was acting and wished the Green Curtain to drop.'[8] That afternoon William attended a council to swear in the remaining Privy Councillors and Lords-Lieutenant. The review had taken longer than anticipated so the ceremony was delayed, much to the annoyance of the lieutenants who had arrived on time and were furious at being kept waiting. The Duke of Wellington was sworn in as Constable of the Tower of London and Lieutenant of Hampshire, then the Earl of Jersey and the new privy councillors took the oath, followed by the lieutenants, six or seven at a time. To expedite the process and avoid holding them up even longer, the customary kneeling was dispensed with. The king had been told their name or their county beforehand, and he had a civil word to say to each one of them. He invited some people to come to dinner, and reminded others of visits he had made to their locality in the past. When it came to George Wyndham, Earl of Egremont (one of whose daughters, Mary, had married George FitzClarence), who owned a large estate at Petworth in Sussex, he caused some amusement by telling him that he had a home nearby at Brighton, and asked his Lordship for permission to live in his county.

After the ceremony was over, or as some sources suggested, once the king had grown bored with the lengthy task of swearing in the officials, and had endured enough, he walked out, changed his clothes, and went for a gentle stroll down St James's Street, where he met an old friend, Watson Taylor, and they walked along arm in arm. He was deemed 'quite alone, the mob following him, & one of the common women threw her arms around him & kissed him. However, I hope he will soon go out of town & be quiet.'[9] Members of White's Club, who had been astonished to hear a noisily enthusiastic crowd coming past their windows, looked outside and to their astonishment saw the very public kiss. Thinking he might be in danger, they rushed out to form an improvised bodyguard and escorted the king, still holding on to Mr Taylor, safely to his palace. The king was a little startled, but unconcerned, and in thanking them for their assistance, assured them that he had walked around the streets a few times, and that people would get used to it and take no notice.

The Duke of Wellington and Queen Adelaide were among those who tried to persuade him this was not the way for a king to conduct himself. They pointed out that it was unwise, undignified and, above all, most unsafe to behave in such a way. The queen, with some concern, told one of her ladies-in-waiting about his activities and the way he was followed, and said that in future he would need to take his stroll early in the morning, or else confine it to somewhere far less public. After all, it was only thirty years since the last attempt on the life of his father. At length he reluctantly accepted that such behaviour could possibly jeopardize his personal safety, and that he was no longer at liberty to live like a private citizen. Yet his natural informality and an endearing sense of ordinariness were ready to cut their way unashamedly through the traditions of etiquette that had been beloved, or at least taken for granted, by the court for so long. Pomp and ceremony for their own sake simply bored him.

There would be more instances of the refreshing spontaneity that often startled those around him. On the following day, while he was at dinner, it occurred to him on the spur of the moment that it might be a good idea to invite his nephew William, King of Württemberg, who was then at Boulogne, to come and visit them – and ought to do so immediately, so that he could come and watch the prorogation of parliament on 23 July. Before they had finished their meal, he despatched George FitzClarence, without allowing him to change out of his silk stockings and cocked hat, to go to Boulogne immediately so he could deliver the invitation to his fellow sovereign. George did as he was bidden and was back in fifty-six hours, bringing their guest with him, and arrived in time to see the ceremony at the House of Lords.

Greville had a certain amount to say about the occasion, not least about how delighted King William IV was to find himself in a state coach surrounded by all his pomp. Yet he was determined to try and do everything on his own terms. He delivered his speech very well but he did not wear the crown, which was carried by the Marquis of Hastings, his Gentleman of the Bedchamber:

> Etiquette is a thing he cannot comprehend. He wanted to take the King of Württemberg with him in his coach, till he was told it was out of the question .... Yesterday, after the House of Lords, he drove all over the town in an open calèche with the Queen, Princess Augusta, and the King of Württemberg, and coming home he set down the King (dropped him, as he calls it) at Grillon's Hotel. The King of England dropping another king at a tavern! It is impossible not to be struck with his extreme good-nature and simplicity, which he cannot or will not exchange for the dignity of his new situation and the trammels of etiquette; but he ought to be made to understand that his simplicity degenerates into vulgarity, and that without departing from his natural urbanity he may conduct himself so as not to lower the character with which he is invested, and which belongs not to him, but to the country.[10]

Ministers and members of parliament were pleasantly surprised at what they saw of the new monarch. Earl Charles Grey, one of the leading Whig politicians, wrote to his confidante, Princess Lieven, that 'there really was in his manner at the *levée* this morning a degree of composure and propriety which one could not have expected'.[11] Queen Adelaide was also much admired by those around her, and about three months later Princess Lieven noted that the consort was 'a far cleverer woman than they generally give her credit for; above all, she shows much determination of character.'[12] The princess had not always been too charitable about William, but then she thought that the phrase 'happy as a king' might have been made with their new monarch in mind. She was particularly impressed 'by his manners, his good nature, and cordiality, a sense of gratified nature which is quite contagious.'[13]

King William was renowned for his off-the-cuff speeches which could be lively, amusing, downright tactless, and sometimes all three. A month after his accession, on 25 July, he was present at a dinner at Apsley House in Piccadilly, the Duke of Wellington's London residence. The dinner was being held in Wellington's honour to mark the anniversary of the battle of Vimiero in 1808, one of the war hero's most decisive victories over the French during the Peninsula War. When William proposed a toast to the duke's health, he offered some good-intentioned but rather clumsy congratulations on his successes over the French. Suddenly he remembered that the French ambassador, the Duke of Laval-Montmorency, was also present, and attempted to remedy what he had said. The ambassador understood no English and immediately walked forward to King William and thanked him for his compliments. Thoroughly gratified, the monarch concluded his address with the remark that as long as he reigned, he would continue to give his confidence to the Duke of Wellington. When his rather embarrassed Lordship was congratulated by Princess Lieven afterwards, he said gravely that 'he would far rather the King had not made the speech.'[14]

Under the new king and queen court life underwent a rapid change and became more respectable, even though some might find it rather dull after the splendours of the reign of his brother, King George IV. At the queen's request, people who had a reputation as gamblers and drunkards or who had apparently committed other misdemeanours were not made welcome at court. She declined to receive the very rich, fashionable Duchess of St Albans, widow of Coutts the banker, who had previously been 'an actress of doubtful reputation'. In view of the theatrical career of Dorothy Jordan, it was a stricture which her husband may have found a little embarrassing. The Countess of Ferrers also found herself cold-shouldered, on account of having lived openly with the Earl for some years as his mistress, before they were married in 1829. When she presented herself at a court reception, Queen Adelaide discreetly turned away and refused to greet her.

The licentiousness of George IV's days had given way to a new era. The standards set by King William and Queen Adelaide, including welcoming only those who could be expected to conduct themselves in their private lives with absolute propriety, suggest that Queen Victoria and Prince Albert of Saxe-Coburg, who would preside over an equally unblemished English court life ten years hence, were not 'the first Victorians' after all.

Since Dorothy Jordan's death, the then Duke of Clarence had been kept informed of whenever any portraits of her came up for sale, so he could purchase them for his private collection. Now that he was king, he still had one private act of atonement to carry out. He sent for Francis Chantrey, the leading portrait sculptor of the day, and commissioned him to produce a statue of Dorothy Jordan with two of her children, carved in marble, 54 inches (137 cm) high. The king asked that it should be placed in St Paul's Cathedral but the chapter declined to accept it and it remained in his possession until his death. It then passed to his eldest son George, by then Earl of Munster, and was subsequently left by his descendants to the Royal Collection.

At Brighton, King William and Queen Adelaide were always the kindest of hosts, although anything but extravagant. The king was generous to all, unfailingly outgoing, and always adept at making his guests feel welcome. It was by no means unusual for them to have thirty or more to dinner in the evening, and sometimes there would be more than a hundred. When they were at Brighton the king strolled along the streets and grasped the hand of any former naval officer whom he recognised. Sometimes he sent a message to the local hotels for a list of their guests, so he could invite anybody whose name, with his excellent memory, he might remember. His naval friends from years past were always especially welcome. When the wife of a particular friend tried to excuse herself from an invitation because she did not have a smart enough gown, the king told her not to worry and to come along anyway; 'the Queen and myself are quiet people and indeed she does nothing after dinner but embroider flowers.'[15] Every evening after the king and queen and their guests had dined, they left the table to find armchairs and make themselves comfortable. Adelaide took up her knitting or embroidery, while her husband regaled them with conversation and old anecdotes, often of his service life. Some of these – to use an appropriately nautical figure of speech – sailed a little too close to the wind. Whenever he was feeling the weight of his sixty-something years and particularly tired after a long day, he would nod off gently in his chair, occasionally waking to mutter, 'Exactly so, Ma'am,' to guests, and then go back to sleep. It may not have made for the most exciting of dinner parties, but it was cosy, friendly, by royal standards pleasantly informal, and above all very agreeable to his guests, most of whom were much the same age as he was.

Some of them were not always quite so easy to please. After one of her visits to Brighton, Lady Wharncliffe admitted that her kingly host had been 'in very good spirits and good fun', although everybody had to be careful not to 'encourage' him, as he was inclined to be carried away on such convivial occasions, when his jokes often verged on the improper. Princess Lieven deprecated what she called the total lack of 'informed conversation', with never a word about politics. It can only be assumed that she had missed some of the more entertaining, if questionable, occasions when William, having drunk well, was obliged to give full rein to his oratorical powers. His speeches frequently could be as verbose, even undiplomatic, as they had when he was younger. He had never liked or admired the French, as befitted a man whose formative years had been during an era when his country was at war with France, where the experiment in republicanism from 1789 onwards had been mired in revolution and a reign of terror. Though the monarchy had been restored on the other side of the English Channel, William was no admirer of King Louis-Philippe who, he asserted, had taken the crown of his cousin, King Louis XVIII. Although the Government in London had observed diplomatic niceties and duly recognized the new regime, one night at dinner the king referred to the new monarch as 'an infamous scoundrel', an unfortunate turn of phrase. Afterwards Wellington warned him firmly that is was not to be repeated, in the interests of amicable Anglo-French relations. At a subsequent occasion at Windsor, a military banquet, William startled his guests by saying that he hoped, if the guests ever had to draw their swords, it would be against the French, whom he called 'the natural enemies of England'. For William, the nation that had given Europe a character such as Napoleon Bonaparte was not to be trusted.

In the first few months of his reign, King William gave orders for part of the Royal Lodge at Windsor to be demolished, while the East Terrace and the private drives through the park were opened to the public, although he was annoyed when he found that some of the visitors were scribbling their names on the statues. Turning his attention to the capital, he authorised the demolition of the Royal Mews in the environs of Buckingham Palace, to clear part of what would subsequently become Trafalgar Square, and had a public passage opened between Waterloo Place and St James's Park.

Recognizing the need for economy after his brother's extravagance, he cut the numbers of the castle staff and dismissed the French cooks, provoking a complaint from the gourmet Lord Dudley, a regular guest at court, about 'cold pâtés and hot champagne', and replaced the German band with a smaller English one. The more exotic and expensive animals in the royal menagerie, which had so captivated the previous monarch, were sent to the London Zoo, the number of horses in the royal stud was halved, and three of the five royal yachts were taken out of service as they were deemed unnecessary. Yet he was anything but mean. On his birthday he gave a banquet, including a roast beef meal, for 3,000 of the town's poorer inhabitants. Having no taste for grandeur, he could afford to entertain his subjects on a large scale without over-burdening the civil list.

A large collection of paintings and other treasures – which he dismissed as 'damned expensive taste' or 'knick-knackery' – was presented to the nation. Although nobody would have called him a particularly devout or saintly man, he held strong views about the paintings of religious subjects, saying they were improper and ought to be destroyed. King George IV had been regarded as one of the most discriminating and well-informed art connoisseurs ever to occupy the throne, but his successor was the very opposite. Fanny Kemble, the writer, actress and abolitionist, remarked disdainfully that 'The poor, dear king ... knows as much about painting as *una vacca spagnuola* [a Spanish cow].' As if to endorse this point of view, King William allowed himself, his family, and family animals to be painted by anybody who begged to be allowed such an honour. On a day when the pictures were being rehung at Windsor Castle, in the presence of Sir William Beechey, President of the Royal Academy, someone 'discovered in a wretched daub close to the ceiling a portrait of Lady Falkland [Amelia, one of the FitzClarence daughters], and another of His Majesty's favourite cat, which were immediately lowered to a less honourable position'. Beechey tactfully removed some of his own paintings, which everyone else knew were far superior.[16] It seemed that William concurred with his great-grandfather, King George II, who once exclaimed that he 'hated all boets and bainters'. Not surprisingly, William's additions to the royal collection were mostly naval scenes and portraits.

For a man of his age, with no previous political experience, widely regarded as a buffoon if not of questionable sanity, William quickly established a good relationship with his ministers, who knew that he had his faults but above all was anxious to be a conscientious king and do his best for his subjects. Accordingly, there is good reason to consider King William IV as the first truly constitutional British monarch. Unlike his autocratically minded predecessors, he believed it was the sovereign's duty to support his ministers, whether he agreed with their policies or not, unless they were evidently out of touch with the mood of the nation. As his change of heart at the time of Catholic emancipation had proved, he was not so stubborn as to cling doggedly to opinions that he had held for many years if he could see and appreciate another view. Although nobody could ever call him particularly clever, he had sufficient common sense to grasp with some speed the essence of problems concerning matters of state, giving his own views 'with perfect candour and fairness'. When meeting his councillors, he would listen patiently to all arguments and listen carefully to those who had reason to disagree with him. He perceived his role as that of an arbitrator between political rivals. In this he was ably assisted by Sir Herbert Taylor, his private secretary, a post he had formerly held with King George III, Queen Charlotte and the Duke of York. Taylor's letters to senior members of the Government on the king's behalf would play a significant role in maintaining good relations between majesty and ministers.

This was accompanied by a determination to show all due diligence in discharging his duties as a sovereign. During his last few months, King George IV had become too lazy to sign state papers at all, leaving his brother a backlog of several thousand. Queen Adelaide sat beside him as he laboriously worked through piles of documents, helping him at intervals to bathe his cramped fingers in a bowl of warm water. Wellington would claim that he had done more business with King William in ten minutes than with his predecessor in as many days.

At the time of his accession, William's three younger brothers were all, like him, in robust health. The mild-mannered, incorrigibly eccentric Augustus, Duke of Sussex, had always been distrusted by King George IV because of his sometimes alarmingly radical opinions, but at once he found himself back in favour at court. Greville noted approvingly that the king was 'very well with all his family, particularly the Duke of Sussex.'[17] He was appointed Chief Ranger of Hyde Park and St James's Park, which was little more than an honorary position but still the first honour he had received from the Crown since being granted his dukedom.

Adolphus, Duke of Cambridge, remained in Hanover as viceroy. Like Augustus he was an easy-going, gentle-minded prince, who had that rare gift of being liked and respected by almost everyone. This was certainly not the case with Ernest, Duke of Cumberland, who was now heir to the throne of Hanover. Ernest had been a courageous soldier on the field of battle during the wars against Napoleon. He had lost an eye in action and bore a severely disfiguring facial scar as testimony to his service to king and country. He may have been brave but he was disliked and even feared by many, because of his right-wing views. His reputation for blunt speaking and a sometimes-abrupt temper were not undeserved, although the rumours that he was an ogre in human shape who had fathered a child on one of his unmarried sisters, and also murdered his valet, might have excited the gutter press elements of the day but had no basis in sober fact. His relations with King George IV had been excellent, but this was mainly due to the latter having been too tired, weak and ill for the last few years of his life to try and argue with a strong-minded younger brother. He had been prepared to let him have things largely his own way in return for a quiet life.

King William was made of sterner stuff and they got on well with each other only because they agreed to differ. William was keenly aware of the duke's faults, and was not afraid to say no to him when the occasion demanded. 'Ernest is not a bad fellow,' he is said to have remarked, 'but if anyone has a corn, he will be sure to tread on it.'[18]

Ernest had persuaded King George IV to appoint him the Gold Stick, an honour that included the right to command the Windsor household cavalry, and to rule that he was thus directly responsible to the monarch and only the monarch. When he ascended the throne, King William ruled that in future the Gold Stick was to be responsible to, and would take his orders from, the Commander-in-Chief of the army, like any other regimental officer. As far as Cumberland was concerned, this stripped the post of any military significance. He informed the king through his private secretary that, as senior Field-Marshal of the Army, after the Duke of Wellington, he was unable to accept a situation which obliged him to take orders from an officer of lower rank than his own. Not for the first time in his life, the Duke of Wellington tried to mediate and effect a compromise, but neither of the royal brothers would give way. The duke wrote a lengthy letter in which protest was mingled with regret. He said he had made every effort conscientiously to fulfil his duties to their late brother and regretted that he would no longer be able to do the same for the present king, but the changed status of his office was not compatible with his honour as a prince of the blood royal. The king replied bluntly that he regretted his brother should consider it necessary to resign his office in consequence of the new arrangements, but it was his prerogative to make or approve any such changes. Consequently, after more than thirty years, the Duke of Cumberland was no longer on the active list of the British army.

Ernest was equally annoyed when King William sought to rescind an agreement whereby the duke's horses occupied the queen's stables at Windsor, there having been no queen during most of the previous reign. In response to a civil request that he take the animals elsewhere, the duke retorted with fury that he 'would be damned if they should go', but again he had no alternative but to obey his sovereign. Yet these disputes did not result in any lasting ill-feelings between them. Not long afterwards, the duke invited the king to come and dine with him at his house at Kew, a small bachelor dwelling that was unsuitable as a home for himself, his family and suite [retinue]. William subsequently allowed the Duke and Duchess of Cumberland and their son, George, to move into a spacious empty house on Kew Green, beside the entrance to the gardens.

Apart from these occasional issues with the brother who was next to him in age, King William had a relatively untroubled relationship with most of his family. The main exception to this rule was his relationships with his sons, the FitzClarences. Led by George, the eldest, they complained of the 'cruel position' in which they were 'placed as natural children' in the eyes of the law. They were nameless, they insisted, denied many rights and advantages that were granted to their fellow subjects, and should be enabled 'to take that reasonable rank in society' that they were entitled to expect. They incessantly made demands of the king, on the grounds that as sovereign their father was well placed to give them anything for the asking, within reason. At one stage George threatened to take his own life, while Frederick, adopting a tactic that his father himself had once resorted to, in order to get his own way from his own father, announced that he was intending to seek a seat in the House of Commons. His sons knew that the king was genuinely fond of them and felt a sense of guilt on their behalf, something which they were ever ready to exploit.

About six months after the king's accession, Greville reported that there had been 'a desperate quarrel between the King and his sons' at Court one evening. George, was hankering after a peerage and a pension, and had asked his younger brothers to support him, but the king had refused. 'They want to renew the days of Charles II, instead of waiting patiently and letting the King do what he can for them, and as he can,' said Greville.[19] In June 1831, the king wearily gave in and, anxious to put an end to what he called George's 'inordinate ambition and vanity', created him Earl of Munster, Viscount FitzClarence and Baron Tewkesbury, at the same time. William also gave his other sons and daughters the rank of children of a Marquis. Two years later,

George was also made a Privy Councillor. A scathing comment in the *Morning Post* suggested that the FitzClarences did not deserve any place in public life, opining that 'the by-blows of a King' should not be his bodyguard. 'Can anything be more indecent than the entry of a sovereign into his capital, with one bastard riding before him and another by the side of his carriage?' it asked. 'The impudence and rapacity of the FitzJordans is unexampled even in the annals of Versailles and Madrid.'[20]

Privately King William might have agreed with this judgement. His second surviving son, Frederick, had inherited William's early extravagance and seemed to think nothing of running up debts of about £12,000 and sending the bills to his father. The king told Frederick that if he were to sell his house to pay off part of his debt, he (William) would make up the difference, Frederick did not even bother to reply. The youngest son, Augustus, who had entered the Church and had been appointed as chaplain to his father, before his accession to the throne, once complained angrily to Fanny Kemble that he had been trained as a sailor, but after the death of his elder brother, Henry, he had been taken from his ship and despite his reluctance, had been compelled by his father to enter the Church.[21]

There were no such problems with the FitzClarence daughters. They had made successful marriages into the aristocracy, had no need to beg their father for money, and he had excellent relationships with them all. Lady Wharncliffe thought they were 'pretty and lively, and make society in a way that real princesses could not'.[22]

King William IV and Queen Adelaide divided their time between St James's Palace in London, Windsor Castle, and Brighton Pavilion. Though they retained Clarence House, their main home in the capital was the neighbouring St James's Palace. When William ascended the throne, he had not been particularly familiar with Windsor. On the day following the funeral of King George IV, he undertook a thorough tour of the building and admitted afterwards that he had seen several of the rooms for the very first time. Windsor had long been the official seat of the British monarchy and, as he sensed the public expected it of him, he was prepared to respect historical tradition and spend a certain amount of time there. Nevertheless, he admitted that he much preferred spending his time at Bushy, which had been his home for so many years as an adult. He and Queen Adelaide also liked Brighton Pavilion and found the town pleasant enough, although the sea air tended to make the king drowsy. The Pavilion was the only place, one of his granddaughters thought, where he could cast off 'the trammels of royalty' and live more like an ordinary citizen.

Buckingham Palace was William's least favourite residence, despite the alterations that had been begun by his father and continued by his elder brother, which at long last were close to completion, although the costs had exceeded the original estimate by about half a million pounds. He found it too flamboyant and called it 'a most ill-conceived house'. Throughout his reign he was anxious to get rid of it and frequently suggested that it might be better used by somebody else. Shortly after his accession he suggested that it could be converted into a barracks, as suitable accommodation for about 1,500 foot guards, but Earl Grey vetoed the idea on the grounds of expense.

In an age long before the advent of opinion polls, it is impossible to estimate just how unpopular the British monarchy was in 1830. While it is all too easy to make sweeping statements about whether the country was on the verge of abolishing the institution for the second time in less than two centuries, or not, one can hardly argue that the previous two monarchs were outstandingly popular with the nation at large. George III was a pious, well-meaning man who, despite his domestic virtues, went down in history as 'the king who lost America'. This failure was only partly mitigated when he was pitied for the melancholy of his last years, as he descended into a twilight world ascribed to madness. While King George IV, a patron of the arts *par excellence*, had his defenders, not least the Duke of

Wellington who could always be relied on to see the best in anyone or anything. A few days after the king's death, Wellington praised him in the House of Lords as a man acknowledged by all as 'the most accomplished man of his age'.[23] Not long after, he spoke of his late sovereign even more warmly as 'the most extraordinary compound of talent, wit, buffoonery, obstinacy, and good feeling that I ever saw in any character in my life.'[24] This did not alter the fact that when he passed away, King George was little mourned, and in retrospect he was probably one of the most disliked kings ever to sit on the British throne. As Roger Fulford opined more than a century later, in view of his unpopularity and the abuse and ridicule heaped on him in his last years, 'the reputation and authority of the Crown were severely damaged'.[25] The last thing the throne needed, if its survival was to be ensured, was a reincarnation of King George IV in his brother William.

It was just as well that Prince William Henry had proved to be a man of a very different stamp when he succeeded to his inheritance. He had already given evidence of his affability, his refusal to stand on ceremony, and his endearing if less than dignified informality. When it came to working with the Government, it was soon apparent to those around him that he had every intention of avoiding the slightest appearance of intrigue against his ministers. He was critical to friends, albeit discreetly and only in trusted company, about the errors his brother had sometimes made regarding having been insufficiently supportive of his government. They soon realized that William would be far more likely to act according to the principle that his duty was to support the prime minister until parliament determined, usually through a vote, that the minister no longer possessed the nation's confidence. Long before the term was widely used in British political parlance, William had shown pronounced democratic tendencies that were unusual for the time.

These observers were not mistaken, but they had not taken into account two factors that would distinguish William's reign from that of the previous monarch. First, William was determined that he was going to take more interest, and participate more fully, in the business of government than George IV had done, and his willingness to interfere with his ministers' course of action was far greater than that of his predecessor. Secondly, it was not clear that an active king would behave quite in the way predicted, should he confront a constitutional issue that he thought would affect the position of the monarchy. William combined an old-fashioned distrust of party with fears of radical republicanism, and saw his role as that of a conciliator, favourable to the idea of a coalition government that would enable the most adept politicians to serve together, irrespective of party, to safeguard the established order. It was an ideal that he continued to cherish at various times throughout his reign, especially later when he thought the Whigs were failing to provide strong government but suspected the Tories would not have the support of the country. He never completely grasped the rivalries and resentments of political leaders, or their need to retain a reputation for consistency. Of the complex currents of political life outside parliament he knew little, if anything, and he shared the view of most of his brothers that leaders of popular movements were generally troublemakers. Nevertheless, William was far shrewder, and even moderate, to a degree, in his general outlook. It was fortunate that he possessed such qualities, for within a few months of his accession he would be called upon to face a tough challenge – the demand for parliamentary reform that had been growing steadily over the previous few decades.

It was convention that a new House of Commons had to be elected after the death of a king. Accordingly, in July 1830 parliament was dissolved. The ensuing general election coincided with the abdication of King Louis XVIII in France, and the accession of his more democratic Bourbon rival, King Louis-Philippe. This was a striking reminder, if not a warning, of the new forces of reform afoot in Europe. King William was highly critical of the new French ruler, and in matters of foreign policy he rarely deferred to his ministers.

He had never had any love for France and could be quite outspoken on the subject, and the French sovereign – as he often was about anything or anyone who irritated him. Earl Grey remarked, somewhat unguardedly, to Princess Lieven that this behaviour was 'very unfortunate, and still more improper,' and everyone had known for a long time that discretion was not among the king's good qualities.[26]

Electoral reform would prove to be a prominent issue on the hustings. When the results were counted, fifty seats had been gained by the Whigs, and when parliament met again in September, Wellington remained in office as prime minister, but with a small Tory majority. His position was vulnerable as the party had been deeply divided, particularly as the more conservative element had not forgiven him or Sir Robert Peel for having introduced Catholic emancipation at the end of the last reign. He had lost further support when the opposition raised the issue of reform in one of the first debates of the year, to which he responded with a stout defence of the existing system of government, much to the dismay of some of the more far-seeing members of his own party.

Throughout the tribulations of the Napoleonic wars and their aftermath, the changes wrought by the Industrial Revolution, and an approximate doubling in the population of mainland Britain between the mid-eighteenth century and 1830, the antiquated British electoral system had remained completely unaltered, and the number of voters and geographical distribution of seats became more anachronistic with each passing year. For example, Cornwall returned forty-four members to Westminster, while cities such as Manchester, Leeds and Birmingham, and expanding industrial centres in the midlands and farther north, where many people lived in order to satisfy the labour demands of new factories, had no members in Westminster. The most extreme instance of this archaic system, which was clearly no longer fit for purpose, was that of the borough of Old Sarum in Wiltshire. Initially it had been based on the original ancient settlement which had long since moved to the town of Salisbury. Since the fourteenth century it had consistently elected two members to the House of Commons, although for several centuries it had not had any resident voters, only landowners who lived elsewhere.

The need for parliamentary reform had been discussed regularly since early in the reign of King George III, and increasingly so since the example of the French revolution had motivated radicals to seek a change to the existing order. Successive prime ministers, all of whom were to some extent content with matters as they were, had avoided the issue. The Duke of Wellington had been foremost among them. In a debate at the opening of the new parliamentary session on 2 November in 1830, he had remarked on Grey having 'alluded to the propriety of effecting parliamentary reform', although the Government was just as unprepared with any plan as Grey was himself, while adding that he had been candid enough to acknowledge that he had not prepared for any measure of reform. Wellington himself was 'fully convinced that the country possesses, at the present moment, a legislature which answers all the good purposes of legislation, and this to a greater degree than any legislature ever has answered in any country whatsoever. I will go further and say that the legislature and the system of representation possesses the full and entire confidence of the country.'[27] He sat down to silence, with many of his colleagues dismayed at his blunt defence of the present order. The Whigs regarded it as the greatest gift to their cause that they could ever have imagined.

One week later the king and his ministers were due to dine at the Guildhall, when they were warned that there was likely to be an organised protest in London, and the authorities could not guarantee their safety. Wellington assured William that he had 'no desire to be massacred ... I would have gone if the law had been equal to protect me, but that was not the case.'[28] The Government promptly cancelled the dinner. Lord Brougham, who had been appointed Lord Chancellor in the new government, was planning to table a motion on parliamentary reform. It would have proved unnecessary, for on 15 November, during a debate on the civil list, Wellington was defeated. The motion of no confidence was carried by a majority of twenty-nine votes and Wellington was forced to resign as prime minister the following day. The king regretted his departure from government but, it was said, 'accepted the ministers' resignations without remonstrance'. All of them, except characteristically Wellington himself, assured their sovereign of the need for some degree of reform. It gave the king some indication that he and his new government were likely to face an uncertain future.

In spite of this, William saw no reason to fear the advent of a slightly more radical government, for he had long known and respected several of the senior Whigs. Having consulted several of them, it was evident that Grey was the person who would command most respect in the party and the country, and the King sent for him on the afternoon of 16 November. King George IV had cordially disliked Grey, but his brother had never shared his views. The transition was quite seamless. Grey accepted office and undertook to form a new ministry, on condition that he would introduce some measure of reform, a commitment that the king was happy to accept. At the conclusion of their meeting, both men evidently had been very pleased to be able to do business with each other. Greville was particularly impressed with the way the sovereign had presided over a change of administration. It was unanimously considered that he had acted with the greatest circumspection, 'no intriguing or underhand communication with anybody, with great kindness to his Ministers, anxious to support them while it was possible and submitting at once to the necessity of parting with them. The fact is he turns out an incomparable King … he is as dignified as the homeliness and simplicity of his character will allow him to be.'[29]

When the new ministers came to St James's to receive their seals of office, King William received them with his customary informality and a short speech which assured them that, as members of the new government, they would receive from him the most cordial, unceasing and devoted support.[30] That he had not inherited a government of revolutionaries or radicals in sheep's clothing became reassuringly evident when one of Grey's first communications with him was a cabinet minute addressing the subject of taking action against unlawful assemblies and civil disobedience. William and his prime minister were united in the need to preserve order, with sterner measures if necessary. The present state of the country was volatile, and new legislation might be needed to maintain law and order. Yet the king questioned the wisdom of a scheme to create vigilante groups from units of discharged soldiers, to maintain law and order. He told Grey that this might provoke violence rather than restrain it, and his words of wisdom were readily taken on board.

Despite this harmonious overture to their working relationship, it was inevitable that before long there would be sources of disagreement. One of the principles maintained by the Whigs, particularly at a time when the economy was not in a good condition, was that of economy in public life. The court was therefore firmly in their sights, particularly after King George IV's lavish expenditure on himself and his favourites. His successor, they may have sensed, might well understand and appreciate the need for some form of retrenchment, as he would make clear in a few months' time when the matter of his coronation was under discussion. Before this, there was the business of the queen's outfit. Sir Herbert Taylor (the king's secretary) felt himself obliged to inform the Government that certain expenses pertaining to the royal household, specifically that of Queen Adelaide's outfit, should be met by government expenditure, otherwise Her Majesty would be considerably in debt at the beginning of her husband's reign.

Grey considered it a reasonable demand, but admitted he was uncertain as to how the House of Commons would view the matter. Before he was able to take it any further, Baron Glenelg, President of the Board of Control, threatened to resign if the queen's outfit were to be paid for by the nation. Grey then had to admit to the king that he hardly dared to raise the matter in parliament, as it would be a contentious issue. He was sure that when the Civil List was debated, Viscount Althorp, Chancellor of the Exchequer, would make arrangements for the cost to be met in a satisfactory manner. The king was grateful for his reply and requested that Althorp make no reference to the subject, as he did not wish to claim any merit for relinquishing an assertion to which an objection could be made.

Financial issues continued to pose something of a problem. Althorp proposed that certain expenses, which had been paid from the Civil List as a matter of course, should now be put under parliamentary control, to which the king fully agreed. The Government saw this as an opportunity to scrutinise expenditure in the Royal Household, and to propose reduction of the salaries paid to certain court officials. This annoyed the king, but as it involved no more than roughly £12,000 a year, Grey did not intend to risk any confrontation over what he saw as a relatively trivial matter. When Althorp was entrusted with the question in the House of Commons, he acknowledged that he too, when he had first considered costs incurred in the Royal Palace, had found it strange that though the prices of most commodities had recently decreased, overall expenditure was higher. Even so, he maintained, it would be difficult to make any reduction without compelling the king and queen to alter their style of living or to incur debt, and he was sure the House also had no wish to compel them to do so. It was a state of affairs that the House was content to accept.

Chapter 6

Reform Proposed

Shortly after Earl Grey took office in November 1830, a committee of four was established. It comprised two cabinet ministers, the Earl of Durham, Lord Privy Seal (and husband of Grey's eldest daughter), and Sir James Graham, First Lord of the Admiralty, as well as two senior Whigs, Lord John Russell, Paymaster of the Forces, and Viscount Duncannon. Although the latter was not yet a minister, he was chosen partly for his proven ability to help organise elections, partly because he was a friend of Daniel O'Connell, who was recognised as the champion of Ireland's Roman Catholic majority in the first half of the nineteenth century and whose support would be needed, and also partly on account of his detailed knowledge of Irish matters. He was appointed chairman, and all four met at his house in Cleveland Row, where they received regular deputations seeking their views on what needed to be done, and collaborating on a measure of parliamentary reform that culminated in the Representation of the People Act. This would increase the franchise, eliminate the most glaring anomalies in representation, and take measures to correct abuses and fraud in the election of members of parliament. The aim was to satisfy public opinion, while still maintaining the essential character of the Constitution.

Sir Herbert Taylor was anxious to reassure Grey that the king was uneasy about the impending proceedings in parliament, and not surprised that his prime minister was approaching it with dread. His Majesty was satisfied that nobody could be 'more strongly opposed in sentiment, in principle, in judgement, and firm solicitude for the preservation of the constitutional monarchy of this country, and for its welfare and security, against the wild and mischievous projects of the Radicals.' He had total confidence in Grey, and was anxious not to embarrass him 'by objections which can be considered frivolous or captious'.[1]

Grey was relieved but not completely satisfied. He suspected that the king was still surrounded by a number of diehard Tory adherents, intent on trying to convince him that Whig proposals would be ill-conceived and dangerous, and who would not hesitate to pass mischievous gossip to the press in the interests of frustrating any further progress towards reform. When Grey complained that members of the household were doing so, Taylor assured him that Their Majesties were 'accessible at all hours', the king saw several people throughout the day, 'and converses freely with them on subjects on which they may give him information', but he never conversed with them on any matter that might be the subject of government or official information. He forbade any discussion on politics at dinner or evening parties, and he never spoke about them with the queen. As time would show, the last statement was not accurate, and Queen Adelaide's Tory prejudices would ultimately do the king's reputation for impartiality no good at all, as did those of the Duke of Gloucester and the FitzClarences.

Despite everything, Grey was slightly apprehensive when the time came for him to visit the king at Brighton and propose the reform draft. He told the Marquess of Anglesey, Lord Lieutenant of Ireland, that if King William agreed to it, he was sure they would be supported by public opinion. 'If he does not – what next?'[2] He need not have worried. The King examined it thoroughly, asked several questions and assured Grey that he intended to support it in every detail.

Yet a few days later it seemed that royal approval might not be quite so unequivocal after all. On 4 February the king sent Grey a long memorandum setting out his views on the principles of the bill, rather than the details. He said he could foresee dangers in introducing the measure, and that they outweighed any possible advantages. This did not detract from his acceptance of the fact that his ministers were committed to a measure of reform, and, as he appreciated that the present system was by no means perfect, he would support it, albeit with reluctance. He felt duty-bound to warn Grey that he feared a substantial reform would be passed by the Commons, but then be rejected by the Lords, and that any ensuing quarrel between both Houses would be disastrous for the country. The monarch, Grey realized, was the Government's ally, but his approach was less than steadfast.

Grey informed the Lords that the bill would be introduced in the Commons at the beginning of March 1831. William's fears concerned not an extensive reform measure in itself, but what might need to be done to put it on the statute book. He dreaded any election that would follow its rejection by the Commons because of the disorder it might engender, especially in Ireland. The prospect of the Lords rejecting a bill that the Commons had accepted seemed to him even more alarming, but Grey was ready to reassure him. The previous month, he had told Taylor, that if what they were proposing would meet with His Majesty's agreement, he was certain he could carry it through parliament. This was good enough for voters who believed that many of the noblest families in the country, headed by the king himself, supported the Government and the bill. Yet the king still had his doubts, and told Grey so, urging that, while the principle of the bill could not be abandoned, it ought to be 'remodelled'. Although the Government had won a comfortable majority and therefore a mandate for the measure, the modifications drafted by the ministers were not enough to satisfy the king, or to win over the more moderate Tory peers. Reshaping the bill did not seem feasible, and Melbourne later told Taylor that he thought it would be wrong to proceed by taking a course of action which suggested the Government was reneging on its commitment to major change, especially one that was moving with the times and clearly would be very popular. In spite of his misgivings, the king was still fully prepared to give his support to the Government.

The original motion for reform as proposed by Brougham, who was regarded as one of the most passionate advocates of reform, had suggested that about five boroughs were likely to be disenfranchised. During the previous three or four weeks there had been much speculation as to the extent of the amendments the Government planned to undertake. The general assumption was that only about a dozen seats, at most, would be affected. On 1 March, Lord John Russell, one of the four cabinet ministers who had helped to draft the Reform Bill, presented it in the House of Commons on behalf of the Government. His proposals came as a rude shock to the Tories. He began by reading out a schedule of sixty boroughs, with less than 2,000 inhabitants each, that were to be abolished, followed by a second round of forty-seven boroughs each of which would lose one of their two members. There would be a transfer of 168 seats from small boroughs to large towns and counties; eight would be given to London, thirty-four to large towns, fifty-five to English counties, five to Scotland, three to Ireland and one to Wales. These new measures would provide every constituency with at least a minimum of resident voters and an increase of nearly fifty per cent (about half a million people) in the franchise, which would be extended to those who lived in houses rated at £10 per annum, and to leaseholders and copyholders of counties. Half-measures, he said, would not suffice, 'no trifling, no paltry reform, could give stability to the Crown, strength to the Parliament, or satisfaction to the country.'[3]

Grey feared the bill would not be passed if it was left to the discretion of the existing membership of the Commons, and that a dissolution leading to another general election would be the only answer. He knew that the king would be certain to reject the proposal, as he thought that elections at such a contentious time would lead to violence. When he asked the king, His Majesty responded that he would do what he could to help the Government with its problem, but gave no hint that he would allow such a course of action.

On 18 March the Tories defeated the Government by forty-six votes on a separate matter, a bill concerned with the imposition of timber duties. It was a crucial defeat, signifying their likely intention to give no quarter to the administration in voting against the Reform Bill as well. The king was alarmed, for he believed that the Tories had to allow the Whigs to govern responsibly. Preparing for the worst, Grey asked Taylor to find out what the king's reaction would be. to going to the country. The king made it clear to Grey that he would deeply regret 'anything that would shake the stability of the present Government' and deprive him of his services. He was 'convinced that, by perseverance, they will overcome opposition and combinations; and they may depend upon his utmost support in maintaining their ground, provided His Majesty be not called upon to dissolve Parliament at this period'. Yet Grey continued to press the question, until the king told him firmly that if a general election were to take place at that moment, as a consequence of his administration

> being defeated in the attempt to carry the Bill of Reform,
> thereby throwing back, upon an excited population, a
> measure which is considered by that population to have
> been brought forward in deference to the expression of its
> opinion; if what is called an appeal to the people be now
> made upon a popular question so strenuously advocated
> by those who have been supported by popular clamour,
> when a spirit of agitation which has been so long in
> progress has been so much increased by the introduction
> of the bill and the discussion upon it, this country would
> be thrown into convulsion from the Land's End to John
> O'Groat's.[4]

The Tories, who knew they had most to lose from the abolition of rotten boroughs that had so long been theirs for the taking, agreed to let it pass unchallenged on the first reading, but they and their allies in the House of Lords were determined to defeat it on the second. This came close to happening when the Reform Bill was carried by only one vote on 22 March 1831, thanks to support from some of the more moderate Tories. Thomas Macaulay, at that time a newly elected Whig Member of the Commons and later an eminent historian, was thrilled. He wrote to a friend of the moment the vote was announced.

> We set up a shout that you might have heard to Charing Cross, waving our hats, stamping against the floor, and clapping our hands. The tellers scarcely got through the crowd: for the house was thronged up to the table, and all the floor was fluctuating with heads like the pit of a theatre. But you might have heard a pin drop as Duncannon read the numbers. Then again the shouts broke out and many of us shed tears. I could scarcely refrain.[5]

The first battle had been won, but the predictably close result of the vote was ample warning to Grey and his ministers that it was only the first, and that not all the goodwill in the world from his sovereign could hide the fact that subsequent progress could not be taken for granted. King William was as good as his word in giving the Government all reasonable support. Two junior Tory members of the Commons who were attached to the King's Household, Henry Meynell and Horace Seymour, voted against the bill and were dismissed from their positions. All the same, the Tory opposition was determined to halt the reform movement in its tracks. When the bill went into committee on 18 April, an amendment was introduced by Isaac Gascoyne, a Tory who had been noted for his support of reactionary policies, regarding the slave trade, Catholic emancipation and the practice of bullbaiting. Now he moved that the total number of members representing seats in England and Wales should not be reduced. The cabinet insisted that this would run counter to the spirit of one of the bill's main proposals and was therefore quite unacceptable. Grey thought that the division on this issue would be favourable, but warned the king that if not, it would call for 'immediate and anxious consideration'[6] on the part of the ministers – in other words, the dissolution that King William was anxious not to grant. After two nights' debate, Gascoyne's motion was carried by eight votes. With this Grey realized that there was no alternative to dissolution, and on 22 April 1831 the king reluctantly agreed to come and do so in person, accepting such a course of action as the lesser of two evils. The Whigs were overjoyed, and the Tories furious. The Duke of Wellington was particularly aggrieved, convinced that his sovereign had been extraordinarily rash. He confided to the Duke of Buckingham, a former Lord Steward of the Household, that he did not think the king of England had 'taken a step so fatal to his monarchy since the day that Charles I passed the Act to deprive himself of the power of proroguing or dissolving the Long Parliament.'[7] The Duke of Gloucester was equally annoyed, and allegedly taunted his cousin, 'Who is Silly Billy now?'

Having been forced to intervene against his instincts, King William was displeased by the obstructive tactics of the parliamentary opposition. To him, this was tiresome mischief-making for its own sake without any sensible motive in mind, and the only result would be to accentuate division throughout the country. Knowing what the likely result of any forthcoming general election would be, Lord Wharncliffe threatened to sponsor a motion in the House of Lords against dissolving parliament. If he succeeded, this would immediately widen the breach between both houses, something the king was anxious to avoid at all costs. In order to prevent the motion from being introduced, Grey and Brougham went to St James's Palace

Prince William and Prince Edward, who were born two years apart and were always close during childhood. Benjamin West, 1778, Royal Collection.

King George III.
Thomas Frye, c.1762.

William, Duke of
Clarence, aged 30 but with
his active naval career
now behind him. Thomas
Lawrence, 1795.

Right: Dorothea Jordan, renowned actress and for several years the Duke of Clarence's mistress. John Hoppner, 1791.

Below: 'The Disconsolate Sailor': Catherine Tylney-Long's choice between the Duke of Clarence (right) and William Wesley-Pole. Caricature by Charles Williams, 1811.

THE DISCONSOLATE SAILOR or Miss LONG ING for a POLE.

Queen Adelaide. Sir William Beechey, c.1831.

George FitzClarence, Earl of Munster. Engraving by Richard Austin Artlett, after Thomas Phillips, 1839.

King George IV. Sir Thomas Lawrence, 1821.

Charles Grey, 2nd Earl Grey, Prime Minister during the passage of the Great Reform Bill. Sir Thomas Lawrence, c.1828.

Cartoon supporting the Reform Act. King William sits above the clouds, surrounded by Whig politicians, while looking down, the British lion disperses the Tories and Britannia slays the dragon. Unknown artist, 1832.

William IV in Masonic insignia, shortly after his accession. James Lonsdale, 1830.

Victoria, Duchess of Kent, and her daughter Princess Victoria, later queen. Samuel Denning, c.1825.

King William IV, one of the last known portraits, by his daughter Sophia De L'Isle and Dudley, shortly before her death in childbirth, 1837.

William IV, granite statue by Samuel Nixon, 1844. Originally placed in King William Street near London Bridge, it was moved to Greenwich Park, near the National Maritime Museum, in 1936 (© Sue and Mike Woolmans)

at once to ask the king to come and prorogue parliament in person, thus putting an end to any further discussion.

In the words of Greville, the result was a *coup d'état* that came on them so suddenly that nobody was aware of it until two or three hours before it happened, and some not at all. When Brougham made it clear that the Lords were resorting to any tactics they could to prevent dissolution, the king was angry at what seemed to be wilful infringement with his exercise of the prerogative. Instantly grasping the urgency of the situation, he was so intent on acting at once that he did not appear surprised when Brougham told him that he had already ordered an escort of the Horse Guards to be prepared. Getting the state coach ready proved more complicated. Legend has it that an attempt was made to stop him when The Master of the Horse tried to warn him that the horses' manes for the royal coach would take five hours to plait, to which he retorted that he would go to Westminster with 'anybody's else's horses', or in a hackney coach if all else failed. When he arrived at parliament, he found the Lords in chaos, with several members trying to obstruct dissolution in any way they could. Startled by the noise as he entered the robing room, he asked what was happening, to which Brougham told him that the Lords were debating. Some doubt the truth of this story, although it is quite credible, as a characteristic of his impatience, and determination that time-honoured but time-wasting ritual could not be allowed to get in the way of immediate action if necessary.

Somebody had been sent in a coach to collect the crown from the Tower. In theory the king should not have worn it yet, as he still had to be crowned, but this he believed was no time for meaningless niceties. When he was in the robing room, he sent for it and when the Marquess of Hastings was about to place it on his head he stopped him, saying, 'Nobody shall put the Crown on my head but myself.' He did so, and then turned to Lord Grey with a look of triumph, saying that his coronation was over.

George Villiers said later that he had never witnessed such a scene, and as he looked at the king on his throne, with the crown loose on his head, with Lord Grey standing grimly beside him with the sword of state in his hand, it looked almost as if His Majesty had his executioner by his side, 'and the whole picture looked strikingly typical of his and our future destinies.'[8]

It is doubtful whether such an uncertain situation involving parliament and the monarch in person had been seen in England since the turbulent days of King Charles I, and King William found himself something of a national hero after his decisive action. Polling for the subsequent general election was held from 28 April to 1 June, with the reformers exhorting people to 'vote for the two Bills'. The king was displeased, fearing that it would call his impartiality into question. He believed the Lord Mayor of London was wrong to order illuminations to mark the dissolution, and furious when told that pro-reform mobs were going around London breaking windows of darkened houses, notably those of the Duke of Wellington at Apsley House, evidently signifying their political sympathies. In spite of this he was anxious to continue supporting Grey as far as he could, and in May he conferred the Order of the Garter on him, although there was no vacancy at the time. It provoked a complaint from Wellington that to do so was 'a gross impropriety ... not justified by services or by precedent'.[9]

As a brief respite from politics, the king was granted a diversion in the first week of June by going to Ascot, where he was joined by some of the FitzClarences. He evidently did not enjoy himself, as the races bored him, and his own horse broke down while running. At the end of the week he and the queen threw a dinner at Windsor Castle, to which they invited about forty people. As was his regular practice, Greville left an interesting commentary on the proceedings in which irony, praise and criticism were finely balanced. He found the room insufferably hot and not nearly large enough for the assembled company, although the dinner was not bad. The king drank wine with everybody, he observed, and fell asleep after dinner. Immediately after coffee, a band consisting mostly of violins and other stringed instruments began to play; the queen and the whole party sat there the whole evening, 'so that it was, in fact, a concert of instrumental music'. He found it all 'exceedingly magnificent, and the manner of life does not appear to be very formal, and need not be disagreeable but for the bore of never dining without twenty strangers. The Castle holds very few people, and with the King's and Queen's immediate suite and *toute la bâtardise* [all the bastardy] it was quite full.' The contrast with similar occasions during the previous reign struck him at once. He considered the present circumstances much the better, although, bearing in mind his host's advancing years, he wondered how long this would continue:

> What a *changement de décoration*; no longer George IV, capricious, luxurious, and misanthropic, liking nothing but the society of listeners and flatterers, with the Conyngham tribe and one or two Tory Ministers and foreign Ambassadors; but a plain, vulgar, hospitable gentleman, opening his doors to all the world, with a numerous family and suite, a Whig Ministry, no foreigners, and no toad-eaters at all. Nothing can be more different, and looking at him once sees how soon this act will be finished, and the same be changed for another probably not less dissimilar. Queens, bastards, Whigs, all will disappear, and God knows what replaces them.[10]

In the face of political and popular pressure for reform, the result was a foregone conclusion. The pro-reform Whigs won a landslide majority of 136 over the Tories and won almost all constituencies with genuine electorates, leaving the Tories with little more than the rotten boroughs. Gascoyne was among several members from the previous parliament who had lost their seats.

If anything, the victory had been a little too decisive for the king's liking. Conventional wisdom has it that large powerful governments, even if democratically elected, tend to be over-confident, complacent and do not necessarily make good administrations. Would Lord Grey be sufficiently magnanimous to compromise with his political adversaries, or would it be a case of 'winner takes all'? Throughout the weeks in which polling had taken place, the king continued to remind Grey that he was sure there were few members of the House of Lords who did not admit that some measure of reform was vital, but that the majority of them objected to the extent of the proposed bill, and he was fearful that they would persist in their relentless opposition to its passage. He strongly believed, as he was sure his government did, 'as *all* must feel who value the peace and prosperity of this country, and take an interest in the maintenance of that Constitution which has hitherto ensured both, amidst the convulsions and the desolation of other states, the extreme importance of preventing a collision between the two Houses of Parliament.' It was only fair to remember that King William had sacrificed his own prejudices and scruples regarding the issue; he had abandoned his personal objections which were deeply seated and had been strongly urged that:'... claims from those whom it has been his study to support, throughout the perilous struggle in which they have engaged, that they will so shape their further course as to relieve him, if possible, from the serious embarrassment in which they may place him, by a too close and too rigid adherence to all the features of the bill.'[11] When the bill came again before the House of Commons on 7 July, it was again passed with a majority of 136.

Meanwhile, convention and the kingly trappings of state required a new sovereign to give some thought to the unavoidable question of a coronation for the new reign. If he had really supposed that placing the crown on his head prior to dissolving parliament earlier in the year would have been accepted as adequate, he was doomed to disappointment. With his now already well-known distaste for grand ceremonies of any sort, he would willingly have dispensed with one altogether, especially as he thought the rituals of the previous one in 1821 had been a complete waste of time and money. A full dress affair with the customary fripperies, he was convinced, would be far too costly. The country was in an unsettled state, and would they risk unleashing a wave of protests against the extravagance of what amounted to little more than a magnificent but unnecessary circus of pomp and splendour? Moreover, at the age of sixty-six he was no longer as strong and fit as formerly, and the potential strain and fatigue of such a business did not appeal to him in the slightest.

When he consulted legal opinion as to the possibility of dispensing with it altogether, he was told that some such ceremony would be required for swearing the oath before the Lords and Commons. His solution was that a simple service would be adequate for the purpose. Yet his subjects, particularly the Tories with their reverence for time-honoured tradition, told him firmly that this would be inadequate. He also had to take into account the views of the Duke of Cumberland who, as ever, was determined to have his say and insisted on a proper coronation as some compensation for having given his very reluctant support to the Reform Bill. As always, the Duke of Wellington argued succinctly for the traditional view. 'In my opinion, we cannot meddle with the ceremony,' he wrote to the Duke of Buckingham. 'All that we have a right to expect is that the King shall be crowned in the usual manner before his people.' He also knew that it would be an occasion for creating more peers, much to the advantage of the Whigs, and there was much talk every day that this would be done. 'I confess that I concur with you in thinking that Lord Grey will stick at nothing. There can scarcely be a question about the King, considering what His Majesty has done by dissolution.'[12]

Yielding to the inevitable, King William was still determined that any such proceedings would be considerably curtailed. The Tory peers had been looking forward to another magnificent spectacle and insisted that a coronation – and a grand one at that – was a necessity. When they heard that they could expect only a somewhat trimmed-down affair, they threatened to boycott the 'half-crownation', to which William retorted that he could therefore expect 'greater convenience of room and less heat'.[13] Much to his annoyance, a few Tory peers did absent themselves from Westminster Abbey on the day, and although his eyesight was far from perfect, he noticed. It did not endear the Tories in general to him. He was even more angry when his eldest son, George FitzClarence, recently created Earl of Munster and Baron Tewkesbury, asked him if he would let him carry his crown at the ceremony. It would only be fair, he said, on the grounds that nobody was more fit to do so than his own flesh and blood. Moreover, he suggested that the Order of the Garter would be an acceptable reward for such a service.

The ceremony that took place on 8 September 1831 was therefore a humble affair that offended some of the traditionalists. Yet in some matters they did have their way. A few days earlier, a copy of the ceremonial was submitted to him for his approval. When it came to the homage paid to him by the spiritual Peers, led by the Archbishop of Canterbury, William Howley, he was informed that they all had to kiss him on the cheek. William retorted indignantly that he was not going to be kissed by the bishops, and ordered that part to be struck out. The Archbishop insisted that this section was not negotiable, and the king gave in, said Greville, 'and so he must undergo the salute of the spiritual as well as of the temporal Lords.'[14]

The total cost was a little over £30,000, comparing favourably with £240,000 for the opulent affair that had been staged for King George IV, but the hard-pressed nation appreciated the fact that due economy had been observed. Fears that the occasion might have been greeted with protesting pro-reform mobs were never realized. When the king and queen arrived in their carriage they were enthusiastically cheered. The Duke of Cumberland arrived a little later, initially to groans and cat-calls, but he refused to be daunted, and by the time he entered the abbey he was hailed as well, if less vociferously. All but his most unforgiving opponents had to admit that their battle-scarred war hero, who had fought so fearlessly thirty or forty years before, was the last man in England likely to be intimidated by a few noisy demonstrators.

As for the bearing of the sovereigns at the centre of proceedings, Macaulay thought that Queen Adelaide 'behaved admirably, with wonderful grace and dignity. The King very awkwardly.' The Duke of Devonshire, Lord Chamberlain of the Household, upstaged him completely by giving every appearance of looking as if he had come to be crowned instead of his master. The king's bearing, he continued, 'made the foolish parts of the ritual appear monstrously ridiculous and deprived many of the better parts of their proper effect. Persons who were at a distance perhaps did not feel this; but I was near enough to see every turn of his finger and every glance of his eye. The moment of the crowning was extremely fine.' At the moment the archbishop placed the crown on the king's head, the trumpets sounded, and everyone cried out 'God save the King.' All the peers and peeresses put on their coronets, 'and the blaze of splendour through the Abbey seemed to be doubled.' Next the king was conducted to the raised throne, where the peers successively did him homage. Some of them were cheered as they did so, 'which I thought indecorous in such a place and occasion.' Macaulay noticed also that the Tories cheered the Duke of Wellington loudly, while the Whigs took revenge by doing likewise for Lords Grey and Brougham. Despite the grandeur and solemnity of the occasion, he found the ceremony much too long, carelessly performed in parts, and complained that the archbishop mumbled.[15]

Lady Wharncliffe pitied the king, thinking that he appeared 'very infirm in his walk, poor man, and looked oppress'd with the immense weight of his robes and crown'.[16] Nevertheless Greville agreed with Macaulay that it had been a superbly organised triumph for all concerned; 'the coronation went off well, and whereas nobody was satisfied before it, everybody was after it.' Although the king was able to dispense with the customary Westminster Hall banquet afterwards, he had to give a private feast at St James's, at which he asked his guests to join him in a toast to 'the land we live in'.[17] With one eye on the Duke of Cumberland, William said that he personally thought the coronation had been unnecessary, but he was anxious to watch over the liberties of his people.

Meanwhile the reform legislation proceeded on its fitful parliamentary progress. During the previous few months, political unions throughout the country had maintained pressure on parliament, ensuring their voices would be heard, with regular mass meetings, pamphlets and petitions to both Houses. Eighty petitions in favour of reform were presented on one day alone. The opponents of reform deliberately slowed its progress at committee stage through lengthy and detailed arguments, but it was passed on 21 September 1831 by a margin of more than a hundred votes and sent to the House of Lords, with its inbuilt hostile majority. After the Whigs' decisive victory in the election, some speculated that opponents might abstain, rather than openly defy the public will.

Their predictions were realized to an extent, when, after further debate, the Lords voted on 7 October on the second reading of the bill. Many Tory peers refrained from voting, but it was still defeated by 41 votes. The following day, the king wrote to Grey that in his view he had no need to recapitulate his reasons why he should have deprecated, and now lament, a state of affairs that would be so detrimental to national interests. He also considered it equally pointless to state that 'the evil cannot be met by resorting to measures for obtaining a majority in the House of Lords, which no Government could propose and no Sovereign consent to, without losing sight of what is due to the character of that House, to the honour of the Aristocracy of the country, and to the dignity of the Throne.'[18] He believed that the Whigs were not making any concessions or compromises, and under the circumstances felt he could not create any further peers to force reform through.

On this rejection, public violence ensued with riots breaking out in several cities and industrial towns. That same evening in Derby a mob attacked the city jail and freed a large number of prisoners. Elsewhere, in Nottingham, the castle, home of the Duke of Newcastle, was set alight, and the nearby Wollaton Hall, Lord Middleton's estate, was attacked. At the end of October, the arrival in Bristol of the Recorder of the city, Charles Wetherell, another noted opponent of reform, led to protests that soon escalated into the worst unrest seen in an English city since the Gordon riots in London, more than fifty years previously. The forces of law and order were temporarily overwhelmed as rioters took control for three days, breaking into prisons and destroying several buildings, including the bishop's palace and the lord mayor's mansion, as well as various private properties. Order was eventually restored by the cavalry. At least twelve people were killed in violent clashes, and more than a hundred bodies were later recovered from the remains of burned buildings. Feelings ran high in these places, all of which had most to gain from the increase in the franchise proposed. The royal family themselves were not immune from popular protest, with mobs surrounding and attacking the carriages of the king and queen, travelling separately, as they returned to St James's Palace. Genuine concern at the threat of major unrest throughout the country, if not outright revolution, grew apace. Wellington was particularly alarmed, and on 5 November warned the king that 'a great crisis' was approaching, with the unions being trained to arms along the same lines as the national guards of France. 'Nothing has appeared from authority against such dangerous, unconstitutional, and illegal schemes.'[19]

The king did not share his apprehension, replying later that week that he himself also viewed with considerable anxiety and uneasiness the establishment and growing presence of political unions, to say nothing of their intention of assuming arms and forming National Guards. He assured the duke that there was no cause for alarm, as his government had the power and the means to afford protection to the lives and property of His Majesty's subjects, 'and he is aware that if the military force, acting under the direction of the magistrates, being not sufficient, the King has the power of augmenting it to any extent according to law'.[20] William forwarded the letter to Grey, adding that he was sure that the duke had 'very unnecessarily taken alarm', and assured him that as king he had never suspected his confidential servants of inattention or indifference to the formation of armed bodies, incompatible with his prerogative and with the acknowledged laws and constitutions of his dominions'.[21]

Greville believed that 'the Bristol business' had done some good in that it had helped to alert those in government and power as to the depth of feeling, 'but if we are to go on as we do with a mob-ridden Government and a foolish King, who renders himself subservient to all the wickedness and folly of his Ministers, where is the advantage of having people's eyes open, when seeing they will not perceive, and hearing they will not understand?'[22] Ministers were convinced that the only way to restore peace and stem the tide of anarchy throughout the land was to grant reform at once, while the king maintained that his responsibility was to bring about an understanding between both major parties in parliament, thus facilitating an amicable solution and enabling reform. If he was worried by the riots, what he dreaded even more was the increasing strength of the political unions, supported wholeheartedly by the radical press, and threatening to become more powerful than the Government itself. After the forces of law and order were restored in Bristol, he asked Taylor to inform Grey that he firmly believed the only solution was to ban the unions altogether. While Grey was equally alarmed by the riots and promised to do his best to discourage such organisations, he was sure that the only reason they were so successful was because of the obstinate behaviour of those in the House of Lords who strenuously opposed any change.

Nevertheless, a proclamation issued on 21 November made it illegal for political unions to have recourse to arms.

Meanwhile the House of Commons responded to the Lords' move by passing a motion of confidence affirming support for Lord Grey's administration. As parliamentary protocol prohibited the introduction of the same bill twice during the same session, the ministry advised King William to prorogue parliament. When the new session began in December 1831, the Third Reform Bill was brought forward, reflecting data that had been collected during the newly completed census, and no longer proposing a reduction in the total membership of the House of Commons. The bill was passed on 12 December with a majority of 162 votes.

As the passage of the bill wore on, the king's patience wore thinner, and his attitude to his ministers steadily became less conciliatory. It did not help him that the whole situation had become more complicated by the actions, during the previous few months, of Earl Howe, a Tory Lord of the Bedchamber for King George IV, and subsequently Lord Chamberlain to Queen Adelaide. As a result, Howe wielded considerable influence over king and queen, both of whom liked him and respected his judgment. Gossip suggested that the queen was besotted with him and that he was her lover. Those people who knew her well recognised this as a politically motivated falsehood, but it did not help her standing in the kingdom that he and she were both fervent Tories who were hostile to the whole concept of reform.

If Howe had kept his opinions to himself, Grey and the Government would have tolerated him, but his indiscretion proved his undoing as well as seriously damaging the reputation of Queen Adelaide. In May 1831 he had signed an address from the people of Kent protesting against the Reform Bill, and Grey asked King William to reprimand him. On his royal master's behalf, Sir Herbert Taylor assured him that this would be done. Yet Howe did not learn his lesson and proceeded to repeat this action a few days later when he was presented with a similar petition from the people of Warwickshire. Anxious to call him to heel, Taylor wrote him a letter informing him of the king's annoyance. At the same time, he advised Grey that Queen Adelaide was gravely concerned that if Howe continued to behave in this way, he would be dismissed, and she did not want to lose such a valued member of her staff. Suitably chastened, Howe considered resigning his post at once in order not to cause the queen any further embarrassment. He spoke to the Duke of Wellington, who told him there was no need for such drastic action but said he had to be more circumspect in his behaviour in future. Howe would have heeded this advice had Taylor not informed the press that he had reprimanded the erring chamberlain. Angrily, he wrote to Wellington that there was a Whig plot intent on separating the king from his true friends. He had been astonished to find his sovereign shedding tears with him, lamenting the indiscretion of his confidential servants, 'and actually advising his private friend to consult the political enemy of these ministers'. Howe continued that his beloved master's kindness and liberality was 'beyond all praise. Would to God I could say as much for his moral courage!' Nothing, he vowed, would now induce him to resign. 'I have the King's leave to vote as I like; my opinions are firmly but temperately declared.'[23]

Obligingly Howe kept quiet for the next few months. All was well until October, when a letter strongly attacking the Government appeared in the *Standard*, and everyone believed it to have been his work. When he did not deny its authorship, Grey advised the king that he would have to be dismissed, and Howe's resignation was accordingly accepted. Queen Adelaide was furious. In her diary, she bemoaned the fact that she could hardly believe it, for she had fully trusted 'and built firmly on' the king's love for her, but now he had given in to the wishes of his ministers. 'May God support us and protect and shield this country and save the King from ruin ... I felt myself deeply wounded both as wife and Queen.'[24] She was particularly annoyed with Lord Grey, whom she treated coldly whenever he went to Windsor to consult her husband.

By the end of 1831, the king was resenting the fact that all the reassurances given him had proved unreliable. He refused to commit himself about the committee stage, or even to allow an immediate creation of peers in the increasingly unlikely event of a second-reading defeat. His confidence in his ministers had diminished, and his wife was encouraging him to spurn reform and give as little ground as possible, if indeed any at all. Meanwhile there had already been unrest in parts of the country. There were limits to the extent to which the authorities could contain such a volatile situation. King William began to fear the worst, and was sure the country faced an uncertain future.

Chapter 7

Reform Carried

On 3 January 1832, Lord Grey arrived at Brighton to ask King William for the immediate creation of ten or twelve peers, and maybe more – in other words, as many as would prove necessary – at a future stage, if the first intake was unable to bring the Tory peers to heel. He warned the king that under present circumstances there was likely to be a majority of about twenty votes against the bill in the Lords. Even if it was carried on the second reading, there would be good reason to fear that many who would vote with the Government would be likely to support alterations in the Committee 'as would be fatal to the efficiency of the Bill, and consequently impossible for the Government to consent to'.

The king said he had long foreseen such a proposition would eventually be made to him, and that he had given it serious consideration. His objections to the creation of peers for such a purpose had already been stated to his ministers, Grey himself had acknowledged their validity, and that he still contemplated the danger of such a precedent. He was prepared to listen to any advice the ministers might think it their duty to offer him, but he would prefer the advice in writing and also to give a written reply. If it should ultimately be determined that he should make an addition to the peerage, in order to increase the strength of the Government on the question of reform, he trusted that it would be managed in such a way as to affect the permanent character of the House of Lords as little as possible. The king asked for Grey's views on the matter and Grey replied that he had been anxious to avoid the situation altogether if possible, and that in any new creations he would strive to make the least possible permanent addition to the numbers of the peerage.[1]

Meanwhile, on the previous day, the Duke of Wellington had written to the Duke of Buckingham, suggesting that he ought to go and see the king, and advise him to refuse to create any new peers. Wellington would offer to form a government himself, in order to protect His Majesty from any such demand, but it would be impossible for them to carry on without a new parliament. 'This House of Commons is formed purposely to carry parliamentary reform. It is part of a conspiracy against the House of Lords; [that] it would not hear of a Minister who should found his authority on the basis of protection of the independence of the [House of] Lords.' If he should go to the king, he had to make it clear that he could not look for the support of the present House of Commons, and at the moment he could not advise him to dissolve parliament. It was a dangerous situation for all of them. 'The great mischief of all is a weakness of our poor King, who cannot or will not see his danger, or the road out of it when it is pointed out to him; and he allows himself to be deceived and trifled with by his Ministers.'[2]

The king could see for himself that it was impossible for a new government to be formed, any more than it had been the previous year, and conceded to Wellington's request with some reluctance. To some, the arguments against any new creation of peers seemed overwhelming, not only to him but to many of the Whigs, as well as the Tories. Any deliberate aim to overrule one House of Parliament and materially alter the other to its own advantage looked like flouting the constitution for short-term advantage.

The Duke of Wellington was particularly fearful of the consequences of such a solution. There were two very easy and straight roads for the destruction of the British monarchy, he maintained. One was a moderate Reform Bill, similar to the one defeated the previous October by the House of Lords. 'The other is to destroy even a semblance of independence in the House of Lords by creating peers to counterbalance the majority which voted against the Reform Bill. It is expected and intended to carry the new Reform Bill by this *coup d'état*.' What then, he asked, would become of the independence of the House of Lords? After such a precedent, it could be of no use to the existence of the monarchy, none to the democracy. It would be the ridicule of the public and a disgrace to itself.'

Wellington believed that the king knew all too well 'the mischief' of creating peers. His ministers had told him that he would have an insurrection and civil war in the country if the bill was not carried, and he insisted to them that all he wanted was to have the bill 'fairly discussed in a Committee of the House of Lords'. His ministers had told him as much, but they should also tell him that those who voted for the second reading of the bill admitted its principle, namely, 'the principle of *efficiency* which Lord Grey's *honour* requires, without reference to the consequences to His Majesty's interests of the admission of this principle.' There were some in the House of Lords, Wellington maintained, who would prefer death to such a course. 'But it is said, if this course be not adopted, we shall have insurrection and civil war!! What have we had throughout the year 1831? Is it tranquillity? Is it the British Constitution? Is it security to any man for his property, his rights, his house, or even his life? Nothing can be worse than what we have lost. *Any* change would be an improvement.'[3]

Knowing that some of the bishops and peers had agreed to reverse their votes, and assuming from a remark by Grey that a creation of twenty-one would be sufficient, the king agreed with a heavy heart immediately to create twenty-one new peers. When the cabinet explained a few days later that they did not yet know how many would be needed, on 15 January he undertook to create enough peers to secure the success of the bill at the right time, but not before. As the exact number was not specified, and as it was subject to the king's interpretation, it would be difficult to bring the undertaking into effect for anything except a second-reading defeat. Moreover, the king stipulated that, except for three new peerages that had already been agreed, the creation of new peers must not add permanently to the Lords, but was to be confined to the eldest sons of peers and collateral heirs. Grey told the king the next day that he hoped the necessary creations would not exceed the number of twenty or so that he had already suggested. This, the king told him, would have to be the end of the matter. Yet the prime minister could give no assurances. He had warned his colleagues some weeks earlier, there was always a risk that such a creation [increase in the number of peers] might turn some of their supporters against them. There were already indications in the press that this was likely to happen – and sooner rather than later.

During the next few months, the king found some hope from an olive branch offered by a group of moderate Tory peers, led by the veteran former minister, the Earl of Harrowby and Lord Wharncliffe, dubbed 'the Waverers'. Although they had voted against the bill the previous October, they were now prepared to establish some kind of consensus between the Whigs and Tories. In the interests of breaking the parliamentary stalemate, they would attempt to obtain promises of a majority for the second reading, on the strict condition that no more peers would be created. Their aim was not to prevent the bill, but to have it amended in the Lords committee, as far as possible. At the same time, they made it clear that if any peers were created, all their fellow converts as well as a number of government supporters would oppose the bill at every stage. The king reported all their contacts with him to Grey, and openly lent his support to their efforts.

However, once they appreciated the scale of the entrenched opposition the bill was likely to arouse, the ministers were disillusioned. For them to consider withdrawing it, or reducing it to a shadow of what had been planned, would be bad for them and for the country. Grey admitted to a colleague on 9 February that he wished he had never even introduced it in the first place. Four days later he told Taylor that if the Government could not make the concessions demanded by Harrowby and Wharncliffe, and if the Waverers voted with the opposition after all, the cabinet would be obliged to ask the king for a creation of fifty or more peers.

As matters reached an increasingly delicate stage, King William needed to be seen to tread carefully with regard to the company he was keeping. The Marquess of Anglesey saw him in March and respectfully warned that it would not do for the king to surround himself with Tory relations and courtiers. The king agreed but allegedly said it was all the fault of the queen, and complained he was leading 'a life of the damned'.[4] The queen's open Tory partisanship and aversion to reform were something of an embarrassment to William at this crucial stage of events, and this was hardly to be doubted. Yet for King William to criticise his wife in such blunt terms, and to a public servant rather than a close member of the family who could be relied on to respect family confidences, was extremely unusual. It suggested that either Anglesey was putting words into the king's mouth or he had caught his sovereign at a particularly unguarded moment when he had been exceptionally harassed and irritated by the queen's attitude and behaviour. The situation was exacerbated by the fact that, although he had been dismissed, Howe continued to spend much of his time at Windsor. When he was at his own home, the queen still corresponded regularly with him, not hesitating to confide in him her views on how the king's eyes 'were now open to the perils' of granting reform.

After the bill had been passed in the Commons by even larger majorities, on 26 March it was again sent up to the Lords. Realising that another rejection would not be politically feasible, the opponents of reform decided that the best they could do would be to table amendments that would try and change the bill's essential character, such as voting to delay consideration of clauses in the bill that disenfranchised the rotten boroughs. Efforts were made to persuade some of their lordships to vote in favour, while at least one was happy to name his price. The Earl of Ferrers, whose wife Queen Adelaide had firmly declined to receive at court because husband and wife had made no secret of living together before they married, promised to vote with the Government if his wife was no longer barred from court, but the king declined to accept his offer. The ministers believed that if everything else failed, the only alternative would be to create a large number of new peerages, thus swamping the House of Lords with pro-reform votes. Grey and the Whig ministry were therefore recalled, with a promise wrung from the still hesitant sovereign to create as many peers as necessary to force the measure through the Lords. He saw such a move as unconstitutional and likely to create a dangerous precedent but assented 'if the dreaded necessity arose'.

On 14 April the bill was narrowly passed by the Lords, now clearly anxious at the threat of being overwhelmed with new peerages, by 184 votes to 175. The opposition leaders, who assumed that their followers would be too divided for detailed committee work, adopted obstructionist tactics similar to those used a year earlier by their colleagues in the Commons, and sponsored a wrecking amendment under the guise of an adjustment in the procedure.

Seeing a chance to oust the Government and replace it with a Tory administration that would be ready to pass the Reform Bill barely unaltered, on 7 May Baron Lyndhurst, Lord High Chancellor, tabled a motion for postponing consideration of the clauses for disenfranchisement. It was carried by a majority of 35. Grey informed the king that unless a sufficient number of peers was immediately created, to pass the bill, the ministry would have no alternative but to resign; 'they find themselves deprived of all hope of being able to carry the Reform Bill through its further stages in a manner that would be for the advantage of your Majesty's Government, or satisfactory to the public.'[5] With regret the king accepted their resignations two days later, and asked the Duke of Wellington to form an administration that could carry through a bill that would be more acceptable to the Lords than that devised by Grey.

Wellington had always been opposed to reform in principle and was reluctant to admit otherwise. Would he now have started to see the expediency of such a measure, within moderation? To abandon it completely would unleash national unrest on a scale that neither king nor parliament dared to contemplate, yet he still sounded extremely unwilling to countenance the idea. He was ready to serve king and country, writing to Lord Lyndhurst that he would be very much concerned 'if we cannot at least make an effort to enable the King to shake off the trammels of his tyrannical minister. I am perfectly ready to do whatever his Majesty may command me. I am as much averse to the reform as ever I was ... No private consideration shall prevent me from making every effort to serve the King.'[6]

However, Wellington had underestimated the deep divisions that still ran through his party, and when Sir Robert Peel refused to join him, he realized that he was unable to form a ministry after all. His resignation left King William with no choice but to recall Grey, which was effected on 15 May. The king hoped and expected 'that the difficulties which have arisen may be removed, without resorting to any change of Administration, by passing the bill with such modifications as may meet the views of those who may still entertain any difference of opinion upon the subjects.' Such an arrangement, the king continued, 'would relieve him from the embarrassment under which he has been placed by the proposal to make so extensive a creation of Peers for the purpose of passing the Reform Bill.' Grey found himself obliged to answer that he and his colleagues could not continue in government unless they could be sure of 'sufficient security that they will possess the power of passing the present Bill, unimpaired in its principles and its essential provisions, and as nearly as possible in its present form.' This, he stressed, would be conditional on being given consent to the creation of peers if required.[7]

Pressure throughout the country for speedy reform was growing, and the pamphleteer, journalist and future Member of Parliament,

William Cobbett, was sure that the clamour for a republic was growing. When it became known that the Duke of Wellington was planning to form a ministry, the national situation became increasingly volatile, particularly in the big towns which sought to benefit most from reform. There was a general suspension of work and business, as people stood about in groups awaiting further news. Nevertheless, there were no riots, except for a small one in York. A Whig member, Sir Robert Heron, summed up the approaching storm; 'no breaking of windows, no trifling expressions of discontent; all seemed reserved for a tremendous explosion'. His words were echoed in a feeling among observers that parts of the country were only a step away from anarchy, and that the orgy of violence and destruction seen in Bristol the previous October could be repeated elsewhere. The authorities in Birmingham and other cities were instructed to barricade themselves, to create new municipal authorities if necessary, and close the banks. Elsewhere, it was said that the middle and working classes were prepared to fight if troops were sent against them and would pay no taxes until Grey came back.[8]

It was rumoured that the king had agreed to a plea from the queen that she should be allowed to leave the country and escape to Hanover. A more extreme variation on this theme, which was allegedly mentioned by John Hobhouse, a minister in Grey's government, was that she had actually persuaded the king to leave the country clandestinely and planned to run away with him to Hanover. Once he arrived there, this version continued, he would act as a king over the water, dissolve the English Parliament and call upon one or more of the more authoritarian powers in Europe to restore him to the throne. This had the sound of some almost surreal monarchical adventure which might have happened in bygone times, but which could not possibly occur in the nineteenth century. It would surely never have been countenanced for a moment by a monarch like King William IV, a patriot and a true John Bull to his bones, who regarded foreigners with suspicion at best. Yet the fact that such rumours were widely believed was indicative of the ferment in which the country found itself for a short period of time.

The action of one of the king's brothers that same month might have gained the royal family some popularity, but it risked alienating the monarch himself. The Duke of Sussex had temporarily disgraced himself (or covered himself in glory, from the pro-reform point of view) by attempting to present his brother with a sharply worded petition from the Bristol political union, a local organisation and radical pressure group demanding reform. The king did not take this 'insolent address' seriously, but he was furious with his brother for taking what he thought was an unnecessarily partisan stand at such a crucial time for the country, especially with one of the organisations that seemed to regard themselves more or less above the law of the land. There were fears, noted Hobhouse, that the Duke of Sussex 'means to play the part of the Duke of Orleans', and it was followed by an address from the City of London, asking the Duke to take charge of the city in case of disturbance.[9] Having his brother associating himself so openly with the radicals was too much for the king to stomach, and he temporarily forbade him to come to court. It would be another three months before he was deemed to have learned his lesson and was permitted to return.

At a cabinet meeting on 18 May, the day on which national unrest was said to have been most likely to erupt, Grey and his colleagues decided they could not possibly continue in government without being given some security for insuring the passage of the bill. That afternoon, he and Brougham went to meet the king at St James's. Brougham said it was one of the most painful hours he had ever spent in his life, as the king was suffering so much, yet still behaved with the greatest courtesy. In spite of this it was the only audience he ever had in which the king kept his seat, and did not invite them to sit down as well. Nevertheless, the king gave his promise to create such peers as they both advised. Before they left, Brougham asked with some boldness if, in view of it being 'a most delicate position' in which they were placed, he would consent to giving them his promise in writing. 'Do you doubt my word?' the king asked him angrily. Somewhat taken aback, Brougham replied, 'certainly nothing of the kind,' adding that it would be more satisfactory to them if he would 'add this to his other kindness'. The king promised that he would comply with this request and send him a few lines the next day. As they left the palace, Grey told Brougham he was quite shocked at what he had done and wondered how he could be so unfeeling. Brougham assured him that within twenty-four hours he would see that he was in the right, and that in all probability, such a promise might render the measure of creating new peers unnecessary. 'God grant it may,' Grey answered.[10]

The king was as good as his word, and that evening he confirmed in writing his authorisation of the creation of peers to such an extent as would enable Grey to carry the bill. He took the opportunity to inform Grey that he was 'more concerned than surprised at the irritation which still prevails, and the acrimony of some of the opponents to the Reform Bill; but trusts that, however annoying, it will prove no serious obstacle.' This did not alter the fact that he approved wholeheartedly of 'the temperate course' pursued by his prime minister on this occasion.[11] This persuaded most of the opposition peers to reconsider their position and withdraw. Without informing his cabinet, Wellington wrote to the Tory peers, encouraging them to break the deadlock by altering their course of action, and warning them of the dire consequences if they persisted in thwarting a bill that plainly reflected the mood of the people. Rather than see the peerage cheapened in such a manner, the Tory Lords and bishops followed Wellington's advice. As Brougham had triumphantly told Grey, no creation of peers would be needed.

It had been more than a year since the bill was first introduced in parliament, and to sovereign and ministers at the centre of events, to find that it was about to be passed at last, after so many delays and obstructions, was a source of unbounded relief to all concerned. The king was keenly aware, now that the bill was about to reach the statute books, that it was 'not only unimpaired in its principle, and essential provisions, but wholly unaltered and unimproved', but he was anxious 'to suggest and encourage all that can tend to conciliation, and to diminish the irritation and the acrimony which unfortunately have arisen, and are kept up, in the higher ranks of society in this country, and between the individuals of the greatest respectability and influence.' William's attention had been drawn to recent declarations made in public that the Reform Bill was only a precursor to a programme of reforming legislation being considered that would involve the Church, corporation property, and other institutions. He had good reason to believe that those who had dropped their opposition to the bill, out of deference to his sovereignty 'and in order to relieve him from the painful necessity of creating Peers for the purpose of passing it, have done considerable violence to their feelings, and that they are hurt and disappointed that they have not, by this sacrifice of their opposition, secured even those modifications which it had been understood that you would not have felt unwilling to admit.' He could not decide how far it might be practicable for Grey to introduce any further changes on the report, or on the third reading, but he was satisfied that to do so would help to allay irritation, conciliate many of those in opposition, and eventually to secure their support to the Government.[12]

Grey could not offer any assurance of being able to help. He answered that the feeling in the party and country had now reached such a stage that anything in the way of a concession to the Tory opposition would lead not only to further dissension in parliament, but to national unrest. Ministers particularly wanted the king to come in person to Westminster to give the royal assent, which would demonstrate that he fully accepted the reform which he had supported fitfully, at best. The opposition agreed that he should come to Westminster, in the interests of restoring the king's popularity and that of the crown in general, if nothing else. It would also strengthen his position and mean that his judgment carried more weight with the Government in case of further dissension in the years to come.

Grey wrote to Taylor on 5 June that if the bill was returned from the House of Commons that night, it would probably receive the Royal Assent next day, and then Brougham would communicate directly with the king. 'The manner in which His Majesty spoke to me upon it precluded my proposing that he should go to pass the bill in person; but it would hardly be consistent with my duty not to state that the wish that he should do so is very general, and that I believe it would have a great effect in calming the present agitation.'[13]

Any intention that King William might have had in his more charitable moments of coming to Westminster and passing the bill in person had long since vanished, as Taylor was obliged to make clear to Brougham. He wrote bluntly that in ordinary times, the king would have doubted the propriety and necessity of a step for which there were few precedents, if any. Under the circumstances, nothing would 'induce him to take it in deference to what is called the sense of the people, or in deference to the dictates of the press, its ruler, after the treatment he has experienced from both.' King William had tried his hardest to fulfil his duty to the best of his judgment, and according to the dictates of his conscience, and for his pains 'he had been misrepresented, calumniated, and insulted; that the insults had not been confined to him — they had been heaped upon his Queen, on all belonging to him; and that the law had been declared not to be strong enough to protect him and them against such insults. Was he to cringe and bow? Was he to kiss the rod held out *in terrorem* by the mob?' Any thoughts of playing to the gallery carried no weight with him. He had never attached the slightest value to that ephemeral popularity, here today and gone tomorrow, 'which results from the effervescence of the moment — that which is not felt to be due to, and to arise from, a sense of the correct and honourable discharge of duty.' Had it been in his nature …

> to be misled by applause and acclamations given to his supposed *unqualified* sanction of popular measures, what

has recently passed would have undeceived him, and would have discovered to him how valueless is popular favour; how little deserving of the solicitude of those who are responsible to God and to their conscience for their acts. He is told that his giving the royal assent in person to the Reform Bill would be agreeable to the people — to those who, within the last fortnight, had so grossly insulted him; and that, by this step, he would regain the popularity which he is assured he had enjoyed — that he would set himself right again.' After what had happened, 'he would greatly prefer their continued abuse, to the conviction that he had merited it by degrading himself in courting applause which he has learnt to despise.[14]

The bill, virtually unamended, received the Royal Assent on 7 June 1832. Its net result was to increase the total electorate by about 45%. This was still only a small fraction of the total population, with constituencies that more equitably reflected the centres of population density. Thirty rotten boroughs in Cornwall, eighteen in Wiltshire (among them, naturally, the notorious Old Sarum), fourteen in Sussex, and ten in Hampshire, and the Isle of Wight, all disappeared from the electoral map.

In his memoirs, Brougham later gave his side of the last stages of the drama. He subsequently recalled that the ministers had no further differences with the king in connection with the Reform Bill, except on 'the unimportant part of his giving the royal assent in person, which he refused, probably because he was unwilling to show more favour towards the measure than necessary; perhaps, also as he felt that the Lords would regard it as a mark of disrespect to them after what had happened.' Only sometime later, when it came to making plans for the dissolution of parliament, did he realize that the king still did not regard the bill as settled, 'and renewed his expressions of dislike to it.'

When the king asked Brougham why another proroguing of parliament was necessary, it was explained to him how impossible it would be to have the Commons sitting for another session, 'when it had been declared incompetent by its construction to perform its duties, and when so many great towns, now entitled to send representatives, were still unrepresented.' The king insisted that he would have to see Lord Grey about the matter and, after an audience, he told Brougham 'it was quite necessary to enforce this necessity further, and that I must have another audience, which was only a repetition of the former.' Brougham and Grey later found out from Earl Erroll, Queen Adelaide's equerry, the cause of this attempt to avoid the dissolution. The queen, who could generally be relied on to take 'the Tory view', had urged William to refuse at the last moment, and he had come to town after promising that he would do so. The advice was foolish, whoever had given it; for though the reform excitement had very much subsided, and success had been gained, agitation would have been renewed in great force by so violent a proceeding as precluding those on whom the franchise had been conferred from its exercise. The king was very alarmed at the tendency of the new experiment, as he called it, to fill the House with Radicals; and demanded constant accounts during the election of the kind of men who were returned. He was relieved to find that so many 'moderate men' had been elected, and generally that parliament was of much the same composition as it had been in former elections. As for the Whigs themselves, most of them had been satisfied with the senior ministers' 'conduct of the Bill to its final success', apart from the minority who seemed more concerned with trying to 'obtain a general power of thwarting the Lords than to carry any specific measures, and who greatly lamented the creation of peers in large numbers not having become necessary.'[15]

It might be an exaggeration to call the Reform Act another bloodless revolution, especially when it is remembered that a few people perished in the Bristol riots of October 1831. Estimates vary as to how many, but suggest anything between a dozen and one hundred. What is beyond doubt is that a protracted and sometimes acrimonious campaign at Westminster between two firmly entrenched, sometimes acrimoniously opposed sides, had been peacefully and calmly resolved. King William IV, whose position might have been likened in sporting terms to that of a referee or an umpire, had been faced with difficult decisions, and naturally had found it impossible to please all his ministers all the time.

Yet throughout a very testing eighteen months he had acted with a fairness with which few would have credited him, some years earlier, despite his lack of enthusiasm for the cause of reform, and despite in the last few weeks having felt increasingly that he had been taken for granted, and had been treated with scant gratitude for his efforts. Some historians and biographers have generously praised him for his common sense and calmness, others have been more critical and accused him of being inept if not downright dishonourable. It is only fair to take a balanced view and consider that this was a monarch who had been called upon to act in an almost unprecedented situation, treading an uncertain path, trying hard not to displease one side or the other. Like his senior ministers, he emerged from it not totally unblemished, but with some credit. Lord Grey, Lord Wellington, and particularly Lord Brougham had all walked the tightrope with skill, and the result was a carefully executed manoeuvre from which leading statesmen and their sovereign could walk away with some satisfaction, if not pride.

In retrospect, the monarchy was fortunate that William had been on the throne at the time. Faced with a testing situation such as had not been encountered by his father or his brother, he followed his own largely unerring instinct, and followed it as sensibly as he could. As Roger Fulford would remark a century later, the skill with which he had met the reform struggle can be appreciated by imagining what would have happened if either of his surviving brothers had come to the throne in his place, in 1830. The Duke of Cumberland, as King Ernest, might possibly have allowed Grey to form an administration, but he would never have granted a dissolution in April 1831, and would most likely have relied on an extreme Tory government to stamp out the enthusiasm for reform. This would have resulted in Ernest being driven off the throne in six months, assuming the radical elements had not had their way and there still was a throne. On the other hand, it is conceivable that the Duke of Sussex, as King Augustus, would have sided so completely with the Whigs, by putting the royal prerogative at the disposal of Grey's administration, and risked transforming many of the moderate Whigs into bitter opponents of reform. This would have made it possible for the bill to be passed by a display of arbitrary sovereignty not seen in England since the Stuart era.[16] Instead, King William had taken the difficult middle path.

Not all commentators were quite so ready to praise the monarch for his behaviour. Walter Bagehot, writing some fifty years later, admitted that he was a very conscientious king, but at the same time thought him exceedingly weak, for having agreed 'to make a *reasonable* number of peers if required to pass the second reading of the Reform Bill'. When 'the Waverers' went back on their undertaking, the second reading was carried without it by nine votes, and then the king refused to create an insufficient number of peers, when a vital amendment was carried by Lord Lyndhurst, that would have destroyed, and was meant to destroy, the bill. 'In consequence, there was a tremendous crisis and nearly a revolution. A more striking example of well-meaning imbecility is scarcely to be found in history'.[17] It was a severe and perhaps unnecessarily harsh judgement that does the monarch less than justice.

Chapter 8

European Affairs

Although King William IV had been preoccupied for the first part of his reign with the tortuous processes of the Reform Bill, throughout his seven years on the throne he attached no less importance to the matter of British relations with European neighbours. Having travelled widely in his youth across Europe and North America, as the king he was inclined to regard foreign affairs as a particular interest, and one on which he felt he could speak with some authority. His in principle ingrained dislike and distrust of foreigners had not altered the years and, if anything, his insular prejudices had intensified, with the perfidious French at the top of his list. To him King Louis-Philippe was little better than a usurper, and he hated Talleyrand, the French Ambassador in London, formerly Napoleon's chief diplomat during his early years of success, although he later turned against his former master and supported the restoration of the Bourbon monarchy in France, which brought the Bonaparte era to a close. It had given King William no small pleasure, at the start of his reign, to dismiss the French pastry-cooks who had worked in the kitchens at Windsor during his brother's reign.

Like his father before him, William was particularly suspicious of what he considered to be revolutionary or radical regimes abroad. To him, it was folly trying to export British liberal ideas by expecting them to work in foreign countries not yet ready for them. Most of his countrymen in all classes shared the first of these views at least. His expression of them may have proved an advantage to Viscount Palmerston, who served as foreign secretary under Grey, and his successor Viscount Melbourne, on whom, despite their regular differences of opinion, the king conferred the Grand Cross of the Bath in June 1832.

The first major foreign policy issue of William's reign concerned the matter of the Belgian revolution. This conflict led to the secession of the southern provinces of the Netherlands, mainly the former Southern Netherlands, from the United Kingdom, and the establishment of an independent kingdom of Belgium. The people of the south were mainly Flemings and Walloons, traditionally Roman Catholics, while the largely Protestant Dutch lived in the north. Belgium had been governed by Holland since 1815, but most of the population regarded King Willem I of the Netherlands as a despot. The revolution in Paris in July 1830 inspired similar unrest elsewhere in Europe. On 25 August, riots broke out in Brussels where shops were looted while factories were occupied and machinery was destroyed in other parts of the country, before order was briefly restored. The States-General in Brussels voted in favour of secession and declared independence and in November a conference of major European powers was convened in London, which recognised Belgian independence and agreed that a new king should be found.

In view of his lifelong antipathy to France and its people, King William IV was placed in a difficult position. With French support, the Belgians were defying the legitimate authority and he had little respect for those whom he saw as radicals and revolutionaries. He would therefore have been inclined to take the side of Holland, a nation that had traditionally been an ally of Britain for more than a century. Above all, the sympathies of Queen Adelaide and her family were always staunchly pro-Dutch. However, he recognized that a United Netherlands was not feasible. It fell to the conference to establish how both countries should be equitably divided, and then try to cajole the protagonists into acquiescence.

King Willem of Holland, whom King William IV personally disliked, posed the main difficulty. For a while King William favoured the idea of bringing together the two opposing factions by nominating the eldest son of the King of the Netherlands, Willem, Prince of Orange, as head of the new state. The Belgians made it clear that such a choice would be unacceptable.

Like his sovereign, Palmerston was not by nature sympathetic to nationalist aspirations of smaller territories in Europe, but he believed it was necessary for Belgium to achieve separation from Holland and achieve recognition as an independent state, in order to prevent a Franco-Belgian union, and thus preserve the balance of power in Europe. An over-mighty France would always be a grave threat to peace throughout the continent. In February 1831 the Belgians elected Louis, Duc de Nemours, the second son of King Louis-Philippe, to reign over them. It would have been difficult to find anybody less palatable to King William IV than a son of his *bête noire* in Paris. Grey and Palmerston agreed that Louis would be unacceptable to England. They and their sovereign all thought this was an underhand manoeuvre by King Louis-Philippe to plan for the annexation of Belgium to France.

When Palmerston suggested that Leopold of Saxe-Coburg, the widower of Princess Charlotte of Wales, who might otherwise have become the eventual King of England in all but name, should become King of the Belgians, William was anxious that the Dutch might suspect the British of trying to establish a puppet sovereign who would be completely dependent on his masters in Holland. His suspicions of French intentions soon overrode these scruples, and Leopold became the official British candidate. It was a view with which the Belgian Congress concurred, and in June 1831, by a decisive majority, it elected Leopold king. He had received more than three out of four votes cast. He made his acceptance of the crown conditional on Luxembourg being freed from Dutch rule and becoming part of Belgium. King Willem of the Netherlands was so angered by this that in August he sent his army to invade Belgium.

To King William IV's concern, the French army promptly went to the assistance of the Belgians and drove out all the invading forces, except for a small detachment that remained in the citadel of Antwerp. Ensuing international pressure compelled the French to withdraw their troops as well. The dispute boded badly for European unity, as Russia and Austria, the eastern powers, took the side of Holland, while France became ever more vocal in her championship of Belgium. This put a strain on the relationship between King William IV and his ministers, who were far more pro-French than he was. Palmerston intended to commit himself to the cause of Belgium, while the king felt it could not be right that Britain should act in concert with the French against the legitimate powers of Europe.

Even so, it was evident that a new solution to the Belgian question would need to be found, in order to avoid further conflicts. In October, the London Conference agreed on the twenty-four articles, which included Belgium's separation from the Netherlands, a cessation of the rule of the House of Orange, and a guarantee of the perpetual neutrality and inviolability of Belgium. They formed a compromise arrangement that they hoped would satisfy both countries. To the annoyance of King William of England, King Willem of the Netherlands refused to accept the settlement, despite efforts by Palmerston and the French to persuade him to yield. Even King William IV had to admit that such continued obstinacy was delaying a satisfactory conclusion to the negotiations, but he did not want to force the Dutch to submit by Britain joining the French in applying violent pressure. He feared that this could result in the French occupation of the whole of Belgium.

To William, it was important that the four powers should all appear to France to be mutually supportive. Under pressure from his ministers, he conceded that some kind of cooperation might be necessary with the French, but he remained reluctant to be drawn into war with England's traditional allies, fighting against the excessively powerful state that had long since been their traditional adversary. In September 1832 he wrote to Palmerston that he could not 'for a moment admit the possibility of Britain being forced into a war against Austria, Prussia and Russia, in conjunction with revolutionary France.'[1] Even so, in October Britain and France co-operated by sea and land to coerce the Dutch into surrendering the citadel of Antwerp, under the watchful and hostile eyes on the one side of the French war party, who sent troops to march on the Dutch garrison there, and on the other side the English Tories and the despotic powers of the East, Russia, Austria, and Prussia, which all looked disapprovingly on Belgian independence as a breach in the reactionary system of the treaties of Vienna, and were waiting only for a misunderstanding between France and England to pounce on the small rebel kingdom. In May 1833, after nine months of economic blockade, King Willem agreed to abandon hostilities against Belgium. Against his better instincts, King William IV had to admit that the peace of Europe had been preserved mainly by Anglo-French cooperation.

Once the Belgian question had been resolved, King William focused his attention on Palmerston's policy towards the German states. In the wake of the July 1830 revolution in France, there had been similar unrest not only in Belgium but also in the southern and western German states. As a result, Hesse, Baden and Bavaria were among those that had clamoured for and been granted new, more liberal constitutions, Palmerston and most of the Whigs eagerly endorsed the democratic tide that seemed to be sweeping across central Europe, but which struck fear into the heart of the reactionary Austrian chancellor, Klemens von Metternich. In June 1832, Metternich succeeded in forcing through the German Imperial Diet [the general assembly] six resolutions intended to restrict any further constitutional development in Germany, tightened censorship of the press, and prevented any enlargement of the franchise in the southern states. Palmerston strongly condemned such actions and regarded Metternich as a demonic figure trying to put back the clock throughout mainland Europe. King William found himself more in sympathy with the Austrian position. He thought the South German states were being 'strongly impregnated with Revolutionary Ideas and Feelings', influenced by a 'licentious and unbridled press'[2] that seemed all too similar to its counterpart in Britain.

Palmerston found it unhelpful, if hardly surprising, when the Duke of Cambridge, the viceroy at Hanover and therefore the king's representative, supported the resolutions in the German Diet. Palmerston had no control over Hanoverian policy, but he knew that observers abroad believed this support was according to instructions from the British Foreign Office. William himself affirmed to Palmerston his approval of the six resolutions in July, but early the following month Palmerston decided to make publicly clear his own position, by asserting in the House of Commons that the independence of constitutional states, whether as powerful as France 'or of less relative political importance, such as the minor States of Germany, never can be a matter of indifference to the British Parliament, or, I should hope, to the British public'. He considered such states to be the natural allies of Britain and was sure that no English ministry would be performing its duty if it paid no heed to their interests.[3]

He followed this by bracing himself for King William's disapproval and dispatching a note to the President of the Diet which strongly attacked the six resolutions, taking the Austrian and Prussian governments to task on account of their high-handed policies. The king angrily asked Palmerston whether he really wanted the press in other countries to become tantamount to the governing power, defying the law and every rule of society. The Prussian foreign minister refused to receive the note, a matter of protocol which King William found deeply offensive. Also, it did nothing to ease relations between the sovereign and the foreign secretary, who in general liked and respected each other, although their views were occasionally at variance.

Undaunted, the following year Palmerston, acting at the behest of the French foreign minister, asked King William to instruct his Hanoverian ministers to decline an invitation to a conference of German states convened by Metternich in Vienna. William refused on the grounds that he did not wish to offend Austria, a major European power that Hanover might find a useful ally in the future. In this he had the support of the Duke of Cambridge, who had readily accepted and declared he would attend the conference. The king added that although he hoped the conference would not result in the erosion of existing constitutional privileges in Germany, he did not want to see them expanded. When the conference took place, Palmerston could do nothing to prevent the Hanoverian envoy and delegates from firmly aligning themselves with Metternich's policy and agreeing with all his proposals.

Matters in Portugal and Spain were also of some concern to the English sovereign and his government. Dom Miguel I, King of Portugal, had usurped the Portuguese throne from his niece, the child sovereign Maria II of Portugal, and her father, King Pedro IV of Portugal, Emperor Dom Pedro I of Brazil, was trying to re-establish her rights. Palmerston shared the majority of the Whig party's abhorrence for the cruelty perpetrated by Miguel throughout his realm, but prudence forced him to declare an official policy of British neutrality to the issue. Pedro had proved himself just as corrupt and inefficient a sovereign, although less barbarous an individual than his younger brother. He and Maria were supported by France, who considered that they were the more constitutionally and democratically minded alternative, while the eastern powers of Europe and Spain looked more benignly on Miguel, who was anathema to the Whigs in Britain.

King William took the attitude that there was not a great deal to choose between two very unimpressive factions. As different European powers seemed to be taking different stances on the matter, he thought it prudent to disassociate himself from both factions and support neither. He held the thirteen-year-old Maria in low esteem, but Palmerston was prepared to offer at least token support to assist Pedro's cause. When the latter launched an invasion of Portugal from the Azores in the spring of 1832, the foreign secretary ensured that the nearby British fleet kept a benevolent eye on events, observing the river Tagus, and ensuring that Pedro's fleet could reach land safely. At first the invasion fared badly for King Pedro, but in July 1832, his forces established a foothold in Oporto. He was also helped by the fact that there was a change of policy in Madrid, when King Ferdinand dismissed his ministers and formed a new government intended to win the support of the middle classes. Palmerston was hopeful that such a government would support the constitutionalists in Portugal against Dom Miguel.

The war continued throughout the following year and Miguel launched a major offensive designed to destroy Pedro for once and for all. It was however Pedro's guardian angel, a British naval officer, Admiral Sir Charles Napier, who achieved a spectacular victory at sea that helped Pedro to capture Lisbon. King William regarded Napier as an unprincipled firebrand and rogue and was enraged by what he thought was his interference in favour of Maria. Not long afterwards, he was invited to visit an art exhibition at Somerset House, an event not calculated to interest him. Bowing to duty he went anyway, and the President of the Royal Academy, Sir Martin Archer Shee, showed him around the galleries. When they stood in front of a portrait of Admiral Napier, the King became angry. 'Napier may be damned, Sir!' he exclaimed. 'And you may be damned, Sir! And if the Queen was not here, I'd kick you downstairs.'[4] Ironically, Archer Shee was best remembered for having painted three of the most well-known full-length paintings of the king at various stages of his life.

Whatever his private feelings, the king was obliged to acquiesce in recognition of Maria's government. When Pedro's forces invaded Lisbon, Palmerston urged that it would be politic for Britain to recognise her claim to the throne. King William agreed with some reluctance that Lord George Russell, the British ambassador, should be given discretion to recognise her claim if Pedro was the victor in any action on land or at sea, but insisted that Russell would need to work in tandem with Admiral Parker, who was commanding

155

the British naval units stationed off the Iberian coast. Despite this, Lord William acted on his own initiative and accepted Maria as Queen of Spain anyway. Perceiving that it would be undignified to make difficulties, King William concurred with the decision.

Although he had been inclined to offer Pedro his support anyway, his attitude towards Queen Maria became more favourable when he learned that she had been snubbed by King Louis-Philippe. When she visited England in September 1833, he agreed to accept the niceties of royal protocol and entertain her for a few days at Windsor. She landed at Portsmouth, accompanied by a small suite and her stepmother Amelie, Duchess of Braganza. King William sent his carriage to meet her at Bagshot and bring them to Windsor, where they were guests of honour at dinner on the night of their arrival. Also present that evening were Princess Augusta, the Duchess of Gloucester, and Palmerston. On the night of their arrival, Sir Herbert Taylor, as ever a stickler for the correct procedure, informed Lord Grey that the king had arranged for a guard of honour to receive them in the castle court. Grey deemed this to be incorrect as they were guests of the king in his own personal residence. He added that 'His Majesty, being in a speaking mood I dread his committing himself more than is desirable.'[5] King William admitted later that he thought Maria was very ugly, stupid, and the most uninteresting girl he had ever seen, while his nephew Prince George of Cumberland, who was about seven weeks younger than Maria, thought she looked like a huge doll. Although Grey had feared that the king might not have been very hospitable, or else downright tactless, he happily reported to Brougham afterwards that His Majesty had conducted himself with perfect discretion throughout her stay.

The young queen was probably overawed and shy at first, but after a couple of days she was more at her ease and began to romp around the castle with the king's spinster sister Augusta, a sprightly princess then in her mid-fifties. Lady Charlotte Bedingfeld, a Lady of the Bedchamber, shared the king's unfavourable impression of their guest, thinking her voice terribly ugly and her whole manner rather uncouth. On the other hand, Princess Victoria of Kent, who was about six weeks younger than Maria and destined to be a queen herself within a few years, met her at Portsmouth on board the royal yacht *Emerald* before her departure later that week. Generally inclined to be very charitable in her formative years, and usually starved of friendly company her own age, the young heiress of Kensington Palace wrote in her journal afterwards that Queen Maria was very kind to her, 'very tall for her age, but had a very beautiful figure; she is grown very tall but also very stout. She has a beautiful complexion and is very sweet and friendly.'[6] It seems that she enjoyed the visiting young sovereign's appearance in England more than the elder generation of royalty, who found her rather demanding. After Queen Maria returned to Portugal that week, Princess Augusta became ill with gout, while an exhausted Queen Adelaide took to her bed and slept for fifteen hours.

By January 1834, Dom Pedro realized that he could not continue to fight without assistance from any of the other powers, and he appealed to the British to intervene in favour of his daughter's cause. Grey was strongly in favour of the idea and prevailed upon the king to agree to a favourable response. King William took the attitude that if Britain was to help, then it must be done effectively and there had to be a good chance of success. On this occasion it was not William's attitude, but dissension within the cabinet that prevented the sending of aid to Pedro. Althorp spoke against the scheme, mainly on the grounds of finance, and the project was temporarily abandoned. Grey threatened to resign but when he went to Brighton to tell King William of his decision, he was told firmly that it was his duty to remain in office, and assured of his sovereign's complete trust. As a result, he rescinded his resignation, but Dom Pedro did not get the help he had requested.

In April 1834, a solution was found at last when a treaty was signed between England, France, Spain and Portugal, pledging to restore peace in the Iberian Peninsula. Miguel agreed to a cessation of hostilities and surrendered, Pedro's regency ended, and Queen Maria's throne was guaranteed by the interested powers. Palmerston insisted that the treaty would be strengthened if France was a signatory and King William IV, who was initially reluctant to agree, was soon persuaded of the advantages of a cooperation that would probably avert the need for the use of armed force. Miguel was exiled from Portugal for life, while Pedro was allowed to remain but died of tuberculosis later that year.

The Quadruple Alliance signed in April also drew England into the Civil War being fought in Spain, the First Carlist War of 1833–1840, where Infante Carlos was trying to wrest the throne from his young niece, Isabella. Britain agreed to afford her assistance, albeit with reservations, and Palmerston arranged for a force of British volunteers to fight in Spain. His choice as commander of the British Legion fell on Colonel George de Lacey Evans, the radical MP for Westminster, an individual of whom King William strongly disapproved. This, and the fact that the policy of assisting Isabella had come about partly through an agreement with France, contributed to the king's lack of interest in Spanish affairs, a detachment that bordered on contempt for the country. A more liberal constitution was forced on the young queen in the summer of 1836 after a *coup d'état*, an attempt by the old royalist elite and the more moderate representatives in government, in an effort to hold back the forces of radicalism by widening the franchise and introducing economic reforms.

Melbourne and Palmerston welcomed such developments, seeing in them a more stable future for the nation, but King William was furious. When Melbourne sent to him a draft speech from the throne, with an expression of goodwill to the reformers, the king indignantly struck it out, saying he had 'not the least confidence in the Queen's government, no opinion of the patriotism of the Spanish nation.'[7] Such a business, he declared, rendered null and void all existing treaty obligations towards Spain, much to the annoyance of the prime minister.

There was little they could do to dissuade him from his deeply entrenched opinion that all Spanish governments were utterly incompetent, and it was pointless for Britain to become involved in their affairs, as long as they posed no threat to the political balance of Europe. In William's view Spain was a nonentity and, unlike France, far too ineffectual to pose any genuine threat to the British government's peace of mind. To the end he remained stoutly xenophobic when it came to comparing his kingdom with the rest of Europe, but it was a prejudice unashamedly shared by many of his subjects. For all its faults, and despite the troubled passage of the Great Reform Bill, there was much to be said for the English government. John Bright, shortly to be elected to the House of Commons, some thirty years later referred to it as 'the mother of parliaments'.

Chapter 9

A New Parliamentary Era

Once the Reform Bill had been passed, King William assumed that parliamentary affairs would enter a more peaceful phase. He was not to know that it was obvious to the ministers that the country needed a dissolution of parliament and a new general election. The old House of Commons had been returned under a system that was now obsolete, and the electorate had to be permitted to exercise their rights under the new one. The king was convinced that all general elections were periods of disorder and upheaval, with the potential to lead to discord and outrage. In May 1832, as the Reform Bill was in the final stages of its tortuous progress through parliament, William asked his ministers whether it contained provision for an automatic dissolution. If it did so, he thought that this would infringe his prerogative. Melbourne assured him that this would not be the case.

A little later, Brougham dropped a casual comment about the forthcoming election, which was immediately queried by the king. He had assumed that there would be an interval of maybe two years, if not more, until the country went to the polls once again. Brougham and Grey then had to explain that the House of Commons needed a new mandate to reflect the will of the people in the new post-reform era. His ministers complained that on this point the king was more obstinate and wrong-headed than they had ever found him before, and it took the threat of a mass ministerial resignation to make him submit to their demand for dissolution. He did so ungraciously, telling them that he would yield, but against his personal inclination.

The king continued to feel that matters in the country were unsettled, and that the mood of the populace was far from what it should be.

In August, a month after the bill had been passed, while at Ascot, he was hissed at and stones were thrown at him. Only the padding in his hat saved him from injury. On 16 August Hobhouse was present when parliament was prorogued, and thought the king seemed rather out of sorts. His speech, he said, was 'a poor performance', with reform being referred to in brief, but without any particular notice. He spoke very loudly, 'in some sentences ludicrously so', at odd moments 'with a sudden roar and emphasis that made me start'. Afterwards he watched the king return to the palace, and thought it 'like a funeral procession: scarcely a hat taken off, and positively no cheering.'[1]

It was about this time that Grey extended an olive branch to Queen Adelaide, who had never looked too kindly on him. That same month, August, he suggested that now that the Reform Bill was out of the way, it would be perfectly in order for Howe to resume his duties as her Chamberlain. The only condition he would make was that he should not overtly oppose the Government in the Lords, and with this the king was reassured. Negotiations were left to Taylor, which was perhaps not the wisest choice as he and Howe thoroughly disliked each other. Taylor wrote Howe a rather pompous letter which offended the latter's sense of his own dignity, bringing forth a reply saying that the queen's household should not depend on the whim of a minister. Taylor treated it as an outright rejection of the invitation, but this was not Howe's intention in the least. He now began to climb down and to Taylor's concern the king seized the opportunity, suggesting that Howe should be allowed to vote against the Government provided he maintained some cautious reserve in his opposition. With some trepidation Taylor informed Grey, admitting that the compromise was not precisely the way he had planned it, but he said he was sure matters would turn out for the best. It was a vain hope, and both men had cause to regret that they had reopened the matter in the first place. Howe attempted to increase his demands, before finally giving up in disgust towards the end of the year and refusing office.

An unfortunate aspect of the reopening of a business that everyone had thought belonged to the past was a recurrence of rumours about the former Chamberlain's relationship with Queen Adelaide. Greville described Howe's conduct 'towards her like an ardent young lover' who seemed never to be out of the Pavilion at Brighton, dined there almost every day or every evening, rode with her, never leaving her side, and never taking his eyes off her. The queen did nothing to try and keep him at a sensible distance, perhaps assuming that it was a perfectly innocent friendship and she had nothing to feel guilty about. Greville readily admitted that there was absolutely no evidence that she was treating Howe as a lover, if she did the secret would be out at once, as she was surrounded by enemies. 'All the FitzClarences dislike her and treat her more or less disrespectfully. She is aware of it, but takes no notice. She is very civil and good-humoured to them all; and as long as they keep within the bounds of decency, and do not break out into actual impertinence, she probably will continue so.'[2]

Grey went to Brighton towards the end of November, but found the atmosphere unusually chilly, with Howe clearly restored to favour. There seemed to him an overwhelmingly Tory flavour in the company at the Pavilion that initially made him feel he was rather out of place. It was not until after the general election, which assured him that he had a very strong mandate from the country, which placed him in a position of strength, that he felt more secure in their company. Although she had initially treated him with coldness, Queen Adelaide now made a point of speaking kindly to him, and the king went out of his way to make him feel at ease. It may have occurred to them that in recent months their faithful prime minister had been made to feel less than comfortable.

The major difficulty for Grey was that, at around this time, the king reverted to his old demand that the Government ought to suppress the political unions. He conceded that so far, they had made little mischief, but it was the principle of tolerating such societies to which he objected, and they had the potential to create a good deal of damage if left to flourish and propagate their venom against the state. They posed a threat to the future that could not be taken lightly by anyone who valued law and order and the Constitution which, he maintained, was the object of these self-constituted organisations 'to resist, to undermine and to destroy'.

Although Grey thoroughly disliked and distrusted the political unions himself, he knew it would be counter-productive to give them an opportunity for martyrdom, by suppressing them. His views provoked a longer and still more intemperate letter from King William. Taylor sadly told the prime minister that, if anything, the king was understating his views, saying he was convinced that he would consider the threat of a French invasion the lesser evil. It was as if the king, having been more liberal than expected towards his Whig ministers in the first two years of his reign, had started to wonder whether he had given too much away, and was being asked to give even further ground, while he felt he had been quite generous enough. Alternatively, he was perhaps assuming the mindset of the ageing authority figure who thought the modern world was deteriorating before his very eyes, standards were lowering all the time, and it was all much better 'in the good old days when I was young'.

This time the elections, held over a four-week period covering much of December 1832 and the first few days of January 1833, were not noted for any violent excesses. The Whigs achieved two-thirds of the votes and seats, but not the total monopoly of the Commons which some, including the king, had predicted or feared.

Having overseen reform during a particularly turbulent eighteen-month period, Grey was now exhausted and increasingly gave the impression of having lost his former zest for leadership. The king was proving ever more intractable and difficult to work with, the reform legislation and the Belgian question had involved him in exceptionally hard work, and the ill-health of his son-in-law Captain

George Barrington, a former naval officer who had briefly sat as a Whig in the House of Commons, gave him cause for anxiety. Nearly eighteen months older than his sovereign and approaching the age of seventy, Grey appeared increasingly ready to resign and retire into private life after a series of setbacks that a younger prime minister would normally have taken in their stride. Despite their differences William had come to respect and trust him, and the entreaties of his monarch and colleagues kept him in office to serve king and country a little longer, somewhat against his personal inclinations.

King William had hoped for a cessation in hostilities post-reform, and a less adversarial parliament, much as he had done about the situation in Ireland following Catholic emancipation in 1829. Once again, he had been too optimistic, for he and the ministers had reckoned without the inevitable participation of Daniel O'Connell. His mobilisation of Catholic Ireland had been instrumental in the cause of emancipation, and he had then become a fervent ally of the Whigs, devoting himself to the cause of parliamentary reform. He had demanded an additional twenty members for Irish seats in the House of Commons, although representation was increased by only five. His next objective was the restoration of a separate Irish Parliament through repeal of the Acts of Union in 1800, which had brought the United Kingdom of Great Britain and Ireland into existence the following year. He did not yet envisage complete independence or separation from the crown, and for all his nationalist aspirations, he always treated the royal family with respect if not tenderness.

In spite of this, King William was no admirer of the man. For him the union was as inviolate as everything else he had sworn to uphold in his coronation oath, and the name of O'Connell was anathema to him. In January 1831 O'Donnell was arrested on a charge of conspiracy to violate and evade a proclamation under the law for the Suppression of Dangerous Associations, much to the king's joy, but soon released without any further charges being brought, to corresponding royal disgust.

In 1833 the Whigs introduced a Coercion Bill, in full the Suppression of Disturbances Act, in response to agrarian unrest in Ireland and the Tithe War disturbances when Catholic tenant farmers resisted paying compulsory tithes to the Protestant Church of Ireland. It empowered the Lord Lieutenant to proclaim a district 'disturbed' and then to try suspects by military court martial, with penalties that included whipping, transportation for life, and even death. King William was satisfied at first but thought it did not go far enough. Soon he was asking firmly for any attempt to repeal the Irish union should be made an act of high treason, punishable by death.

Reform and the reworking of existing legislation relating to the Church of Ireland were also required. The tithe system meant that poverty-stricken Catholic peasants were forced to give part of what little they had to support Anglican clergyman in luxurious idleness. Naturally, not all Anglican priests lived in luxury, and the inefficiency of the system meant that the expense of extorting tithes from the peasantry was often more than the resulting income. In February 1833 Althorp's bill for the reform of the Church of Ireland proposed the radical overhaul of the whole tithe system, and a reduction of the number of bishoprics by ten. It was sufficiently radical for even O'Connell to support, but the king was less enthusiastic. He was aware that reform was overdue and had assured Grey that he approved of it in principle, in his speech from the throne. Yet he thought it went too far, as it might be betraying the most loyal of his subjects, as if the Anglican establishment was being deprived of rights that it had enjoyed for a long time. It also reawakened possibilities of another clash between the Commons and the Lords. He suggested to Grey that it might be feasible to suspend the measure, and that the interval preceding its introduction could be used to establish by what modifications its opponents might be reconciled to it. In June 1833 Brougham wrote to Taylor, asking him to submit to the king a request for the immediate creation of four or five peers who were known to favour reform, and a commitment that as many more would be created as needed, to 'discomfit the scheme now brought to the very point of execution'.[3] Taylor's reply came as no surprise.

No person could view the effects of a collision between both Houses of Parliament with greater apprehension than His Majesty, Taylor wrote, 'but he dreads also in a yet greater degree, the effect of any measure which may degrade the House of Peers and the aristocracy of the country. The former evil must be temporary, and may yield to measures of prevention before its prejudices can be seriously felt, but the latter would be lasting'.[4] Grey had known instinctively that the old tactic of requesting the creation of more peers, employed as a last resort a year earlier, could not be used again.

Always placing great importance on the sovereign's duty to defend the established church, the king wrote to Archbishop Howley, urging the bishops not to undermine the Government by outright opposition to the Irish Church Bill, on the grounds that it was not for the bishops to intervene in party politics. Greville was quite angry when he learned of what he called with some restraint 'this puzzling document'. He confided in his diary, 'Never was there such a proceeding, so unconstitutional, so foolish; but his Ministers do not seem to mind it, and are rather elated as such a signal proof of his disposition to support them. I think, as far as being a discouragement to the Tories and putting an end to their notion that he is hankering after them, it may be of use.'[5] It was indeed bad news for the Tories, but most of them realized that it would be pointless to put up any resistance. Yet the king was determined not to take any risks. His letter to the Archbishop had not achieved the outcome he had hoped for, because he had kept the contents more or less private, so a copy was sent also to the Archbishop of York, the Reverend Edward Venables-Vernon-Harcourt, and the opposition leaders were made aware of its contents. When the bill reached the House of Lords, none of the

Tory leaders were in any doubt that the king desperately wanted to see it passed. He had won his point, but it gave Whigs and Tories alike food for thought in that the Government was looking increasingly accident-prone and experiencing problems at getting its legislation passed. Sooner or later their good fortune was liable to run out.

The king thought the only solution for this difficulty lay in a coalition government, 'the union of men of talent, influence and property who have a common stake in the country and the common interest in its happiness and safety and in the maintenance of its monarchical institutions'. Brougham wrote to Taylor, asking him to tell his master that a coalition would be 'wholly impracticable, while men are in their present state of hostility; and if attempted at this time, would inevitably produce the most disastrous consequences, utterly destroying the character of all public men, and placing the country in the hands of the enemies of all good government.'[6] The king accepted his decision, though he was annoyed that it his solution had been rejected without any discussion. It lowered the standing of the Whigs, in his estimation, and he felt increasingly that the Whigs were less and less capable of providing the country with security and stable government.

Wellington might have distanced himself from the political fray for a while, but he could still provide invaluable services for his sovereign. About three years into the reign, there was a particularly delicate business that could have provided major embarrassment to the crown if not carefully checked. Mrs Fitzherbert, who had been unofficially married to the then Prince of Wales in 1785, held the secret in her papers. On the death of King George IV, they became the joint property of his executors, Sir William Knighton and the Duke of Wellington. Mrs Fitzherbert hated Knighton, and more importantly, did not trust him not to betray her and his late Majesty by publishing them for his own financial advantage, or using them for the purposes of blackmail, if he so chose. As Mrs Fitzherbert was a Catholic, if it was proved beyond a doubt that any form of marriage had taken place, it would be a matter of supreme embarrassment to the crown. King William had always been a good friend of hers and shared her detestation of Knighton.

About eighteen months after the death of King George, she requested Wellington to hand the letters over to her or else destroy them. As joint custodian of the material, Knighton adamantly refused to allow this to happen, on the grounds that he would be betraying a 'sacred trust' if he acquiesced. As long as the papers remained within Knighton's reach, there was a genuine risk that the secret would be brought into the open. The duke suggested, with King William's wholehearted approval, that all the letters and documents exchanged between Mrs Fitzherbert and her late husband should be destroyed in the presence of a third party. Mrs Fitzherbert refused this suggestion, on the grounds that she wanted to hold onto one love letter, her marriage certificate and a few other select documents. At length, thanks to the duke's perseverance and negotiating skills, it was arranged that two other peers should be appointed to act with the duke and Knighton. All four agreed that they should destroy all the papers except for the few that she wished to retain. One of the group was prevented by illness from taking part in the final rites, so it fell to the Earl of Albemarle and the duke to carry out the destruction of the great mass of material at Mrs Fitzherbert's house in Tilney Street, in Park Lane, in August 1833. After several hours' burning, the duke remarked that 'we had better hold our hand for a while, or we shall set the old woman's chimney on fire.'[7] Accordingly they waited until the next day to complete the destruction of the documents.

Early in May 1834, Lord John Russell announced that 'the revenues of the Church of Ireland were larger than necessary for the religious and moral instruction of the persons belonging to that Church'[8] and said he would like to see part of them used for lay purposes. The reaction from various sources was hostile, particularly a group of

Irish bishops who presented a petition of protest from the clergy with more than 1,400 signatures. The king had waited for some time to make his views known and delivered a lengthy impromptu speech that was widely reported in the press. He said that he had been 'led to support toleration to the utmost extent of which it is justly capable; but toleration must not be suffered to go into licentiousness; it has its bounds, which it is my duty and which I am resolved to maintain. I am, from the deepest conviction, attached to the pure Protestant faith which this church, of which I am the temporal head, is the human means of diffusing and preserving in this land.' He said he was speaking more strongly than usual, because of the unhappy circumstances that had been forced on them all. 'The threats of those who are enemies of the church make it the more necessary for those who feel their duty to that church to speak out.' His words, he said in conclusion, came from his heart.[9]

Grey was horrified when he heard the reports of this address, and even more so when it was quoted verbatim in the papers. He did not object to the contents, but to the tone and timing of the king's intervention. Taylor likewise admitted that his master had not been entirely discreet. Feelings ran high among members of the Government, not only at the king's words, but also after Russell's declaration of policy. Edward Stanley, a former Secretary for Ireland, said that Russell had 'upset the coach'. He and three other cabinet moderates resigned three weeks later, rather than accept what they saw as the misappropriation of funds belonging to the Irish church. The group included Stanley, the Earl of Ripon, who as Viscount Goderich had served as prime minister under King George IV for five months, Sir James Graham, First Lord of the Admiralty, and the Duke of Richmond.

The following month the renewal of the Coercion Act was debated in parliament. Some of the more draconian measures were to be repealed, but on the matter of restricting public meetings the ministers failed to agree. It was the end for Grey, who had had enough of public life and on 7 July he told the king that he was resigning, and recommended that Melbourne should be his successor. It was a wise suggestion, for apart from Grey himself, King William had very little liking or respect for most of the other senior Whigs. Melbourne was one of the very few whose company he liked, whose judgment he appreciated, whom he respected as a fellow conservative – not to say almost a Tory in all but name – and above all a politician whom he could regard as a gentleman. For his part, Melbourne realized that the king was not well-disposed towards the Whigs as a party, and 'it was a bitter dose for him to swallow … to have to take [accept] us again', but whatever his personal feelings, he was always very civil. With Queen Adelaide, his relations were less cordial; 'I used never to go near her, but used to talk to the Maids of Honour.'[10] It was perhaps fortuitous that Queen Adelaide was away on a family visit at the time. To her, Melbourne was a man without principles and with an improper sense of humour, and she might have tried to dissuade the king from summoning him.

When Brougham came to call on the king shortly after Grey's resignation, he found him determined that the Whigs should not remain in government without some reinforcement. What exactly went on between the sovereign and his Lord Chancellor is open to doubt, but there is speculation that Brougham may have left the king with the impression that he saw himself as the new leader of the Government and would immediately promote several radicals to the ministry, the very last thing the king would have been prepared to accept. William thought that the more responsible members of the party were too weak to keep the more radical wing under control. The Whig majority could not last long, he thought, as they seemed divided and moving from one crisis to another, and in the present circumstances he still thought that a coalition would be far better placed to rule the country.

Melbourne insisted that the senior Tories would have no part in such an administration, but to satisfy the king he agreed to ask

Wellington and Peel whether they would be willing to serve under him. As he had foreseen, they refused, Wellington declaring that a union of men who could not agree in any single principle or policy, whether home or foreign affairs, would be unable to serve His Majesty. He believed that '[we] cannot conciliate the confidence of the public or acquire the support of Parliament, and [this] must lead to the most disastrous results.'[11] It left him with no alternative but to suppress his doubts and appoint Melbourne to lead a reconstructed Whig government. Matters were not helped by the fact that the king had been ill during the autumn, exhausted and depressed. The Duke of Wellington thought he might be going 'mad' like his father, while the Duke of Cumberland, possibly not without personal interest, said that a Regent would have to be appointed as the king was insane and unfit to govern the country.

At such a troubled time, there was to be no escape for the king from political arguments at home. The queen, the FitzClarences and the king's surviving sisters in England were all equally fervent partisans of the Tories. It may have been a combination of stress and a severe bout of asthma that year, but everyone thought the king had behaved very oddly when Queen Adelaide went on a family visit to Germany. Shortly before her departure, he talked with some excitement of the bachelor joys that he would relish during her absence, then his mood immediately changed to grave despondency, and it was as if he could hardly bear to let her go away after all.

Though Queen Adelaide might have found some common ground with her political allies, her stepchildren and their spouses, they often treated her with scant consideration despite the kindness she had always showed to them. Lady Frederick FitzClarence had some understanding of her difficult position, but still regarded her as incorrigibly foreign in her ways. She told Creevey that she had seen a great deal of the consort, whom she thought 'sensible and good natured, but that after living fourteen years in England she has not a single English notion. The Queen's fix'd impression is that an English

Revolution is rapidly approaching, and that her own fate is to be that of Marie Antoinette, and she trusts she shall be able to act her part with more courage'.[12]

Though the king's sisters knew better than to attempt to influence their brother unduly, at heart he was a family man who had always enjoyed good relations with his siblings and this enabled them to put any political disagreements aside. It distressed him that he should seem so out of step with them simply by doing his duty. To Princess Mary, Duchess of Gloucester, he admitted tearfully that he felt the crown tottering on his head.[13] Like his predecessor, he particularly liked to have Mary close to him in times of stress. The duchess had spent much of her time with the dying King George IV, and William found her company sympathetic. It was noticed that she seemed fonder of her two eldest surviving brothers than of her own kindly but uninspiring husband.

Despite his offer of Buckingham Palace to the nation having already been gently declined, King William had not given up hope that the palace he had never liked would be put to other uses. In 1833 he suggested that it ought to be turned into a new Houses of Parliament, with the present buildings turned into a residence for the Lord Chancellor, and Courts of Law, and part of the garden offered for sale for private development to help defray expenses, if necessary. Grey pointed out that so much money already had been spent on modernising the palace under King George IV, that the public would be incensed if a change of use was suggested at this stage.

On 16 October 1834, two underfloor stoves in the House of Lords were used to burn a stockpile of old tally sticks, part of an obsolete accounting system that had been used by the Exchequer and required disposal. The fire was soon out of control, and by nightfall several rooms in both Houses of Parliament had been destroyed. Remembering the difficult events of two years earlier, the queen considered it 'divine retribution', while her husband hoped that this would give him the opportunity for which he had long been waiting. John Hobhouse, later Baron Broughton, a cabinet minister in Melbourne's government, visited the king at St James's two days later. It came as no surprise to him that his sovereign did not seem affected by the calamity, but quite the reverse. 'He seemed delighted at having an opportunity of getting rid of Buckingham Palace; said he meant it as a permanent gift for Parliament Houses, and that it would be the finest thing in Europe.' Later that day, King William and Queen Adelaide came in two plain carriages to inspect the smoking ruins. Both seemed quite fearless as they walked through the dust and debris, the king prodding the tottering walls with his stick, as if to have some minor hand in the destruction the flames had already begun, and unable to conceal his immense pleasure at the prospect of divesting himself of his unwanted residence at last. Just before they entered their carriages, he called Hobhouse and the Speaker, and reiterated firmly that he intended the palace 'as a permanent gift'.[14] In an effort to appease his persistent sovereign, Melbourne commissioned an architect to draw up a report on the suitability of such a plan. To his relief he was assured that the plan was totally impracticable, and that there could not be a worse decision than to accept the king's offer. The king was annoyed but had no choice but to accept the report and the ministers' refusal.

Members of the cabinet were not the only ones who distressed the king or incurred his reproaches. His illegitimate children quarrelled, and continually pestered him for favours and money, and they often treated the long-suffering queen with scant respect. Despite the king's best efforts his eldest son, who had been created Earl of Munster in June 1831, rarely remained on good terms with him for long. Other members of the family and in-laws also bore the brunt of his impatience when he was easily roused to anger by trivial matters within the family. Once, when King Leopold of the Belgians called for some water at dinner, William exploded. 'God damn it! Why don't you drink wine? I never allow anybody to drink water at my table.'[15]

Meanwhile, Lord Melbourne's ministry continued to be plagued by problems. The worst was when the king became concerned at the list of some of his cabinet appointments, particularly that of Lord John Russell, whom he regarded as a dangerous radical. Matters came to a head in November when Earl Spencer's death caused his eldest son, the ever-dependable Viscount Althorp, who had been Leader of the Commons, to be moved to the Lords. Althorp had been one of the few Whig ministers whom the king particularly liked. Melbourne proposed Russell as his successor, but he was one of the least suitable choices Melbourne could have made. The king thoroughly resented Russell, thinking him arrogant, offensive and clever, and above all identified with the policy of appropriating the funds of the Irish church for lay purposes. Melbourne had been prepared for such a refusal by the king and recommended several other possible senior Whigs for the position, although with less enthusiasm. The king refused all of them. On 13 November Melbourne called on the king at Windsor to talk about his plans for the future of the administration. The king lacked confidence in him, and Melbourne was unable to give an undertaking that the revenues of the Irish church would be properly protected. The following day the king dismissed Melbourne, personally handing him a letter in which he said it would not be fair to maintain him in so precarious a position. The departing prime minister took it very amiably, probably having been prepared for such an outcome.

On 15 November, before ministers had been informed what was happening, *The Times* announced that the king had taken the opportunity of Lord Spencer's death to dismiss the ministry, 'and there is every reason to believe the Duke of Wellington has been sent for. The Queen has done it all.'[16] Associating Queen Adelaide with this episode was assumed to have been because of information passed to a reporter by Edward Ellice, a junior minister, and the widowed husband of Grey's sister Hannah.

Wellington had indeed been sent for and was in a private meeting at Windsor when Sir Herbert Taylor entered the room, and apologised for calling his royal master's attention to the paragraph in the paper. The king angrily turned to the duke. 'You see how I am insulted and betrayed; nobody in London but Melbourne knew last night what had taken place here, nor of my sending for you; will your Grace compel me to take back people who have treated me in this way?'[17] Wellington knew from experience that he could not be prime minister, as a member of the House of Lords, when faced with a hostile majority in the Commons. Only a member of the Commons could hope to succeed in such a task, and the only possible man was Sir Robert Peel, who was at the time on holiday in Europe. So Wellington agreed to act as caretaker leader of the Government while Peel was summoned to return to England as soon as possible.

On 17 November Wellington was sworn in as Lord Treasurer, then took the oath as Home Secretary, Foreign Secretary and Secretary for War. For a short while, a single statesman held all the executive offices of government.' This was intended as an interim measure only, despite Grey sneering at 'His Highness the Dictator'. At the first meeting of the Privy Council, the outgoing ministers came face to face with the Tories, whom the duke had assembled for the purpose. Greville noticed that perfect, if glacial, civility was observed all round, except in the case of Brougham, who played the role of a bad loser, looked furious and took no notice of anybody. Instead of handing over the Great Seal of his office in person as per the usual procedure, he had it despatched to the king via a messenger, wrapped up untidily in a bag. One bad-tempered action provoked another, and William reportedly said afterwards that he never wanted to see Brougham's ugly face again.

The Whigs had been deprived of office and were crying foul. Queen Adelaide was the favourite target for their abuse, led by the FitzClarences. If members of the Commons thought twice about being disloyal to their elderly monarch, it was easier to denigrate his spouse who was known to be unnecessarily partisan. Every discontented supporter of Melbourne seemed to delight in suggesting that her hand could be detected in what amounted to a constitutional *coup d'état*. Yet while public indignation was not so marked as it had been in 1832, the king's reputation in Westminster had rarely been lower, and it seemed that his popularity had gone forever. To use an analogy, two years earlier he had played a reasonably good if by no means faultless hand. This time, his personal prejudices and hasty temper suggested a high-handed autocratic *diktat* that few apart from his most ardent defenders could explain or pardon.

Dismissal of a popular government by their monarch was not a wise action, and to dismiss a popular government commanding a large majority in the House of Commons was difficult to justify. Those who have sought to explain it have argued that Melbourne had laid such emphasis on the future weakness of his administration as to convince the king that it could never persist, and that in all but the last formal rights, he had indeed resigned. This argument has some validity. Melbourne and Grey both emphasised the difficulties ahead, with the former showing a marked lack of enthusiasm for remaining in office, admitting that there might be secessions. He had accepted his dismissal with alacrity, almost relief, as if he had half-heartedly accepted a poisoned chalice and knew that it could easily fall from his never very secure grasp, at any time.

When he was able to view events from a distance, Grey conceded that he could hardly attach any blame to the king for his decision. He admitted to Russell that the present government was in a difficult position and would find it almost impossible to continue in office. Melbourne took an equally measured view of the situation. He said that the king's decision had come as no surprise, and felt he could not entirely condemn His Majesty's actions. He inferred that most members of the present cabinet could hardly be trusted, he had never liked Lord John Russell, and he had been badly unsettled by issues pertaining to the church. Nevertheless, he had misjudged the state of the Whig Party, at the time. He believed with good reason that the party was bitterly divided, and if allowed to go into opposition, it would have ample time for reflection, free from the pressure of having to govern. Suddenly finding themselves in office could lead to a damaging split. His own dismissal had probably worked to their advantage, as they suddenly became united again, if only on the surface. Moreover, in all good conscience he felt that he could not sanction a government that included Lord John Russell as a senior member, a man whose policy on the Irish Church he had found thoroughly unacceptable.

In what was becoming an increasingly politicised atmosphere at Westminster, the king may have felt that his ministers were taking him more and more for granted. He had been scrupulous in giving every encouragement to the Whigs from the moment that Grey succeeded Wellington as prime minister. He had acknowledged that as politicians they were doing the best they could for their country. While he may not have agreed wholeheartedly with the more radical ministers, William was prepared to place his confidence in them and let them get on with the job. Yet some of their policies were a bridge too far for him. He firmly believed they were pursuing the wrong direction, too far and too fast, and with the natural resistance of the old to change, he disliked having the dawn of a new world thrust in his face. Surrounded by a family who were almost solidly Tories and who intended to preserve the status quo, it was inevitable that sooner or later he would feel that maybe their instincts were correct after all.

After a brief period under the leadership of the Duke of Wellington, on 9 December Peel returned home. Although he thought that King William had miscalculated the situation, as a loyal servant of the crown he felt obliged to stand by the consequences of his sovereign's actions. He hoped he would strengthen his position by including in his government those moderates who had deserted the Whigs earlier in the year. When his overtures to Stanley and Graham were politely rejected, he was left to form an administration of committed Tories that he knew were entirely unenthusiastic about facing a House of Commons dominated by Whigs and radicals.

Hoping to secure a more sympathetic parliament, in January 1835 at the head of a Tory party committed to a new, progressive outlook, Peel made an overture to the country. In what would prove to be a time-honoured address to his Tamworth constituents, he emphasized that his party was prepared to embrace moderate and constructive reform, when necessary. The results of the campaign brought gains for the Tories, at the expense of the Whigs, and emerged as the largest single party in the new House, although the radicals held their ground. The parliament that met on 10 February, the second to follow the passing of the Reform Act, revealed that the Tories still fell short of a majority government. Peel found himself the head of a minority administration for several precarious weeks. The previous Speaker of the House of Commons, Charles Manners-Sutton, had been popular and effective in his post, well-liked by both sides, and it had been assumed that although he was a Tory he would probably have been re-elected unopposed. Despite this the opposition intended to make a show of strength against a new administration that seemed unlikely to survive for long, and nominated a Whig, James Abercromby, as the new Speaker of the House. He was elected by a narrow margin of ten votes.

Having won one victory against the Government, they were quick to pursue further quarry. Charles Vane, Marquess of Londonderry, half-brother of Viscount Castlereagh, a former member of parliament, military commander and diplomat, had been nominated as the next ambassador to Russia. Despite his previous experience at the courts of Berlin and Vienna, it would have been difficult to find a less popular choice than this boorish, drunken, reactionary aristocrat, whose behaviour had provoked the nickname, used only behind his back, of 'Lord Pumpernickel' (an archaic term, probably of German origin, best rendered as 'devil's fart'). The matter was put to a vote and his appointment was overwhelmingly rejected. Further defeats on subsequent matters of government policy followed. It was as if the Whigs, still smarting after having been dismissed from government, were determined to wear down, by small degrees, the Tories who had supplanted them, and therefore make their position untenable.

King William was impressed with Peel's efforts to govern in the face of such odds. In a long letter to the cabinet, he expressed his appreciation of their efforts, and his view that 'the confidence, the countenance, and the support of the Sovereign are indispensable to the existence and the maintenance of the Government, so long as the Constitution of the country is monarchical.' At the same time, he denigrated the actions of what he called 'the present factious Opposition', who gave every appearance of putting party above country. If his confidential servants should recommend a further appeal to the country, he would consider it his duty to yield to their advice, although it was likely that the result 'would offer proof of a further reaction in the public feeling.' The king acknowledged that the last change of administration had been his own immediate and exclusive act, in that he had asked for the resignation of ministers 'whom he considered no longer capable of carrying on the business of the country with advantage, and he called to his councils others whom he considered deserving of his confidence.' He stated that if he were forced to take the opposition back into government, he would find it impossible to give its members his confidence:

> They cannot expect it, nor can they claim a support to which their proceedings would have so little entitled them. His Majesty might be obliged to tolerate them, but he could not meet them cordially, nor communicate with them as with friends. They may become his Ministers, but never his *confidential* servants. He would receive all their advice with jealousy and suspicion. He could not bring himself to affect that which he cannot feel.[18]

Within a few weeks, Peel bowed to the inevitable. On 4 April, he told the Duke of Wellington that they were giving their opponents 'time to mature a new government' that would be formed independently of His Majesty's consent, although it could not assume the actual functions of governments and the offices of government without that consent. The longer the Tories protracted the struggle, the more certain would be the blow at royal authority. It was said by the Whigs that the beleaguered prime minister had every virtue except resignation, but this was not long in coming. On 8 April, he laid down the burden he had not really wished to assume in the first place, with a short, dignified speech to the Commons that was enthusiastically cheered by his political adversaries as well as his own party.

Anxious to keep the radicals from power, the king strongly considered turning to Grey and asking him if he would take on the premiership once more. Failing that, perhaps he would return to the Government as foreign secretary, with Melbourne acting as a go-between. The latter accepted this request with good grace, in the almost certain knowledge that he knew what the response would be and that nothing would persuade his former leader to come out of retirement. It came as no surprise when Grey told him that he would 'sink under a burden which [he had not] strength to maintain'.[19] He advised the king to send for Melbourne as prime minister and the Marquess of Lansdowne as foreign secretary, and offered to be present at any meeting between them if it would help to ensure an orderly transfer of power.

It was a situation which the king had hoped to avoid by persuading the Tories to accept reform, and not wage a campaign of obstruction for its own sake. This had been too much to ask, and there was no alternative but to accept an imminent Whig return to the offices of state. He made it clear that he would do so as a matter of duty, but his support would comprise only the customary civil formalities. Tolerating them as ministers was one thing, but he could not regard them as friends or confidential servants, and any advice they offered would be considered very carefully. The Whigs did not seem unduly perturbed. As independently minded as ever, Russell had no scruples about letting his sovereign have his own way over matters of state, considering that he had brought the risk of any humiliation on himself, having dispensed with the services of his Whig ministry after their irreconcilable differences over the disestablishment of the Irish Church.

The days when the king had been able to confer a majority by offering an individual the post of Prime Minister were no more than a memory. He was forced to recall Melbourne to office, but this did not improve his relations with the ministry. When asked whether he would be entertaining on his customary scale during Ascot week, he remarked irritably that he could not give dinners without inviting the ministers, and he would rather see the devil than any one of them in his house.

Summoned for a second time, Melbourne was cautious enough to assert his conditions before accepting the king's offer. Given what had happened the first time, he had no intention of subjecting himself to a similar experience. He required a firm, unequivocal pledge from the existing royal household members, who were also either in the Lords or Commons, that they would support the Government; and, in the event of vacancies, nobody was to be selected whose principles and opinions were adverse to it.

Melbourne was concerned when the king announced that he would veto certain names if they were to be submitted to him for ministerial appointments. He stated firmly that he would be unable to accept any principle of exclusions, while the king was equally firm in refusing to abandon the principle. Deadlock was avoided by the exercise of common sense on both sides, and with Lord Grey acting as an honest broker. Melbourne let it be known that he would ensure he did not put forward any names to which the king had a particular objection. The king told Grey that he would regard as unsuitable only

O'Connell, his fellow Irish member, Richard Sheil, and the Scottish member, Joseph Hume, all radicals whom he regarded as potential troublemakers. As Melbourne assured him that none of them had ever been under consideration, this gave the monarch no problems whatsoever. Melbourne also had no desire to reappoint Brougham as Chancellor, a man whom the sovereign would probably have accepted with reluctance, but Melbourne now harboured a strong dislike for him. The king grudgingly accepted that, all things considered, Melbourne had made the best of what was, but would likely remain a poisoned chalice.

A majority of members of both the old and the new House of Commons had expressed support for lay appropriation of the Irish church's surplus revenues and the decision that they should be devoted to general education for children of all religions. The Whigs declared that they had undertaken to carry out such a policy, and they would be unable to form an administration unless His Majesty accepted such a commitment. Although the king believed that the Whigs' proposal to appropriate surplus church revenues for lay purposes would in some way violate his coronation oath, Melbourne stated flatly that he would only accept office as long as he was assured of no royal opposition to the measure. As a compromise, the king suggested that he should refer the question to a panel of judges, something that Melbourne said he thought 'highly inexpedient', as the issue was not a question of law, but of conscience. Against his better judgement, he eventually conceded that the king might discuss it with the outgoing chancellor, Lord Lyndhurst. Lyndhurst realized the delicacy of the issue and carefully excused himself from any involvement by pleading total ignorance of the bill and of the whole business. Having realized that this was his last option, the king faced the inevitable and decided that the issue did not trouble his conscience so much as he had thought it might. As he would have to give his consent to the bill in the end, he had nothing to gain by refusing it in the early stages.

Melbourne was satisfied with this, although he must have wondered why his sovereign had not saved them all, all this trouble by reaching this conclusion much earlier. However, his government was now duly installed with full if somewhat reluctant royal assent. In reappointing the ministry that he had dismissed not so long ago, parliament thought the king seemed uneasy but perfectly civil, noted Lord Hall. Nevertheless, the king seemed to have an uneasy working relationship with all the ministers, apart from Viscount Howick, Grey's eldest son, who was appointed Secretary of State for War. Everyone assumed that William was prepared to be accommodating towards him, being the son of his father and also as a new minister, who could not be blamed for any of the recent differences.

The previous two kings might have capitulated under such circumstances, but if so would have probably have given in with bad grace. King William was prepared to make the best of a difficult situation, albeit with reluctance. The administration observed with satisfaction that Britain had taken one more faltering step on the road to democracy. It did not disguise the probability that King William's relations with a government he had distrusted from the start, and had been forced to reappoint, were not going to be easy.

A new bone of contention arose a few months later regarding their Canadian policy. This would become a persistent cause of royal peevishness. In July 1835, after William had spoken about this at a council meeting, Greville recorded that in his opinion this did more to diminish the standing of the monarchy than anything else; he claimed that 'to exhibit the King publicly to the world as a cypher, and something less than a cypher, as an unsuccessful competitor in a political squabble, is to take from the Crown all the dignity with which it is invested'.[20] The king was convinced that his government was planning to grant the legislative body of Canada greater freedom that would lead inexorably to self-government and eventually independence from the crown. William told one of the Canada Commissioners that the Canadas had been won by British valour, bought with British blood, and subsequently improved and enlarged at the expense of Britain. These provinces, he warned, 'must not be lost or given away.'[21]

King William's control of his temper was diminishing with increasing ill-health, and the ministers could never entirely rid themselves of the thought that his mental balance was open to question. Now that he had a cabinet that he had never really wanted, but would have to work with, he subjected its members to continual petty annoyances. He believed they had struck a deal by aligning themselves with Irish agitators and would-be revolutionaries, in order to facilitate their return to office. The prospects for a comfortable working relationship between cabinet and sovereign did not look favourable.

Chapter 10

The Last Years

King William reached the age of seventy fully conscious of his mortality. Elderly men often are inclined to find comfort in dwelling on their personal interests and on happier memories of the past, to an extent that those who do not share their enthusiasms find tedious, and the man so often remembered as 'the sailor king' was no exception. On 11 October 1835 the king and queen attended divine service in the chapel at Greenwich Hospital. From there they went to a dinner at St James's Palace to mark the anniversary of the Battle of Camperdown in 1797, an action in which the British navy had decisively defeated the Dutch during the French revolutionary wars.

Once dinner was over, the king rose to his feet and said he hoped the ladies would stay. He had something to say on this occasion that would elicit recollections among the naval officers present, that the battles which their predecessors and brother officers had fought and won, were 'battles worthy of record as proving that the naval history of this country had not been neglected or forgotten by succeeding generations'. He began with holding forth on the first invasion of Britain by Julius Caesar, which he said must have proved to the natives the necessity of a naval force to prevent and repel foreign invasion. Next, he dwelt at some length on the landing of the Danes and other northern nations on the British coast, and proceeded with his impassioned narrative to more recent times, when the British navy had become great and victorious, from the days of Elizabeth to William III, and up to the present day. When he had finished, the guests rose with some relief and retired to the drawing room, but while they were there the king beckoned to Barrow, his old friend and ally at the Admiralty, and said that he was sure he had

185

neglected to mention an important action in his speech. Dreading that he might summon the company back in order to resume his address, Barrow assured him tactfully that he was not aware of any omission. The king then remembered and confessed he had forgotten to say anything about Admiral George Anson and the triumphant action he had fought off Cape Finisterre in 1747, Adding, 'I am not sure I know the details correctly; pray send me an account of it tomorrow.'[1] Barrow did not record in his memoirs whether he had obeyed the command or not, but he must have been relieved on behalf of all the other guests for this minor lapse in his master's continuing almost encyclopaedic knowledge of naval history. It had undoubtedly curtailed the oratory of a sovereign who all too rarely appreciated the benefits of being concise.

Whenever William became unwell, it reminded him that the time was coming when he would have to bequeath the throne to a representative of the younger generation. Despite his uncertain temper, like his wife, he had never harboured any jealousy towards his niece, Princess Victoria of Kent. It still saddened them both that they were allowed to see so little of her. They were very fond of her and believed that as she was the sovereign-in-waiting, it was only right that they should enjoy some time together so that he might talk to her and give her the benefit of his experience. Yet he had every good reason to dislike her mother, the Duchess of Kent and Strathearn, an elder sister of King Leopold, who had never hesitated to hide her contempt for the king and the FitzClarences. Admittedly, the latter family members continued to regard themselves as privileged and had very few friends or admirers in their day. She was also aware that William's kindly efforts to satisfy the demands of his illegitimate sons for honour and emolument, often a means of atonement motivated by some sense of guilt at 'their peculiar position', did little to enhance the general standing of the crown.

At the start of William's reign the duchess had caused offence by demanding that, as the mother of the heir to the throne she should be treated as the Dowager Princess of Wales, and granted an income that would be commensurate with such a rank. About three years later she began a programme of unofficial semi-royal tours around England, their main purpose being to introduce the princess to her future subjects. The scheme had been devised by John Conroy, who had been appointed equerry to the Duke of Kent before his marriage, and after his death became comptroller to the duchess. As Princess Victoria would ascend the throne before long, these tours would have been a sensible idea, provided the king's approval had been sought beforehand. However, the king had not been consulted had not been given any prior warning, and when he found out he was furious. The breach was widened by the behaviour of Princess Sophia, the fifth daughter of King George III and Queen Charlotte. Sophia was on good terms with the duchess and her household and took malicious pleasure in repeating all the king's impatient criticisms of the duchess to her. Every evening after dinner she would visit the latter's apartments at Kensington Palace and regale her with the latest tittle-tattle.

Having had a poor command of English when she came from Germany to marry the Duke of Kent in 1818, to be widowed eighteen months later, the duchess had always been an unwitting pawn of the scheming Conroy. He acted as her trusted confidant and political agent and, if the gossips were to be believed, her lover as well. Some were even prepared to believe or at least suspect that he was the father of Princess Victoria. Although this sounds quite implausible, it was certainly clear that he had tried to act *in loco parentis*. It had been on his initiative that the adolescent princess had been raised according to the 'Kensington System', which he devised and named after the palace in which they lived. He had intended that Victoria would grow up a weak-willed young woman, completely dependent on him and her mother. If King William IV were to pass away before Victoria reached her majority, the Duchess of Kent would become her regent and Conroy would become the real power behind the throne.

The young princess was deliberately kept isolated from her close relatives in the house of Hanover, from all other children her age except for Conroy's daughter, also named Victoire, and was never allowed to be apart from her mother, her tutor or her governesses, Baroness Lehzen and the Duchess of Northumberland. Throughout Victoria's formative years the Duchess of Kent and Conroy monitored and recorded her every action, and read the journal that she kept faithfully each day. As a result, the princess was careful to ensure that it contained little more than a generally bland chronicle of day-to-day events, free from any serious introspection or expression of thoughts that could lead to trouble.

Because of Queen Adelaide's tragic inability to bear any children who lived for more than a few weeks, the king might well have privately resented the existence of his heiress Victoria. Yet he was a kindly man, and like the queen he was very fond of her. Because she would succeed him on the throne, he naturally took a keen interest in her upbringing. As one of his modern biographers has suggested, if given the chance he would undoubtedly 'have delighted in her almost as if she had been his own child'.[2] He deeply resented the duchess's attitude, and the fact that she thought it unseemly for her daughter to appear at a court presided over by a monarch with so many children born outside a wedding ring. She always did her best to prevent her daughter from becoming 'contaminated', as she saw it, by any contact with them. Within less than a year of the king's accession, she told the princess's state governess. Louisa, Duchess of Northumberland, that she had never 'associated' her in any way with the FitzClarences, and she never would. 'With the King they die; did I not keep this line how would it be possible to teach Victoria the difference between Vice and Virtue?'[3] One morning when the duchess was staying at Windsor for a few days, the Earl of Munster accidentally walked into a room while she was having her breakfast. She perceived this as a gross breach of etiquette and left, immediately, in high dudgeon, and rejected Queen Adelaide's entreaties to return.

When Princess Victoria reached the age of sixteen and was confirmed at St James', several of the royal family, including the Duke and Duchess of Cambridge, the Duke of Cumberland, and Princess Sophia were there, alongside the king and queen, her mother and her governesses. She listed them all faithfully in her journal, but one name is absent. When they entered the chapel, the king counted the duchess's retinue, told her that it was too large, and ordered Conroy to leave. The fuming duchess had no choice but to comply, while the instance completely overshadowed the solemn occasion and embarrassed the princess. She took to her bed in tears on their return to Kensington, noting cryptically in her journal that she was 'very much affected indeed when we came home.'[4]

Princess Victoria was seventeen years old in May 1836, and of an age when it was inevitable that the next generation would be seeking a suitable husband-to-be for her. King William thought that Alexander, second son of William, Hereditary Prince of Orange (who some twenty years earlier had been considered for, but rejected by, Princess Charlotte of Wales) would be an ideal choice. He accordingly invited the prince and his two sons to stay in England for several days that month. On the first evening they dined with the king and queen at Buckingham Palace, a party that also included the Duke of Cumberland, Prince George of Cambridge, and Princess Augusta. Perhaps significantly, the Duchess of Kent was 'prevented by indisposition'.

Later that month the duchess and her brother, Prince Leopold, arranged a similar invitation for their eldest brother, Ernest, Duke of Saxe-Coburg and Gotha, and his sons, Ernest and Albert, to visit them at Kensington Palace, and more especially to meet Victoria. King William did not look favourably on the idea of an alliance with the Coburgs, any more than Victoria did, regarding the 'very plain' Alexander. The king was also angry at the conduct of the Duchess of Kent, whom he suspected of matchmaking. She was evidently blamed more than Leopold, who was more likely to have been the *eminence grise* behind the operation. Perhaps King William found it easier to vent his indignation on her than on her brother, but he told the Duchess of Gloucester that he was very inclined to send their sister-in-law a message forbidding her to lodge the Coburg princes at Kensington, 'for as she had upon pretext of *propriety* kept Victoria from being permitted to see her *cousins of England*, he thought the same was valid for her German cousins.'[5] Lord Melbourne managed to pacify him, and the king invited Ernest and Albert to a *levée*. Once he had met them, he realized that the younger was a very pleasant character and said he was one of the most handsome young men he had ever seen.[6] While he may not have warmed any more to the Coburgs in general, perhaps he was prepared to concede that Albert might make his niece a better husband than Alexander.

As far as his personal relations with the Duchess of Kent were concerned, King William did not quite turn the other cheek; but it was generally agreed that while there were faults on both sides, he was less to blame than she was. In August 1836, the feud that had simmered for so long came to a head. The king had invited his sister-in-law and her daughter to Windsor for the queen's birthday on 13 August 1836, and had asked them if they would stay long enough afterwards to celebrate his own birthday, on 21 August, and attend a celebration dinner the next day. The duchess ignored the queen's birthday and announced that she would arrive on 20 August. Meanwhile she appropriated a suite of rooms at Kensington Palace for her own use, notwithstanding his having previously given orders that she should not be allowed to do so. He was furious at such a lack of respect for his wife, but held his peace until after his health had been drunk at his birthday dinner, attended by more than a hundred guests, with the princess seated opposite him and the duchess on his right.

At that point he rose to his feet and delivered an angry speech in which he announced that it was his wish to be spared for nine months longer, in order to ensure that no regency would take place. Pointing to the seventeen-year-old princess, he said he would thus have the satisfaction of bequeathing the royal authority to the personal exercise of 'that young lady', the heiress presumptive to the crown, 'and not in the hands of a person now near me who is surrounded by evil advisers and is herself incompetent to act with propriety in the station in which she would be placed.'[7] He was aware that his sister-in-law was perhaps more sinned against than sinner, and largely at the mercy of her 'evil adviser', the unscrupulous Conroy, who relished the prospect of becoming the power behind the throne should Queen Victoria ascend before her age of majority. Having declared that the same person had continually insulted him and that he was determined his authority would be respected in future, he ended his diatribe on a more conciliatory note, but the damage had been done. The queen was mortified, Princess Victoria burst into tears, and the stony-faced duchess remained silent. After dinner she took her daughter and announced their immediate departure. Only with some difficulty was she persuaded to stay after all.

King William had never really learnt to control his hasty temper, and his anger was slow to cool. On the following morning he asked his son Adolphus what people had said about his speech the previous evening. Adolphus told him that everyone thought the duchess's rebuke was well-deserved, but to have administered it at table in front of a hundred guests was not the time or the place, and he ought to have spoken to her in private. The King retorted that he did not care in the very least where he said it, or before whom; he had been continually insulted by her, beyond all endurance, and he was not going to stand for it any longer. Nevertheless, his verbal explosion had cleared the air, and although there would be no formal reconciliation, for the remaining few months of his life the monarch and his sister-in-law remained on civil, if distant, terms.

His wish to be spared for another nine months was granted. The court spent Christmas 1836 at Brighton, where the weather was exceptionally cold, with snowdrifts several feet high. When he left the Pavilion for the last time in February, he was laid low with his old enemy, asthma. The queen and others around him noticed with concern that his temper was getting worse, and at times he was increasingly aggressive if not downright rude to his ministers. Sometimes he asked family and friends if they would name for him various people some distance from him, whom he thought he could recognize but could not name, as he felt he was becoming increasingly blind. Those around him who remembered the pitiful decline of King George III in his last years may have feared that his now septuagenarian third son might be about to experience a similar fate.

The king's relations with Melbourne as prime minister were never comfortable, and some thought that his hold on power was precarious in the extreme; he was frequently out of favour with his master, an elderly sovereign married to an unpopular reactionary wife. In the spring of 1836, Melbourne's career was briefly considered to be in jeopardy when he was cited as the guilty party in a divorce case when Caroline Norton, wife of George Norton, a former Tory Member of Parliament, sued for divorce, citing Melbourne as the guilty party. The king urged him to stay on as prime minister, as did his old political adversary, the Duke of Wellington, who presciently assured him that 'these things are a nine-days' wonder'. It would take a long time to come to court, he advised, and 'it will all blow over, and won't signify a straw.'[8] The suit did not succeed, and in any case it would have taken more than a divorce case to topple him. King William IV might have longed to find a reason for getting rid of a prime minister whom he liked and respected, but who had some rather suspect friends and political allies. Had the sovereign been in better health, Melbourne's position might have been less secure.

Yet King William sensed that his days were numbered. On 10 April one of his favourite daughters, Sophia, Lady de L'Isle, a lively if sharp-tongued personality, died a fortnight after she had given birth to her youngest child. One of the last things she did before she passed away was to make a sketch of her ailing father. She had always been a favourite of his, and when the news was brought to him, he was heartbroken. Only the queen's death, his secretary Sir Herbert Taylor averred, could have upset him more. In fact, Queen Adelaide had been at Meiningen that same month, to see her dying mother for the last time, and by the time she returned home the travelling and strain had taken its toll on her. On 20 April she was too ill to hold her regular drawing-room and had to ask her sister-in-law, Princess Augusta, to take her place. For a while the doctors warned that Her Majesty was gravely ill, and she was only just beginning to recover when she learned to her distress that her mother had passed away on 30 April, aged seventy-three.

King William's continued estrangement from his eldest son, George, of whom he had always been fond, despite their regular differences, also affected his declining strength. George had also been very close to his sister, and when he learned of her unexpected death he wrote a sincere letter of condolence to his father, who thanked him for this 'additional proof of that goodness of heart which I know you possess and for which at all times I have given you credit'. Yet even this bereavement that profoundly affected them both, and the king's increasing ill-health, failed to bring father and son closer together. At the same time the king invited him to come to Windsor and see him, as soon as he felt inclined. With some sadness he added a postscript saying that as much as he disapproved generally of his eldest son's conduct, he deeply regretted the estrangement between the two of them. George answered heartlessly that he would not be reconciled until justice had been delivered to him. He added rather tactlessly that, 'Death has already commenced his havoc amongst us, and the time may be short, in which I may yet have the gratification, or possibility of a thorough reconciliation with Your Majesty.'[9] He probably failed to realize just how unwell his father really was, otherwise he would surely have taken some positive step to end the estrangement before it was too late. Death had indeed commenced his havoc and had one further life to claim, all too soon.

Sleepless nights became a regular torment, and the decline in the king's health became increasingly marked. On 18 May he went to St James's Palace to hold a drawing-room as arranged. It was the last occasion on which he appeared in public, and he remained seated the whole time. This deviation from his usual practice did not excite as much alarm as the traces of sickness visible in his face. Afterwards he returned to Windsor Castle, and a slight improvement the following morning revived the hopes and spirits of his anxious friends and members of the household who hoped that his health might improve.

The following day was the anniversary of the battle of La Hogue, fought at sea in 1692 which had resulted in a victory for the Anglo-Dutch fleet against the French. King William had invited several officers in the neighbourhood, as well as field-officers of the garrison, to dinner that evening. During proceedings the king detailed, with great minuteness, the causes, progress, and consequences of the different naval wars in which England had been involved over the last two centuries or so. Everyone present was astonished by the extraordinary accuracy of his memory, and of his remarkable command of English history. His voice, notwithstanding one or two moments when he evidently had breathing difficulties, appeared relatively strong and clear to the assembled company, but everyone present realized that the exertion was costing him dearly.

On 24 May his niece, Princess Victoria of Kent, the heiress to the throne turned eighteen years old. With this her mother's hopes of becoming regent during the next reign vanished. King William gave his niece a grand piano and held a ball in her honour at St James's Palace, and made an offer to her, in writing, of £10,000 a year which, he proposed, would be at her own disposal and independent of her mother. He sent this letter by Marquess Conyngham, Lord Chamberlain of the Household, with orders to deliver it into the princess's own hands. When he arrived at Kensington to do so, the Duchess of Kent held out her hand as she demanded to see the letter herself. He said he had been expressly commanded by the King to deliver the letter directly to the princess and nobody else. The princess took the letter and wrote to the king, thanking him and accepting the offer. Her mother strongly objected, claiming that she herself should receive £6,000 of this sum and the princess only £4,000. There the matter ended.

After a severe attack of asthma, it was apparent that the king did not have long to live. His liver and spleen were enlarged, his lungs were full of blood, and his heart valves ossified. Returning from a *levée* in May, he tried to climb the stairs but collapsed, and was led breathless and exhausted to lie on a sofa until he could get his strength back. A few days later he fainted at luncheon and then at dinner, and never left his private apartments again. At the end of the month he attended his last council meeting, but could barely walk a single step, and arrived in a wheelchair. His sight was failing, and asthma was making sleep almost impossible. At this point the burden of representing him at all public functions and entertaining guests on his behalf fell to Queen Adelaide.

By the beginning of June, Sir Herbert Taylor was privately warning politicians and officials that they should prepare for the end. Even at this stage King William would not allow any bulletins about his health to be issued, on the grounds that as long as he was still able to conduct business it was not necessary to alarm the public unduly. His doctors, Sir Henry Halford and William Chambers, watched over him unceasingly. They had hoped for some time that a change of air might effect a partial cure at least, and on 7 June Taylor suggested a plan that the king ought to go and spend a few weeks in Brighton, where the sea air would surely do him some good. He agreed, saying that he hoped he would soon be strong enough for the journey, and plans were made for them to go and stay at the Pavilion. The poor state of His Majesty's health next morning, exacerbated by a very restless night, immediately dashed any such hopes. Increasing problems with breathing and circulation, and swelling in the legs, all suggested that his condition had deteriorated badly. When the royal cortege did not appear at Ascot as usual, the public immediately realized that the situation must be grave.

Not until 15 June did Lord Melbourne inform the cabinet that the queen had asked for prayers to be offered in the churches for her husband's health. It was very doubtful whether he would survive long, he told the ministers rather cynically, 'but the order may as well be given'. The king knew he was dying but by a supreme effort of will retained his iron grip on life. Early on the morning of 18 June, the anniversary of the battle of Waterloo, he asked Dr Chambers, 'Let me but live over this memorable day – I shall never live to see another sunset.' The doctor loyally if unconvincingly reassured him that he would surely live to see many more, to which it has been said the king gave an appropriately blunt reply.[10] He received the sacrament from the Archbishop of Canterbury, and the Duke of Wellington came to enquire whether he ought to cancel the traditional annual dinner commemorating the victory, in view of His Majesty's condition. He refused to hear of it, saying that it was to take place as usual, and although he could not attend, he hoped it would be an agreeable occasion.

By now his lungs were even more turgid with blood, and his spleen double its normal size. Although he was in agony for much of the time he refused to go to bed, preferring to sit propped up in a leather chair to ease his breathing. Benjamin Disraeli, a junior Member of Parliament, wrote that he was 'dying like an old lion'. The queen knelt by his side, turning over the pages of his prayer book, while the Archbishop of Canterbury read the Visitation of the Sick. He held the queen's hand, tightly, all the time, and when exhaustion overcame her and she began to weep, he remarked gently, 'Bear up, bear up.' Soon after midnight on 19 June, the Duke of Cumberland arrived at Windsor Castle and was met by the Earl of Munster, who assured him that the king did not have long to live. Uncle and nephew had a lengthy conversation, after which the duke went to have what would be a final interview with his brother. While they had often had their differences, at this late stage they made their peace with each other. Three of the king's sons, as well as his daughters, came to see their father for the last time, but the Earl of Munster, who remained nearby, was unforgiving to the last and notable by his absence.

At the suggestion of the queen, the king sent a friendly message to Princess Victoria. Much as he would have liked to invite her to come and take her leave of him, it was inevitable that the Duchess of Kent would insist on accompanying her. Although there had been a slight thaw in relations between both, her presence at the monarch's deathbed would have been rather less than welcome.

Propped up in a heavy leather chair so he could breathe more easily, on the afternoon of 19 June he lost consciousness, and those around him knew that he was sinking fast. Queen Adelaide had sat beside him, nursing him devotedly and not going to bed for several days. For some hours as the end approached, she knelt by his side, gently rubbing his hands to try and keep him a little warmer. He remained in his dressing-room until shortly after midnight, after which he was moved into his sitting-room, where a bed had been prepared for him. William became steadily weaker, his moments of consciousness few and far between, and shortly after two o' clock the next morning he passed away, his hand held by Queen Adelaide. The Archbishop of Canterbury had been called just in time to say a short prayer at the very end. Two hours later, the great bell at Windsor Castle tolled in memory of the late sovereign, and a little later the royal standard on the Round Tower was lowered to half-mast.

Queen Adelaide remained for some time beside her husband's bed on her knees in prayer, and then went to her bedroom for a few hours of well-deserved sleep. At eight o' clock she rose to receive Lord Conyngham, who had just returned from his swift mission to Kensington Palace to break the news to Princess Victoria that she was now Queen Victoria. One of the eighteen-year-old monarch's first actions was to send the Dowager Queen a short letter of sympathy, addressed tactfully to 'The Queen', as she did not wish to be the first to remind her widowed aunt of her new, lesser status. The letter begged Adelaïde to remain at Windsor Castle for as long as she pleased. Queen Adelaide replied later that same day to thank her, telling her that she was much affected by everything she had just gone through, 'but I have the great comfort to dwell upon the recollection of the perfect resignation, piety, and patience with which the dear King bore his trials and sufferings, and the truly Christian-like manner of his death'.[11]

'Our lamented Sovereign's dearest friends could not have denied a happier, calmer, easier death,' the Reverend John Ryle Wood, formerly tutor to Prince George of Cambridge and now Queen Adelaide's chaplain, wrote to his young former charge. 'May the Almighty grant that it may be blessed to him and to ourselves.'[12] *The Times*, which had made no effort to be generous to the memory of King George IV seven years earlier, was much more gentle towards his brother, noting solemnly on his passing that 'the good, the kind, the affable, the companion, and the commander of his people, is now, alas! no greater than the meanest among them'.[13] *The Spectator* was less charitable, writing that 'though at times a jovial and, for a king, an honest man, [he] was a weak, ignorant commonplace sort of person'.[14]

Although she had not had the chance to get to know King William as well as she would have liked, his eighteen-year-old niece, who had just become Queen Victoria, cherished her fondest memories of him. On the day of his funeral at Windsor Castle, on 8 July, she noted how she had heard from all sides that he was really very fond of her, 'and I shall ever retain a grateful sense of his kindness to me and shall never forget him.'[15]

King William IV was buried on 8 July in the vault at St George's Chapel, Windsor, after a none too dignified funeral which seemed to Greville and others 'a wretched mockery'. There was a certain irony in this; William had not been known for the greatest decorum at the funerals of others, and some of those who were present to take their farewell were less than overcome. Two men at the ceremony, the diarist observed, were engaged in animated conversation, one of them laughing heartily at the foot of the coffin as it lay in state.[16]

Queen Adelaide had become the first Dowager Queen in Britain for over a century, and the only queen of the Hanoverian dynasty to outlive her husband. She attended the funeral, sitting in the Royal Closet in St George's Chapel, and was presumably spared any sight of the less elegant scenes taking place elsewhere during the ceremony. Afterwards she made preparations to leave Windsor, and for the remaining twelve years of her life she had the use of her old homes at Bushy and at Marlborough House. Never robust, her health continued to deteriorate, and she stayed as a regular guest at various houses of friends in an unsuccessful attempt to recover her strength a little. She made occasional journeys abroad, partly to visit her family in Saxe-Meiningen and partly so she could take advantage of a milder climate, notably wintering in Madeira which had long been recommended as a suitable venue for semi-invalids. Later she rented Bentley Priory, near Stanmore, where she spent the winter of 1848. The following year she returned to Bushy for a few weeks, and on medical advice she subsequently visited Worthing and Tunbridge Wells. Yet it was to no avail, and by the time she returned to Bentley Priory in September 1849, she and her doctors knew that her strength was failing. Increasingly bedridden for the next few weeks, she died there early on the morning of 2 December 1849, aged fifty-seven.

Yet she had outlived her eldest stepson. George FitzClarence, Earl of Munster, achieved a career of some note when he published a book based on his African and Asian travels. His subsequent interests in intellectual and scholarly activities led to his becoming a member of various learned societies, to some of which he gave regular lectures. However, he also suffered from gout and possibly the royal malady porphyria, which had blighted the last years of his grandfather, King George III, as well as other members of the family. He was well liked and respected at court during the early years of Queen Victoria's reign, but there was some speculation – never proved – that he treasured a hope, as the eldest son of King William IV, that he might be made Prince of Wales and thus heir to the throne one day, should anything happen to the queen if she was to die without issue. Marital problems, gout and financial worries darkened his later years, and he took his own life in March 1842 at the age of forty-eight, shooting himself with a pistol that had been given to him by King George IV. In discussing the melancholy subject with Queen Victoria the following day, Lord Melbourne said that George was always 'as Your Majesty knows, an unhappy and discontented man, and there is something in that unfortunate condition of illegitimacy, which seems to distort the mind and feelings and render them incapable of justice or contentment.'[17] The title Earl of Munster was passed down through his descendants and became extinct when the seventh Earl died in December 2000, leaving no male issue.

None of the nine FitzClarence children who survived their father lived to a great age: two of the sons passed away in their fifties, and two daughters in their sixties, while all the others had died somewhat younger. However, the third daughter, Elizabeth, Countess of Erroll, would be remembered for some of her more famous descendants. One of her grandsons, Alexander Duff, first Duke of Fife, married Louise, Princess Royal, the eldest daughter of King Edward VII and Queen Alexandra. Other descendants from the same line included the author and historian, John Julius Norwich, the publisher and author Rupert Hart-Davis, his son Adam, also an author and broadcaster, and David Cameron, the only British Prime Minister ever to be able to claim a degree of royal blood in his ancestry, as a fifth cousin twice removed of his sovereign, Queen Elizabeth II.

Having succeeded William as King of Hanover, Ernest Augustus went to settle in his new kingdom. In September 1837 a statue to

William IV was erected in Göttingen, and it was alleged that after 'much ostentatious praise' of him for his supposedly liberal views, King Ernest Augustus attended the ceremony but deliberately turned his back at the precise moment of the unveiling. This has been ascribed to a rumour put about by a historian who was 'misinformed.'[18] Over the next few years Ernest returned to visit England from time to time. His relations with Queen Victoria and Prince Albert, whom she married in February 1840, were far from amicable at first, as he had never had any love for the Coburg family as a whole, but the feelings on both sides mellowed with time. Having been invited to dinner at Buckingham Palace one evening in June 1843, he shared some kindly memories with the queen of his brother's generosity. 'Poor dear William was an excellent good soul, but he gave away everything – he would have given away his coat at last!'[19]

For all William's shortcomings, the monarchy was supremely fortunate in its last Hanoverian king. George IV, the arch-reactionary whose self-indulgence and gross extravagance had made him one of the least popular monarchs at the time of his death, once said complacently that his brother William's accession would lead to revolution. In a sense he was right, but it was not a revolution of the kind that he had imagined. The changes that had taken place during William's reign were peaceful and accompanied by very little violence. He had achieved a temporarily unstable but successful transition which had begun to change what had been a quasi-autocracy into one of the most democratic countries in Europe. This had bequeathed his young successor a fund of goodwill that had been conspicuously lacking seven years before.

Few if any of George III's other sons could have presided over such a period of change without being provoked to disastrous interference. William was no politician or schemer, and had never laid claim to these abilities, but his straightforward honesty, shrewd judgment and common sense won him widespread respect from politicians and public alike. His moderation of the reform legislation was a delicate balancing act which this most plain-speaking of men had managed remarkably well. Despite having been king of England, he had shown a refreshing lack of arrogance, and had never pretended to know better than the politicians, or insisted to them that things were to be done his way or not at all. He had been good at reading the mood of the country, as a good listener was always ready to hear differing points of view, and to a certain extent he was prepared to let the ministers get on with their job. Admittedly his popularity had declined by the time of his death, but public esteem can be a fickle creature, and it would be less than fair not to acknowledge that he had enjoyed moments of relative popularity at the start of his reign, and again two years later when the Reform Act was passed. How well-deserved that popularity was is a subject that can be argued endlessly, with reasons for and reasons against a-plenty.

Thirty years after the death of King William IV, Walter Bagehot published *The English Constitution* in which he summed up the role of the monarch as 'the right to be consulted, the right to encourage, the right to warn'. Where the role of the Hanoverian kings was concerned, he noted that the first two, both of whom had been born in Germany, had no knowledge of English affairs, George III '[had] interfered unceasingly, but he did harm ceasingly', while George IV and William IV 'gave no steady continuing guidance, and were unfit to give it'.[20] King William may not have provided his prime ministers consistently with steady continuing guidance, but unlike his predecessors, where the rights to be consulted, to encourage, and to warn were concerned, for much of his reign he strove to satisfy and fulfil the criteria of all three 'rights'.

As for William as a prince, with all his faults – and since when has any prince been perfect? – his weaknesses had contributed towards his popularity. Few people really like paragons of virtue, and like many another monarch, be it Charles II before him, or his great-nephew King Edward VII less than seventy years on, William had never pretended to be a model of excellence. It is perhaps worth remembering that his successor's husband, Prince Albert of Saxe-Coburg Gotha, was one of the most virtuous of men, and although he was much admired and respected for his upright character, sensitivity, brain, intellectual facilities and above all a devotion to duty that contributed to his death at the age of forty-two, he was never really loved outside his family circle.

King William was certainly anything but handsome, and had a short temper, and until his wife almost transformed him, he was noted for his coarse manners and an indelicate turn of phrase. Yet his often comic tactlessness, xenophobia, instinctive dislike of pomp and ceremony, and complete lack of pomposity had made him the most human of the Hanoverian monarchs. In June 1830, Britain may well have decided, for the second time in little more than two hundred years, that it had had enough of kings, and embraced the more recent example of republican France. Seven years later, few European thrones were more secure than that of England. Queen Victoria had the good fortune to inherit a crown to which the British people were loyal once again.

Endnotes

Chapter 1: The Sailor Prince

1. Stuart, p.81
2. Hadlow, p.246, Queen Charlotte to Charles, Duke of Mecklenburg-Schwerin, 1 June 1779
3. Huish, p.65
4. Thompson, p.20
5. Ziegler, p.32, Prince William to King George III, 26 January 1780
6. Wright, p.47
7. Hadlow, p.285, Queen Charlotte to Charles, Duke of Mecklenburg-Schwerin, 29 February 1780
8. Ziegler, *William IV,* p.33, Prince William to King George III, 3 March 1780
9. Ziegler, *William IV,* p.42
10. Aspinall, *Later correspondence of George III,* Vol. I, p.153, Frederick, Duke of York, to King George III, 1 April 1785
11. Aspinall, *Correspondence of Prince of Wales*, Vol. I, p.219, Prince William to Prince of Wales, 10 February 1786
12. Aspinall, *Later correspondence,* Vol. I, p.264, Prince William to King George III, 21 September 1786
13. Ziegler, *William IV,* p.62
14. Pocock, p. 107, George Wynne's diary, 27 December 1787
15. Aspinall, *Correspondence of Prince of Wales*, Vol. I, p.329, Prince William to Prince of Wales, 16 February 1788

Chapter 2: The Duke of Clarence

1. Hibbert, *George III*, p.258
2. Brooke, p.327
3. Hibbert, *George III*, p.262
4. Aspinall, *Correspondence of Prince of Wales*, Vol. I, p.454, Prince William to Prince of Wales, 24 January 1789
5. Wraxall, Vol. III, p.154
6. Ziegler, *William IV,* p.73
7. Hamilton, Vol. I, p.19
8. Watkins, p.235, Duke of Clarence to Nelson, 6 December 1792
9. Huish, p.474
10. Patterson, p.83
11. *The Times*, 12 April 1793
12. Fitzgerald, Vol. I, pp.81–2
13. *The Times,* 5 April 1800
14. Ziegler, *William IV,* p.101, Duke of Clarence to George FitzClarence, 19 October 1810

Chapter 3: The Regency

1. Bickley, *Diaries of Lord Glenbervie*, Vol. I, p.160
2. Parry, p.110
3. Aspinall, *Mrs Jordan and her Family*, pp.196–7, Dorothea Jordan to Duke of Clarence, 1 August 1811
4. Boaden, Vol. II, p.271
5. Aspinall, *Mrs Jordan and her Family*, p.78
6. Pocock, p.176, Duke of Clarence to Earl of Mayo, January 1814
7. Knight, C., Vol. I, p.282
8. Hamilton, Vol. I, p.18
9. Aspinall, *Letters of Princess Charlotte*, p.207, Princess Charlotte to Margaret Mercer Elphinstone, 21 September 1815

10. Hedley, p.271
11. Willis, p.129, Queen Charlotte to Duke of Cumberland, 13 June 1815
12. Hedley, p.284
13. Hopkirk, p.10
14. Allen, p.65
15. Ziegler, *William IV,* p.122, Duke of Clarence to George FitzClarence, 21 March 1818
16. Hopkirk, p.24
17. *The Times*, 20 October 1819
18. Brooke, p.386

Chapter 4: Brother of the King

1. Parry, p.303
2. Creevey, Vol. I, p.339, 11 November 1820
3. Aspinall, *Letters of King George IV,* Vol. II, p.523, Duke of Clarence to King George IV, 10 April 1822; Hopkirk, p.62
4. Hopkirk, p.58
5. Lyttelton, p.241, Lord Lyttelton to Lady Sarah Lyttelton, 28 January 1832
6. Fitzgerald, Vol. I, pp.130–41
7. Quennell, p.372, Princess Lieven to Prince Metternich, 30 June 1826
8. Gore, p.234
9. Peel, p. 93, Sir Robert Peel to Mrs Peel, 31 January 1827
10. Ziegler, *William IV,* pp.133–5
11. Ellenborough, Vol. I, p.184, 1 August 1828
12. Fitzgerald, Vol. I, p.192, King George IV to Duke of Wellington, 11 August 1828
13. *The Times*, 15 August 1828
14. Barrow, p.369
15. Pocock, p.208
16. Knight, R., p.67
17. Ziegler, *William IV,* p.141

18. Willis, pp.181–2
19. Fitzgerald, Vol. I, pp.145, 147
20. Willis, pp.182–3
21. Fitzgerald, Vol. I, p.210
22. Ziegler, *William IV,* p.143

Chapter 5: King William

1. Pocock, p.210
2. Fitzgerald, Vol. I, pp.214–5
3. Eden, p.198
4. Molloy, Vol. I, p.14
5. Greville, Vol. II, pp.2, 6, 18 July 1830
6. Creevey, Vol. II, p.211, 26 June 1830
7. Robinson, p.224, Princess Lieven to Count Benckendorff, 20 July 1830
8. Molloy, Vol. I, pp.17–18
9. Greville, Vol. II, p.8, 20 July 1830
10. Greville, Vol. II, pp.10–11, 24 July 1830
11. Le Strange, Vol. II, p.27, Earl Grey to Princess Lieven, 21 July 1830
12. Le Strange, Vol. II, p.110, Princess Lieven to Earl Grey, 19 October 1830
13. Robinson, p.230, Princess Lieven to Count Benckendorff, 28 July 1830
14. Longford, *Wellington,* p.213
15. Molloy, Vol. I, p.35
16. Kemble, p.393
17. Greville, Vol. II, p.5, 18 July 1830
18. Victoria, *Letters,* Vol. I, p.8
19. Greville, Vol. II, p.95, 16 December 1830
20. *Morning Post,* 14 May 1832
21. Kemble, pp.228–9
22. Wharncliffe, Vol. I, p.358

23. *The Times*, 29 June 1830
24. Molloy, *Court Life Below Stairs,* p.426
25. Fulford, *Hanover to Windsor*, p.15
26. Le Strange, Vol. II, p.49, Earl Grey to Princess Lieven, 13 August 1830
27. Wilson, Vol. II, pp.512–3
28. Dunckley, p.140
29. Greville, Vol. II, pp.63–4, 17 November 1830
30. Greville, Vol. II, p.72, 23 November 1830

Chapter 6: Reform Proposed

1. Grey, Vol. I, pp.54–5, Sir Herbert Taylor to Earl Grey, 14 January 1831
2. Ziegler, *William IV,* p.177, Earl Grey to Marquess of Anglesey, 29 January 1831
3. Reid, pp.71–72
4. Grey, Vol. I, p.158; p.164; p.179, Sir Herbert Taylor to King William IV, 21 March 1831
5. Macaulay, Vol. I, p.203, 30 March 1831
6. Grey, Vol. I, p.215, Earl Grey to King William IV, 19 April 1831
7. Buckingham, Vol. I, p.296, Duke of Wellington to Duke of Buckingham, 21 May 1831
8. Greville, Vol. II, pp.135–7, 24 April 1831
9. Wellington, Vol. VII, p.449, Earl Howe to Duke of Wellington, 29 May 1831
10. Greville, Vol. II, pp.147–8, 5 June 1831
11. Grey, Vol. I, pp.274–6, King William IV to Earl Grey, 28 May 1831
12. Buckingham, Vol. I, p.333, Duke of Wellington to Duke of Buckingham, 22 July 1831
13. Grey, Vol. I, p.332, Sir Henry Taylor to Earl Grey, 15 August 1831

14. Greville, Vol. II, p.185, 28 August 1831
15. Trevelyan, *Lord Macaulay*, Vol. I, pp.244–5, 9 September 1831
16. Wharncliffe, Vol. II, p.83
17. Greville, Vol. II, pp.193–4, 17 September 1831
18. Grey, Vol. I, p.363, King William IV to Earl Grey, 8 October 1831
19. Wellington, Vol. VIII, p.30, Duke of Wellington to King William IV, 9 November 1831
20. Wellington, Vol. VIII, pp.43–4, King William IV to Duke of Wellington, 9 November 1831
21. Grey, Vol. I, p.417, King William IV to Earl Grey, 8 October 1831
22. Greville, Vol. II, p.209, 11 November 1831
23. Wellington, Vol. VII, p.445, Earl Howe to Duke of Wellington, 25 May 1831
24. Ziegler, *William IV,* p.199, Queen Adelaide diary, 10 October 1831

Chapter 7: Reform Carried

1. Grey, Vol. II, pp.68–71, Minute of Conversation with the King, 4 January 1832
2. Buckingham, Vol. I, pp.385–6, Duke of Wellington to Duke of Buckingham, 2 January 1832
3. Wellington, Vol. VIII, pp.155–6, Duke of Wellington to Viscount Strangford, 12 January 1832
4. Anglesey, p.257
5. Grey, Vol. II, p.304, Minute of Cabinet, 8 May 1832
6. Wellington, Duke of Wellington to Lord Lyndhurst, 10 May 1832, Vol. VIII, p.304
7. Grey, Vol. II, pp.406, 410–1, Earl Grey to King William IV, 15 May 1832
8. Trevelyan, *Lord Grey*, pp.345–7
9. Broughton, Vol. IV, p.235, 19 May 1832

10. Brougham, Vol. III, pp.198–200
11. Grey, Vol. II, p.438, King William IV to Earl Grey, 19 May 1832
12. Grey, Vol. II, p.448–50, Sir Herbert Taylor to Earl Grey, 5 June 1832
13. Grey, Vol. II, p.462, Earl Grey to Sir Herbert Taylor, 5 June 1832
14. Brougham, Vol. III, p.198–200, pp.211–2, Sir Herbert Taylor to Lord Brougham, 5 June 1832
15. Brougham, Vol. III, pp.198–200
16. Fulford, *Royal Dukes*, p.152
17. Bagehot, pp.246–247

Chapter 8: European Affairs

1. Ridley, p.58, King William IV to Lord Palmerston, 18 September 1832
2. Ziegler, *William IV*, p.230, King William IV to Lord Palmerston, 18 June 1832
3. Lord Palmerston, *Hansard*, 2 August 1832
4. Fitzgerald, Vol. II, p.5
5. Ziegler, *William IV*, p.232, Sir Herbert Taylor to Earl Grey, 9 September 1833
6. Victoria, *Girlhood*, 16 September 1833, Vol. I, p.86
7. Ziegler, *Melbourne*, p.253, Lord Melbourne to King William IV, 18 August 1836

Chapter 9: A New Parliamentary Era

1. Broughton, Vol. IV, p.251, 16 August 1832
2. Greville, Vol. II, p.338, 31 December 1832
3. Brougham, Vol. III, p.281
4. Brougham, Vol. III, p.287, Sir Herbert Taylor to Lord Brougham, 16 June 1833
5. Greville, Vol. II, pp.383–4, 28 June 1833

6. Brougham, Vol. III, p.292, Sir Herbert Taylor to Lord Brougham, 16 and 18 June 1833
7. Albemarle, p.377; Longford, p.288
8. Trevelyan, *Lord Grey*, p.362
9. *The Times*, 30 May 1834
10. Victoria, *Girlhood*, Vol. II, p.148, 7 April 1839
11. Ziegler, *William IV*, p.248, Duke of Wellington to King William IV, 12 July 1833
12. Creevey, Vol. II, p.300, 25 November 1834
13. Fulford, *Hanover to Windsor*, p.36
14. Broughton, Vol. V, p.23
15. Greville, Vol III, p.370, 7 November 1836
16. *The Times*, 15 November 1834
17. Fitzgerald, Vol. II, p.307
18. Parker, Vol. 2, pp.287–9, 22 February 1835
19. Ziegler, *Melbourne*, p.192
20. Greville, Vol. II, p.277, 7 July 1835
21. *The Times*, 8 July 1835

Chapter 10: The Last Years

1. Barrow, pp.274–5
2. Ziegler, *William IV*, p.268
3. Tomalin, p.22, Duchess of Kent to Duchess of Northumberland, 7 February 1831
4. Victoria, *Girlhood*, Vol. I, p.126, 30 July 1835
5. Willis, p.341
6. Ziegler, *William IV*, p.280
7. Greville, Vol. III, pp.309–10, 21 September 1836
8. Greville, Vol III, p.349, 11 May 1836
9. Ziegler, *William IV*, p.287, King William IV to George FitzClarence, 16 April 1837; George FitzClarence to King William IV, 3 May 1837

10. (Wood), pp.25–6
11. Victoria, *Letters*, Vol. I, p.96, Queen Adelaide to Queen Victoria, 20 June 1837
12. Sheppard, Vol. I, pp.39–40
13. *The Times*, 20 June 1837
14. *Spectator*, 27 June 1837
15. Victoria, *Girlhood*, Vol. I, p.208, Journal, 8 July 1837
16. Greville, Vol. III, p.382
17. Victoria, *Letters*, Vol. I, p.486, Lord Melbourne to Queen Victoria, 21 March 1842
18. Willis, pp.287–8
19. Willis, p.345, Queen Victoria's Journal, 14 June 1843
20. Bagehot, p.83

Bibliography

Albemarle, George Thomas, Earl of, *Fifty Years of my Life* (Macmillan, London, 1877)

Allen, W. Gore, *King William IV* (Cresset, London, 1960)

Anglesey, Marquess of, *One-leg: The Life and Letters of Henry William Paget, 1st Marquess of Anglesey, 1768-1854* (Jonathan Cape, London, 1961)

Aspinall, A. ed. *Correspondence of George, Prince of Wales, 1770-1812*, 8 vols. (Cambridge University Press, 1963-70)

_____ *Letters of King George IV, 1812-1830*, 3 vols. (Cambridge University Press, 1938)

_____ ed. *The later correspondence of George III, 1783-1810*, 5 vols. (Cambridge University Press, 1962-7)

_____ *Letters of the Princess Charlotte, 1811-1817* (Home and Van Thal, London, 1949)

_____ *Mrs Jordan and her Family: The unpublished correspondence of Mrs Jordan and the Duke of Clarence, later William IV* (Arthur Barker, London, 1951)

Bagehot, Walter, The English Constitution (Kegan Paul, London, 1926)

Barrow, Sir John, *An Autobiographical Memoir of Sir John Barrow* (John Murray, London, 1847)

Bickley, Francis, ed. *The Diaries of Sylvester Douglas, Lord Glenbervie*, 2 vols. (Constable, London, 1928)

Bird, Anthony, *The Damnable Duke of Cumberland: A Character Study and Vindication of Ernest Augustus, Duke of Cumberland and King of Hanover* (Barrie & Rockliff, London, 1966)

Boaden, James, *The Life of Mrs Jordan*, 2 vols. (Edward Bull, London, 1831)

213

Brooke, John, *King George III* (Constable, London, 1972)

Brougham, Henry, Lord, *The Life and Times of Henry, Lord Brougham*, 3 vols. (Blackwood, London, 1871)

Broughton, John Cam Hobhouse, Lord, *Recollections of a Long Life*, 6 vols. (John Murray, London, 1910-1)

Buckingham and Chandos, Duke of, *Memoirs of the Courts and Cabinets of William IV and Victoria*, 2 vols. (Hurst & Blackett, London, 1861)

Butler, J.R.M., *The Passing of the Great Reform Bill* (Longmans, Green, London, 1914)

Creevey, Sir Thomas, *A Selection from the Correspondence and Diaries of the Late Thomas Creevey, MP,* 2 vols. ed. Sir H. Maxwell (John Murray, London, 1903)

Dunckley, Henry, *Lord Melbourne* (Sampson Low, London, 1890)

Eden, Emily, Miss Eden's Letters, ed. Violet Dickinson (Macmillan, London, 1919)

Ellenborough, Law, Edward, Lord, *A Political Diary, 1828-1830,* 2 vols. (Richard Bentley, London, 1891)

Fitzgerald, Percy, *The Life and Times of William IV*, 2 vols. (Tinsley Bros, London, 1884)

Fulford, Roger, *Hanover to Windsor* (Batsford, London, 1960)

_____ *Royal Dukes: The Father and Uncles of Queen Victoria* (Collins, London, 1973)

Garratt, G.T., *Lord Brougham* (Macmillan, London, 1935)

Gillen, Mollie, *Royal Duke: Augustus Frederick, Duke of Sussex (1773-1843)* (Sidgwick & Jackson, London, 1976)

Gore, John, ed., *Creevey's Life and Times: a Further Selection from the Correspondence of Thomas Creevey* (John Murray, London, 1934)

Greville, Charles, C.F., *A Journal of the Reigns of King George IV and King William IV by the late Charles Greville*, ed. Henry Reeve, 3 vols. (Longmans, London, 1874)

Grey, Henry, Earl, ed., *The Reform Act, 1832. The Correspondence of the late Earl Grey with H.M. King William IV and Sir Herbert*

Taylor, November 1830-June 1832, 2 vols. (John Murray, London, 1867)

Hadlow, Janice, *The Strangest Family: The Private Life of King George III* (Collins, London, 2014)

Hamilton, Richard V., ed. *The Letters and Papers of Admiral of the Fleet, Sir Thomas Byam Martin*, 3 vols. (Navy Records Society, London, 1903)

Hedley, Olwen, *Queen Charlotte* (John Murray, London, 1975)

Hibbert, Christopher, *George III: A Personal History* (Viking, London, 1998)

_____ *George IV: Regent and King, 1811-1820* (Allen Lane, London, 1973)

Hopkirk, Mary, *Queen Adelaide* (John Murray, London, 1946)

Huish, Robert, *The History of the Life and Reign of William IV* (William Emans, London, 1837)

Kemble, Frances Ann, *Records of a Girlhood* (Henry Holt, New York, 1879)

Knight, Cordelia, *Autobiography*, 2 vols. (W.H. Allen, London, 1861)

Knight, Roger, *William IV: A King at Sea* (Allen Lane, London, 2015)

Le Strange, Guy, ed., *Correspondence of Princess Lieven and Earl Grey*, 3 vols (Richard Bentley & Son, London, 1890)

Longford, Elizabeth, *Victoria R.I.* (Weidenfeld & Nicolson, London, 1964)

_____ *Wellington: Pillar of State* (Weidenfeld & Nicolson, London, 1972)

Lyttelton, Sarah, *Correspondence of Sarah, Lady Lyttleton*, ed. Mrs Hugh Wyndham (John Murray, London, 1912)

Molloy, Fitzgerald, *Court Life Below Stairs, or London Under the Last Georges, 1760-1830* (Ward & Downey, London, 1885)

_____ *The Sailor King: William the Fourth and his Subjects*, 2 vols. (Hutchinson, London, 1903)

Parker, Charles Stuart, *Sir Robert Peel, From his Private Papers*, 3 vols. (John Murray, London, 1899)

Parry, Sir Edward, *Queen Caroline* (Ernest Benn, London, 1930)

Patterson, M.W., *Sir Francis Burdett and His Times* (Macmillan, London, 1931)

Peel, George, ed. *The Private Letters of Sir Robert Peel* (John Murray, London, 1920)

Pocock, Tom, *Sailor King: The life of King William IV*, 2 vols. (Sinclair-Stevenson, London, 1991)

Quennell, Peter, ed., *The Private Letters of Princess Lieven to Prince Metternich, 1820–26* (John Murray, London, 1937)

Reid, Stuart, J., *Lord John Russell* (Dent, London, 1895)

Ridley, Jasper, *Lord Palmerston* (Constable, London, 1970)

Robinson, Lionel G. ed., *Letters of Dorothea, Princess Lieven, during her Residence in London, 1812-1834* (Longmans, London, 1902)

St Aubyn, Giles, *The Royal George, 1819-1904: The Life of HRH Prince George, Duke of Cambridge* (Constable, London, 1963)

Sandars, Mary, *The Life and Times of Queen Adelaide* (Stanley Paul, London, 1915)

Sheppard, Edgar, *George, Duke of Cambridge*: *A Memoir of His Private Life Based on the Journals and Correspondence of His Royal Highness*, 2 vols. (Longmans, London, 1906)

Somerset, Anne, *The Life and Times of William IV* (Weidenfeld & Nicolson, London, 1980)

Stuart, Dorothy Margaret, *The Daughters of George III* (Macmillan, London, 1939)

Thompson, Grace, *The Patriot King* (Hutchinson, London, 1932)

Tomalin, Claire, *Mrs Jordan's Profession: The Story of a Great Actress and a future King* (Viking, London, 1994)

Trevelyan, George Macaulay, *Lord Grey of the Reform Bill, being the Life of Charles, Second Earl Grey* (Longmans, Green, London, 1920)

Trevelyan, George Otto, *The Life and Letters of Lord Macaulay*, 2 vols. (Longmans, Green, London, 1876)

Van der Kiste, John, *George III's Children* (Sutton. Stroud, 1992)

Victoria, Queen, *The Girlhood of Queen Victoria: A Selection from Her Majesty's Diaries between the years 1832 and 1840,* ed. Viscount Esher, 2 vols. (John Murray, London, 1912)

_____ *The Letters of Queen Victoria: a Selection from Her Majesty's Correspondence between the years 1837 and 1861,* ed. A.C. Benson and Viscount Esher, 3 vols. (John Murray, London, 1907)

Watkins, John, *The Life and Times of England's Patriot King, William the Fourth* (Fisher, Son & Jackson, London, 1831)

Wellington, Arthur Duke of, *Despatches, Correspondence and Memoranda,* ed. [his son the] Duke of Wellington, 8 vols. (John Murray, London, 1867-80)

Wharncliffe, Caroline, *Baroness, The First Lady Wharncliffe and Her Family (1779-1856),* ed. Caroline Grosvenor, Charles Beilby, 2 vols. (Heinemann, London, 1927)

Willis, G.M., *Ernest Augustus, Duke of Cumberland and King of Hanover* (Arthur Barker, London, 1954)

Wilson, John Marius, *A Memoir of Field-Marshal the Duke of Wellington: With Interspersed Notices of his Principal Associates in Council and Companions and Opponents in Arms,* 2 vols. (A. Fullerton, London, 1853)

(Wood, J.R.), *Some Recollections of the Last Days of His Late Majesty William IV* (Hatchard & Son, London, 1837)

Wraxall, N.W., *Posthumous Memoirs of His Own Times* (Richard Bentley, London, 1836)

Wright, G.N., *The Life and Reign of William the Fourth,* 2 vols. (Fisher, Son, London, 1837)

Ziegler, Philip, *King William IV* (Collins, London, 1971)

_____ *Melbourne: A Biography of William Lamb, 2nd Viscount Melbourne* (Collins, London, 1976)

Hansard, Parliamentary Debates
The Times
Spectator

Index

Marie of Hesse-Cassel, Princess
(1796–1880), 53
Marie-Antoinette, Queen of
France (1755–93), 34
Martin, Sarah, 15
Martin, Sir Thomas Byam
(1773–1854), 30
Mary, Duchess of Gloucester
(1776–1857), 60, 83, 156,
172, 190
Mayo, John Bourke, Earl of
(1766–1849), 46
Melbourne, William Lamb,
Viscount (1779–1848), 148,
158, 176
and parliamentary reform,
114, 160
recommended as Prime
Minister to succeed
Grey, and relations
with William and
Adelaide, 170
appointed Prime Minister,
171
and William's efforts to
get rid of Buckingham
Palace, 173
dismissed by William as
Prime Minister, 174–5
re-appointed, 180–3
ad Coburgs' visit to
England, 190
and Norton divorce
case, 192

informs cabinet on prayers
for William's health, 196
on Earl of Munster's
death, 200
Melville, Robert Dundas,
Viscount (1771–1851),
70–1, 81
Merrick, William, 12
Metternich, Klemens von
(1773–1859), 69, 152–3
Meynell, Henry (1789–1865),
117
Michaelis, Johann (1717–91), 14
Miguel, King of Portugal
(1802–66), 154–5, 157–8
Moodie, George, 5
Munster, Mary, Countess of
(1791–1842), 64

Napier, Captain, 11
Napier, Sir Charles
(1786–1860), 155
Napoleon, Emperor of the
French (1769–1821), 38, 41,
47, 97, 100, 148
Nelson, Horatio (1758–1805),
18–9, 34, 38
Newcastle, Henry
Pelham-Clinton, Duke of
(1811–64), 127
Nisbet, Fanny (Frances Nelson)
(1768–1831), 18
Norfolk, Bernard, Duke of
(1765–1842), 82, 89

Acknowledgements

I would like to place on record my thanks to the editorial staff at Pen & Sword, notably Alan Murphy, who first suggested this book; to Claire Hopkins, Laura Hirst, Chris Cocks, and Joan Cameron; to Sue and Mike Woolmans, for their invaluable assistance with photography of the king's statue in Greenwich Park; and to my wife Kim, for her inestimable support throughout the months of writing.